The Major Satires of Alexander Pope

The Major Satires of Alexander Pope

ROBERT W. ROGERS

NORWOOD EDITIONS
1978

The Major Satires of
Alexander Pope

ROBERT W. ROGERS

ILLINOIS STUDIES IN LANGUAGE AND LITERATURE: *Vol. 40*

THE UNIVERSITY OF ILLINOIS PRESS

URBANA, 1955

Copyright 1955 BY THE UNIVERSITY OF ILLINOIS. MANUFACTURED IN THE UNITED
STATES OF AMERICA. *Board of Editors:* HARRIS F. FLETCHER, JOHN R. FREY, AND JOSEPH
R. SMILEY. LIBRARY OF CONGRESS CATALOG CARD NO. 55–7371.

For

JEANNE

Preface

Many books have been, and are being, written about Alexander Pope, who is one of the more controversial English poets. The nineteenth century denied that he ever wrote poetry; it asserted that he was "a mean, spiteful little wretch" whose character prevented his being given serious consideration as a moralist. In our own times a saner approach to Pope has fortunately emerged. The discovery through historical research of new facts has modified the easy indictments which the nineteenth century tiresomely reiterated. Changes in sensibility combined with a more realistic understanding of human character have permitted us once again to appreciate the poetic qualities that Pope sought to achieve in his own time.

In nearly all recent efforts to evaluate Pope's merits certain phases of his achievement have, however, been neglected. He has been commended because he has quality in common with Keats and quality in common with Milton; but in the process his major satirical work has not been given sufficient attention. We may still agree with Pope's young admirer George Lyttelton that among the Muses, satire is the "least attractive of the nine" (1730); but we need to remind ourselves that satire may nevertheless be a very great art. Consequently we do wrong to neglect the *Dunciad Variorum,* the *Ethic Epistles,* and the *Imitations of Horace,* especially since these are the poems in which the poet took greatest pride. The rhetoric, the method of his work, has in recent times been scanned: we have become well informed on the manner in which Pope said things; but the question of what he was trying to say has been too much ignored. What were the ethical assumptions on which his satire was based? What sort of ethical achievement did he consider possible to man? Was he, in his satires, merely venting his spleen upon unfortunates who had offended him? Was he writing Tory propaganda designed to unseat the government of Sir Robert Walpole? Was he seriously attempting to improve standards of public and private morality? These are only a few of the questions that Pope's later work poses and that so far have been approached indirectly.

The following book represents an attempt to discuss at length these neglected but important questions. It does not purport to present the final word; it endeavors to open up an important avenue of discussion that has been infrequently travelled. To accomplish my purposes I have deliberately accepted certain premises which may be challenged and which should be mentioned at this time. I have, for example, assumed without question that Pope was a great poet and that satire can be a form of great poetry. I have also assumed that Pope's moral character cannot be explained by easy generalizations and formulae. He had a large capacity for growth and development; and basically he was sincere and honest. He may occasionally have acted from mean motives, but personal animus alone will not do much to explain why he wrote as he did. He may sometimes have been guilty of distortion and misrepresentation, but he was not an inveterate liar. I have accepted throughout this book the hypothesis that his own remarks, treated with little more than ordinary caution and imagination, are the most reliable index to his aims and desires. Such assumptions, although at variance with those sometimes accepted in treatments of Pope, do, I think, lead to fair and profitable comments upon the satires.

In preparing this book I have imposed in various ways upon many friends, colleagues, and libraries. My debt to those who have already written of Pope is apparent on every page. Mr. James M. Osborn, Mr. Arthur A. Houghton, Jr., and the Duke of Devonshire have generously allowed me to quote from manuscript materials in their possession. The authorities of the Harvard College Library, the British Museum, the Henry E. Huntington Library, the New York Public Library, and the Pierpont Morgan Library have been more than cooperative in granting me permission to make use of, and to quote from, manuscripts relevant to my work. Friends who have read my typescript or who have contributed materials— William H. Bond, Arthur W. Secord, Edward H. Davidson, Robert Halsband, and Robert M. Schmitz—should know of my gratitude. The preparation of this book would have been long delayed without generous grants from the Research Board of the University of Illinois and the good offices of Professor Harris F. Fletcher. Every chapter of this book has been improved by the critical acumen and editorial hand of my colleague, Gwynne B. Evans, who has bestowed more time upon my work than friendship demands. My debt to Professor George Sherburn is embarrassingly great. Without his counsel and substantive contributions I could not have completed this book.

ROBERT W. ROGERS

Urbana, Illinois

Contents

Abbreviations

For the sake of brevity I have used the following abbreviations in the footnotes for sources most frequently referred to:

E-C   *The Works of Alexander Pope,* ed. by Whitwell Elwin and W. J. Courthope, 10 vols. London, 1871–1889.

Sutherland   Alexander Pope, *The Dunciad,* ed. by James R. Sutherland. New York, 1943.

Mack   Alexander Pope, *An Essay on Man,* ed. by Maynard Mack. London, 1950.

Bateson   Alexander Pope, *Epistles to Several Persons (Moral Essays),* ed. by F. W. Bateson. London, 1951.

Butt   Alexander Pope, *Imitations of Horace,* ed. by John Butt. London, 1939.

Griffith   Reginald H. Griffith, *Alexander Pope: A Bibliography.* Austin, Texas, 1922–1927.

Anecdotes   Joseph Spence, *Anecdotes, Observations, and Characters of Books and Men,* ed. by Samuel W. Singer. London, 1820.

Ball   *The Correspondence of Jonathan Swift,* ed. by F. Elrington Ball. 6 vols. London, 1910–1914.

Unless otherwise noted all quotations from Pope's poetry are drawn from the texts provided in the volumes of *The Twickenham Edition of the Poems of Alexander Pope* listed above; and the line numbers, unless otherwise indicated, are those given in the texts appearing in these volumes.

CHAPTER ONE

Incentives to Satire

In 1725 Alexander Pope declared to Jonathan Swift that his future poetry would contain a "useful investigation of my own territories . . . something domestic, fit for my own country, and for my own time"; and in 1729 he told Elijah Fenton that he intended thereafter to "write nothing but epistles in Horace's manner." [1] Such poetry had not always been Pope's dream. Had he gone on to fulfill the promise implicit in his earlier work, produced as it was in the shadow of the Virgilian tradition, he might have composed an epic, or at least a tragedy. Indeed, at one time he contemplated projects of an even more un-Horatian character. He told Joseph Spence that he had once thought of writing American pastorals; [2] and as late as 1723 he confessed to Miss Judith Cowper that he had "long had an inclination to tell a fairy tale, the more wild and exotic the better." [3] But he wrote no epic, no tragedy, no American pastorals, and no fairy tales. Instead, he fashioned a great philosophical poem and a number of brilliant satires distinguished by hard realism and concerned with the moral temper of England in the 1720's and 1730's.

Pope himself later came to stress how much his interests had changed. To Swift in 1736 he confessed that his poetry had gained in ethical import while losing something on the side of fancy. [4] He publicly stated that what he had written earlier had come to seem inadequate and unsatisfying. Addressing Lord Bolingbroke in the *Essay on Man,* he declared:

> That urg'd by thee, I turn'd the tuneful art
> From sounds to things, from fancy to the heart;
> For Wit's false mirror held up Nature's light; . . .
> (IV, ll. 391–93)

In the *Epistle to Dr. Arbuthnot* he again wrote of his development as a poet, boasting:

> That not in Fancy's Maze he wander'd long,
> But stoop'd to Truth, and moraliz'd his song: . . .
> (ll. 340–41)

And in the same poem he dismissed his early verse in these terms:

> Soft were my Numbers, who could take offence
> While pure Description held the place of Sense?
> Like gentle *Fanny's* was my flow'ry Theme,
> A painted Mistress, or a purling Stream.
> (ll. 147–50)

---

[1] E-C, VII, 50; VIII, 155.
[2] *Anecdotes,* p. 140.
[3] E-C, IX, 431–32.
[4] Pope to Swift, March 25, 1736: E-C, VII, 341–42.

To an extent Pope's descriptions of his earlier work are valid ones. His poetry had been largely experimental, the result of his desire to establish himself in the Virgilian tradition of letters. It was imitative and precocious; and it reflected an intense application to prosody and diction. It was produced by one who had spent his youth in quiet study and who was interested in art primarily for art's sake. His later poetry, on the other hand, was critical and analytic in temper. It was the work of a sensitive and perceptive moralist and commentator upon society. The shift in Pope's literary interests was not, however, quickly or easily made. He had studiously cherished his early aspirations; and he was reluctant to abandon the sort of work which might lead to an epic and to take up a utilitarian kind of poetry which might not endure and which threatened to involve him in perpetual controversy. A variety of circumstances, personal and ideological, conspired to force him, almost in spite of himself, to the decisions which altered the character of his poetry.

His early successes and his own social charm had brought him into contact with men whose enthusiasms were not purely literary. During the years immediately preceding the death of Queen Anne, Pope had known some of the leading Tory statesmen, including Bolingbroke, Atterbury, and Oxford; and he formed lasting friendships with Tory propagandists such as Swift and Arbuthnot. The removal of his family from Binfield to Chiswick in 1716 made it easier for him to mingle with the great of London society, and the lease of a villa at Twickenham in 1718 brought him among people connected with the Court. In time he came to know an unusually varied assortment of influential men. One of his closest friends was James Craggs, who succeeded Addison as a principal secretary of state, with the charge of the southern department; and Pope was introduced to Sir Robert Walpole by William Fortescue, Walpole's private secretary. A mutual interest in gardening secured a friendship between Pope and Lord Bathurst, an important figure in Tory politics; and in 1725, when Lord Bolingbroke returned from a French exile devoted to philosophical pursuits, he settled at Dawley Farm, near Twickenham, where he renewed his acquaintance with Pope. All of these men were men of affairs; some of them had first-rate minds. And none of them, to whom writing was primarily a practical and utilitarian activity, was inclined to encourage him in a continued pursuit of a purely literary correctness.

Pope's early artistic aims were also modified by the rationalism of his times, which presented a tempting challenge to his critical and analytic faculties. Encouraged by the great speculative achievements of the previous century, thoughtful men dedicated themselves to the task of examining inherited opinions and existing institutions in the light of reason and of bringing customs, establishments, and beliefs into conformity with rationally sanctioned ideals. These aims resulted for many in an increased awareness of the disparity between the order which reason attributed to nature and the circumstances of actual life. [And English life after the death of Queen Anne shocked many of Pope's contemporaries. The nation was experiencing the evils that attend a rapid expansion of trade and the accumulation of great wealth; and although society attempted to preserve a veneer of elegance, it could not really conceal the dissipation, corruption, and grossness that everywhere existed. The moral tone of the age seemed not to be improved by the King, the established church, or the leaders of government. The clergy was lethargic; and high appointments were given only to those who actively supported the government. In the pulpits the middle-class virtues of thrift and craft were raised to heavenly ones; and the concepts of sin and redemption which had traditionally afforded Christianity its appeal were ignored or rationalized away. George I, although frugal and prudent, was hardly an apostle of gentility. His treatment of his wife was scandalously brutal. When he came to England in 1715, he brought with him two mistresses, who soon set up a prosperous trade in patronage; and his German counselors proved offensive by their unabashed exploitation of the people. The monarch himself was heavy and dull in society; and he lacked interest in letters. He shocked conservative sensibilities by doing away with much of the pomp and ceremony that had been traditional at the Court; and he alienated large political groups by abandoning even the appearances of impartiality in public affairs. He assumed that he owed his throne to the Whigs and throughout his reign consistently supported their measures. A key figure in the management of the government from the time of George I's accession until 1742, was Sir Robert Walpole. Although he understood public finance and established policies that were to be the basis of England's greatness for over two hundred years, he offended many people. His private life was marked by flagrant disregard of decorum; and his conversation was coarse and cynical. Despite his genuine interest in England's welfare, he loved power and strove unscrupulously to retain it. He believed that effective government was possible in his times only through bribery, purchase of elections, and intolerance of dissent; and, preferring to surround himself with mediocrity, he dismissed from the government many able persons who threatened his dominance.

Even if we hesitate to believe that conditions were significantly worse in the 1720's than they had been during the age of Queen Anne, the existence of corruption was dramatically revealed in the later period, and men were easily convinced that the times were, indeed, degenerate. In 1720 the evils of widespread pecuniary speculation were demonstrated to everyone when the public, which for over three years had been engaged in a speculative orgy, questioned the paper promises of the South Sea Company. The value of stocks declined sharply; fortunes evaporated in the panic, and few escaped major losses. When a report to the House of Commons disclosed the extent to which high officials of the government had been bribed in one way or another by those anxious to promote the schemes of the South Sea Company, thoughtful people had occasion for concern. Five years later, in 1725, a deficiency of £82,000 was discovered in the suitor's money entrusted to the care of the masters in chancery. Thomas Parker, Earl of Macclesfield, was, as lord chancellor, implicated and found guilty of high crimes and misdemeanors. These, and other less sensational evidences of venality, received full notoriety. The *True Briton,* controlled by the Duke of Wharton, made much of the degeneracy of the times and the necessity of "patriotism"; and after 1726, when a strong opposition had been formed by the disaffected William Pulteney, Lord Bolingbroke, and Sir William Wyndham, the *Craftsman* made corruption a primary issue, seizing upon every particular instance of it that could be turned against the government and condemning the manner in which the secret service funds were used, the practice of bribing members of parliament, and the government's pusillanimous conduct of foreign affairs.

The disparity between existing conditions and nature rationally conceived did not lead to questioning of the validity of the ideal; it merely increased the determination of men to bring about conformity to a rational order identified with perfection. To portray the attributes of the good life and expose irrationality seemed to be the primary obligation of enlightened men. As a means of accomplishing this duty satire particularly recommended itself to practising writers, because it offered a means both of setting forth the good and exposing folly and vice wherever they appeared. Furthermore, the conviction that self-love was the strongest of motives promoted faith in the efficacy of ridicule. Ever since the Restoration, satire had been the most prominent single literary genre; and after the death of Queen Anne there was a further increase in its popularity.[5] Such a trend in literary fashion Pope could not easily ignore; and he knew well the kind of triumphs that had been achieved by Swift, Dryden, and Boileau—and by Horace and Juvenal of an earlier age.

By 1720 Pope was thoroughly conscious of the evils which he was eventually to treat in his satires. He had long recognized the follies prevailing among men of learning and writers; and he had come to recognize the evils that distinguished society of his times. In a letter to James Eckershall (March, 1720), he described his age as one of "hope and golden mountains";[6] and in July, 1723, he uttered privately a more pointed protest:

Every valuable, every pleasant thing is sunk in an ocean of avarice and corruption. The son of a first minister is a proper match for a daughter of a late South Sea director, —so money upon money increases, copulates, and multiplies, and guineas beget guineas in *sæcula sæculorum.*

O cives, cives! quærenda pecunia primum est
Virtus post nummos . . .[7]

Meanwhile some of his contemporaries, who had seen his real talent for satire

---

[5] Andrew M. Wilkinson, "The Rise of English Verse Satire in the Eighteenth Century," *English Studies,* XXXIV (1953), 97 n., presents some interesting, if not conclusive, figures on the popularity of satire after the Restoration: "A detailed examination of the poets listed in the *Cambridge Bibliography* inevitably yields only rough figures; one would suggest however that between 1660 and 1680 perhaps 30% of the poets writing produced sufficient invective or burlesque to be classed as 'Satirists'; between 1680 and 1700 the same. The first decade of the eighteenth century has few satirists but there is a considerable increase in the second, giving a percentage of about 21 for the twenty years. The period 1720–40 however has a percentage of 35, after which there is again a decline."

[6] E-C, X, 229.

[7] Pope to William Broome: E-C, VIII, 67.

in his early fugitive writings, urged him to help in the reformation of the times by writing more ambitious satires than he had yet ventured to publish. Bishop Atterbury, after reading Pope's satirical sketch of Addison, encouraged him to attempt more work of a similar sort:

> No small piece of your writing has been ever sought after so much. It has pleased every man without exception, to whom it has been read. Since you now therefore know where your real strength lies, I hope you will not suffer that talent to lie unemployed. For my part I should be so glad to see you finish something of that kind, that I could be content to be a little sneered at in a line or so, for the sake of the pleasure I should have in reading the rest. I have talked my sense of this matter to you once or twice, and now I put it under my hand, that you may see it is my deliberate opinion.[8]

In October, 1722, the author (Matthias Earbury?) of the *Monthly Packet of Advices from Parnassus* wrote of the state of wit, declaring: "*Pope*, indeed, keeps up the Face of an *English* Poet. Oh! could he write what he thinks, in Numbers sweet as those he has already sent into the World; then he would, like *Oldham*, scourge a wicked Age, and trace the Muses Miseries to their Fountain Head." [9] Edward Young, in the first satire of his *Universal Passion*, likewise chided Pope for his failure to treat the vices of the age:

> Why slumbers *Pope*, who leads the tuneful Train,
> Nor hears that Virtue, which He loves, complain? [10]

But Pope was not at once persuaded to abandon his role as a "literary" poet. His direct comments on his times found expression only in remarks uttered privately to friends. He was, after all, a Roman Catholic; and pointed commentary on social and political mores would have been doubtfully acceptable from him. So he continued for a time to cultivate his garden, his poetry, and his friendships. The incentive that finally impelled him to attempt a major satire was provided by his personal literary enemies. From the beginning of his career he had suffered from abusive criticism by men envious of his ability; but attacks upon him became more vicious and intolerable after about 1720, just at the time when public immorality was being dramatically illustrated. In May, 1721, the *Life of the late Celebrated Mrs. Elizabeth Wisebourn, Vulgarly Call'd Mother Wybourn* appeared, and in it the author (Richard Morley?) hinted absurdly that the Duchess of Buckinghamshire had bestowed illicit favors upon Pope. In 1722 or 1723 there was sufficient malicious gossip about his relations with Martha Blount to cause the Carylls to make inquiries of the poet and his friend. In 1725 a story, probably in print, was circulated. This story was mentioned by Pope in a letter to Caryll, December 25, 1725:

> A very confident asseveration has been made, which has spread over the town, that your god-daughter, Miss Patty, and I, lived two or three years since in a manner that was reported to you as giving scandal to many; that upon your writing to me upon it,

---

[8] February 26, 1722: E-C, IX, 39.
[9] Page 28.
[10] *The Universal Passion. Satire I* (London, 1725), p. 3.

I consulted with her, and sent you an excusive alleviating answer, but did, after that, privately and of myself, write to you a full confession how much I myself disapproved the way of life, and owning the prejudice done her, charging it on herself, and declaring that I wished to break off what I acted against my conscience, &c.; and that she, being at the same time spoken to by a lady of your acquaintance at your instigation, did absolutely deny to alter any part of her conduct, were it ever so disreputable or exceptionable. Upon this villainous lying tale, it is farther added by the same hand, that I brought her acquainted with a noble lord, and into an intimacy with some others, merely to get quit of her myself, being moved in consciousness by what you and I had conferred together, and playing this base part to get off.[11]

Although the "villainous lying tale" to which Pope refers has not been uncovered, similarly fantastic stories were published by his contemporaries. Eliza Haywood, in the *Memoirs of a certain Island adjacent to the Kingdom of Utopia* (Vol. I of which appeared in September, 1724), declared, for example, that Martha Blount had been the mistress of James Craggs and of others, had since married "an old servant" of Craggs (i.e., Pope), and had contracted a venereal disease.

Pope's reticence was not encouraged by the fact that in 1725 he was himself detected in what seemed a questionable practice. In that year he published his edition of Shakespeare's plays and the first three volumes of his *Odyssey* translation. In March, as soon as the edition of Shakespeare came out, a group of journalists attacked the publisher Jacob Tonson, who laid claim to a perpetual copyright in Shakespeare's works. Tonson had in effect hired Pope as editor; and the benefits of the subscription were to go to Tonson himself, not to Pope. To writers already sensitive about the tyranny of booksellers this arrangement threatened the whole practice of the subscription subsidy, which from the point of view of authors had proved to be the only feasible substitute for the dying system of patronage. Critics of the edition concentrated upon Tonson's conduct of the venture; but Pope came in for a share of censure because he had allowed himself to be a party to an arrangement which, it was charged, invaded the rights of authors. In April, the next month, Pope brought out the first three volumes of his translation of the *Odyssey;* and he again found himself attacked. He was probably not much disturbed by the effort of critics to revive charges which had been leveled at the *Iliad* translation ten years before—that Pope knew no Greek, that he had used rhyme instead of blank verse, that he had been excessively ornamental—but he was embarrassed by the well-founded charge that he had not contributed as much to the undertaking as public announcements had led readers to believe. Having been discovered in what critics thought an unfortunate arrangement with the bookseller Jacob Tonson, Pope was now found a party with Bernard Lintot in what seemed a deliberate effort to misrepresent the facts of collaboration. Furthermore, he was condemned, somewhat unjustly, for rewarding inadequately those who had collaborated with him. All in all, the publications of 1725 suggested that the poet, like many of his contemporaries, had compromised his principles; and he was placed under some obligation to exonerate himself.

[11] E-C, VI, 287–88.

His first thought was to publish a satire which might cause his enemies to repent of their presumption. As has already been noted, he told Swift, on September 14, 1725, that he planned to write "no more translations, but something domestic, fit for my own country, and for my own time." [12] A month later he again wrote Swift to indicate that he contemplated a satire in which he "endeavoured to correct the taste of the town in wit and criticism." [13] But Swift, who was in faraway Ireland and who may have realized that a satire from one so recently accused of jobbery would be suspect, advised caution: "Take care the bad poets do not outwit you, as they have served the good ones in every age, whom they have provoked to transmit their names to posterity. Mævius is as well known as Virgil, and Gildon will be as well known as you, if his name gets into your verses: and as to the difference between good and bad fame, it is a perfect trifle." [14] Upon receiving this admonition, Pope abandoned his plan for a satire—or at least he so declared to Swift:

... I am much the happier for finding (a better thing than our wits) our judgments jump, in the notion that all scribblers should be passed by in silence. To vindicate one's self against such nasty slanders, is much as wise as it was in your countryman, when the people imputed a stink to him, to prove the contrary by showing his backside. So let Gildon and Philips rest in peace! What Virgil had to do with Mævius, that he should wear him upon his sleeve to all eternity, I do not know, but I think a bright author should put an end to slanders only as the sun does to stinks—by shining out exhale them to nothing. [15]

And he then gave the public an indirect promise that he would attempt poetry of an exalted character. William Broome, who knew his inclinations, hinted, in a congratulatory poem appended to the end of the translation of the *Odyssey* (1726), that now Pope would embark on a noble undertaking:

> This labour past, of heavenly subjects sing,
> While hov'ring angels listen on the wing,
> To hear from earth such heart-felt raptures rise,
> As, when they sing, suspended hold the skies:
> Or nobly rising in fair Virtue's cause,
> From thy own Life transcribe th'unerring laws:
> Teach a bad world beneath her sway to bend;
> To verse like thine fierce savages attend,
> And men more fierce: When *Orpheus* tunes the lay,
> Ev'n fiends, relenting hear their rage away.

Pope did not at once fulfill the promise implied in these lines, for in 1726 irresistible incentives to satire occurred. Swift came over from Ireland during the spring and stayed at Twickenham for three months. He was not inclined in 1726 to encourage any complacency in his friend; and his presence in England revived the dormant enthusiasms which formerly had given the Scriblerus Club its vitality.

---

[12] E-C, VII, 50.

[13] E-C, VII, 57.

[14] November 26, 1725: E-C, VII, 64.

[15] December 14, 1725: E-C, VII, 65–66.

The same year Edmund Curll also published two volumes of *Miscellanea,* the first of which included, among other things, some "Familiar Letters written to Henry Cromwell, Esq; by Mr. Pope." [16] These letters had been written when Pope was young, and they contained some lighthearted and indiscreet sallies which in his maturity he preferred to forget. He had endured much from Curll; but this invasion of his privacy was intolerable. Still another provocation occurred in 1726, when Lewis Theobald published an attack upon the edition of Shakespeare, *Shakespeare Restored; or, A Specimen of the Many Errors, as well Committed, as Unamended, by Mr. Pope in his late Edition of this Poet.* In this work Theobald gave a new turn to the hostile attacks upon Pope's undertaking of the year before: he questioned the poet's competence as an editor, and to support his thesis he presented a number of Pope's readings, chiefly found in *Hamlet,* which Theobald believed incorrect, in some cases naively so. Theobald well understood the usefulness of textual criticism; and he had an abundance of specific information, which he knew how to employ. Even though his criticism was pedantic in its failure to distinguish between the relative significance of trivial mistakes in pointing and vital alterations in meaning, his remarks probably impressed Pope. But they also irritated him; for Theobald's tone was patronizing and his work seemed prompted by malice. Because an indictment of Pope's competence as an editor of Shakespeare recalled directly the similar question which had been raised in connection with his translations of Homer, the poet had good reason to believe that Theobald was not really so much interested in the text of Shakespeare as he was in abusing Pope.

Not long after these events Pope decided to write the *Dunciad,* the first of his major satires. In subject and spirit this work resembles some of his earlier and less pretentious efforts to depict literary folly; but it is also colored by the keener social and intellectual awareness that he had acquired with maturity. The poem is chiefly remarkable, however, as a measure of his progress as a satirist, as a demonstration of the difficulties he had yet to overcome before major achievement was possible. Ultimately, in spite of the rough-and-tumble nature of the times and in spite of his own distracting private affairs, he did discipline himself; and he did eliminate from his satire much of the personal irascibility that in the *Dunciad* stained the moral idealism upon which the merit of satire must primarily rest. He also revealed a more comprehensive grasp of contemporary problems than the limited purposes of the *Dunciad* permitted him to show. Pope's later career as a poet is a fascinating story of one man's successful struggle to create an enduring monument to himself and to his genius, a genius for moral and social analysis which he discovered in himself relatively late in life.

---

[16] Curll had obtained the letters from Mrs. Elizabeth Thomas, Cromwell's onetime mistress, to whom Cromwell had given them.

CHAPTER TWO

The *Dunciad Variorum* of 1729

I

The *Dunciad Variorum* was formally conceived during 1726–1727, but Pope did not at first see all the possibilities of his inspiration. His decision to write the poem was closely connected with his work on the so-called Pope-Swift *Miscellanies,* that collection of fugitive pieces—"not our Studies, but our Follies; not our Works, but our Idlenesses"—which he and Jonathan Swift thought should be owned in view of the freedom with which anonymous pieces had been attributed to them.[1] The plan for the *Miscellanies* was formed during Swift's visit to England in 1726: it called for two volumes—or perhaps three, if sufficient material could be found—of prose compositions together with one volume of verse. During Swift's holiday the two editors, among other things, gathered appropriate selections of their prose for the first two volumes; these Pope saw through the press after Swift left England in August. Although they were printed by February or March, 1727, they were not published until June. In April Swift again came over to England from Ireland, and at this time the two editors turned to the task of preparing the volume of their fugitive verse. They hoped to bring it out in the autumn, but difficulties arose to delay publication until March, 1728.

The point in these preparations at which the *Dunciad* was projected is uncertain. Most biographers of Pope have asserted that he decided to write the poem in 1726; but the spring of 1727 seems a more likely time—at least Pope probably did not work on it before then. His letters do not allude to it, either directly or indirectly, before June, 1727. In the folio edition of the second volume of his *Works* (1735), the poet declared that the *Dunciad* "was writ in 1727."[2] Furthermore, some doggerel verses written by Swift and describing life at Twickenham during the summer of 1727 show that the poem was then in a very fragmentary state:

> *Pope* has the Talent well to speak,
> But not to reach the Ear;
> His loudest Voice is low and weak,
> The *Dean* too deaf to hear.

---

[1] Pope's first reference to the *Dunciad* in his correspondence indicates that it was originally destined for the *Miscellanies:* "As to the poem which I will have to end the volume, it will make three sheets at least, and I will take time till winter to finish it. It may then be published, singly first if proper. I'm sure it will be advantageous so to do—but say not a word of it to any man" (Pope to Benjamin Motte, June 30 [1727]: E-C, IX, 524).

[2] The date in this note was first altered to "1726" in the small octavo edition of the *Dunciad* (Griffith 392), which appeared later in 1735. The alteration could easily have been a printer's error.

A while they on each other look,
    Then diff'rent Studies chuse,
The *Dean* sits plodding on a Book,
    Pope walks, and courts the Muse.

Now Backs of Letters, though design'd
    For those who more will need 'em,
Are fill'd with Hints, and interlin'd,
    Himself can hardly read 'em.

Each Atom by some other struck,
    All Turns and Motion tries,
Till in a Lump together stuck,
    Behold a *Poem* rise! [3]

This evidence would suggest that concentrated work on the *Dunciad* did not begin at least until the spring of 1727, when the two editors were actively preparing the volume for which the poem was originally designed.[4]

Although the *Dunciad* is related to the preparation by Swift and Pope of their joint *Miscellanies,* the exact circumstances which gave rise to it are unknown. Pope provided an account of them, it is true, in the first edition of the *Dunciad Variorum:* "Dr. *Swift* . . . may be said in a sort to be Author of the Poem: For when He, together with Mr. *Pope* . . . determin'd to own the most trifling pieces in which they had any hand, and to destroy all that remain'd in their power, the first sketch of this poem was snatch'd from the fire by Dr. *Swift,* who persuaded his friend to proceed in it, and to him it was therefore Inscribed." [5]

This narrative bears obvious marks of melodrama, but it does hint at a plausible situation. When Pope and Swift were going through their manuscripts looking for appropriate contributions to the volume of their fugitive verse, they may have come across a rough draft of a satire on authors which Pope had composed earlier. Seeing its possibilities Swift may have encouraged his friend to develop it for the miscellany volume; he probably also made some suggestions as to the way in which the subject could be effectively presented. We can only guess at the character of this early sketch and of Swift's suggestions. There are several allusions in the published *Dunciad* to events which were topical long before 1727–28: the action occurs on

---

[3] "Dr. Sw— to Mr. P—e, While he was writing the *Dunciad,*" *Poems of Jonathan Swift,* ed. Sir Harold Williams (Oxford, 1937), II, 405–406. Pope wrote Thomas Sheridan, October 12, 1728, that Swift's attack of deafness during his visit at Twickenham in 1727 had made the *Dunciad* possible: "for had he been able to converse with me, do you think I had amused my time so ill?" (E-C, VII, 137).

[4] One should remark that during the preparation of this volume Pope and Swift had difficulty finding appropriate materials which would make a sizable book. In a letter to Swift, which was probably written February 18, 1727 (Ball, III, 380 n.), Pope hoped to find verses that "have some peculiarity, and may be distinguished for ours, from other writers" (E-C, VII, 95). On July 1, 1727, Swift wrote from Twickenham to Thomas Sheridan in Ireland for a copy of verses that might be used: "Pray copy out the verses I writ to Stella on her collecting my verses, and send them to me, for we want some to make our poetical Miscellany large enough, and I am not there to pick what should be added" (Ball, III, 403).

[5] Sutherland, p. 201.

Lord Mayor's Day, October 29, 1719; and the important role of Elkanah Settle in Book III points to earlier composition, for Settle, who died in 1724, was hardly an interesting figure in 1728. Dennis (in Book II, l. 273) describes himself as being sixty years old, a description which would have been appropriate in 1719–20. Professor Sherburn, in the light of such references, proposes, as a possible hypothesis, that the earlier sketch may have been "a satire on the choice of a city poet (who 'functioned' on Lord Mayor's Day) in burlesque of the recent choice of a laureate (December, 1718)." [6] Thus Swift may have proposed to Pope that he adapt the earlier satire to the circumstances of 1727 when, through Settle's death in 1724, the post of city poet had actually become vacant. It is possible, however, that the early sketch may have been merely a description of a Lord Mayor's Day celebration, in which Settle, as the city poet, prophesies the future triumphs of the city authors. If this hypothesis is just, then Swift may have proposed that Pope utilize the central episode in Dryden's *Mac Flecknoe,* the mock coronation. Whatever the explanation, the events of 1726 and 1727 provided Pope with a hero, Lewis Theobald, who by his performances in *Shakespeare restored* and *The Rape of Proserpine* had shown himself to be a candidate in every way suited for the position which Settle had held and which was currently vacant. Moreover, in the months following June, 1727, a coronation was a topical subject, owing to the death of George I and the approaching coronation of George II.

After June, 1727, Pope began intensive work on the *Dunciad,* hoping that it might be ready for publication in October, the time of the royal accession. [7] There were difficulties, however, for the task proved much more complex and promising than he had at first thought. Indeed, he did not approach the end of composition until early February, 1728, at which time Edward Young reported to Thomas Tickell: "Mr Pope is finishing a Burlesque Heroick on Writers, & ye modern Diversions of the Town, it alludes to Homer & Virgil throughout. The 5th Book of Virgil is burlesqued into Games in which Booksellers run for the Authors & p-ss for Authoresses &^c, as is likewise Part of 6th by a Vision of Heroes in Dullness &^c 'tis near done & what is done is very correct." [8] As the poem grew, important decisions were made that altered the original plans. In February, or early March, 1728, the title was changed from the *Progress of Dulness* to the *Dunciad,* lest the brief title on the spine, "Pope's Dulness," afford sport to hostile critics. [9] Somewhat earlier Pope must have determined to take his poem out of the miscellany volume

---

[6] *The Best of Pope* (New York, 1941), p. 450.

[7] Pope, in a letter to Lord Oxford, August 25, 1727, stated that the volume of *Miscellanies* containing the *Dunciad* was to be related to the royal coronation: "Our Miscellany of poems will be published next October. It is one of the benefits this nation will reap by the coronation" (E-C, VIII, 230).

[8] February 5 [1728]: Richard E. Tickell, *Thomas Tickell and the Eighteenth-Century Poets 1685–1740* (London, 1931), p. 143.

[9] "As for those scribblers for whom you apprehend I would suppress my Dulness (which, by the way, for the future, you are to call by a more pompous name, the Dunciad), how much that nest of hornets are my regard will easily appear to you when you read the Treatise of the Bathos" (Pope to Swift, March 23, 1728: E-C, VII, 123).

and to publish it separately. Before the end of December he had told Swift that he was going to include "a pleasant discourse on the subject of poetry"—the *Peri Bathous*—in the forthcoming volume of *Miscellanies,* even though a prose composition did not belong in it.[10] Although there is no proof that the decision to utilize the *Peri Bathous* in the miscellany volume proceeded from a decision to publish the *Dunciad* independently, a direct substitution was probably involved. And in January, 1728, Pope was clearly thinking of his *Dunciad* as forming a book by itself.[11]

The reasons for this important shift in plan seem quite clear. Even in June, 1727, Pope had hinted to the publisher Motte that the poem might come to deserve separate publication.[12] As it grew, he undoubtedly came to realize that he was engaged upon a major work, not an "Idleness" or a "Folly"; and he was less disposed to obscure its brilliance by including it in a volume given over primarily to minor fugitive verse. Other considerations made the change expedient. The poem, offering possible grounds for a libel action, certainly required anonymous publication, impossible if it was to appear among selections which Pope and Swift had acknowledged as theirs. Borrowing from the miscellany volume meant, however, that another work of sufficient length had to be supplied; and the only suitable composition at hand was the *Peri Bathous*. Although it has been argued that Pope selected this work in order to goad his enemies to abusive retaliation which would justify the *Dunciad,* it is likely that another motive also operated—that he published the *Peri Bathous* because it was available and could fill the gap in the miscellany volume created by the decision to publish the *Dunciad* separately.

Another even more important decision, possibly related to the plan for bringing out the poem independently, was made before May 18, 1728, when the *Dunciad* first appeared on the stalls of booksellers—the decision to extend the range of the satire by including notes and other matter. Although it is conventional to assert that this decision took place immediately after the first edition of the poem came out, Pope had certainly made up his mind earlier. He may even have formulated the plan late in 1727; for a desire to enlarge the scope of the work would explain why he made other plans for the *Miscellanies.* We do know that in January, 1728, he was aware that the materials in his work might well be commented upon: "And it grieves me to the soul that I cannot send you my *chef d'oeuvre,* the poem of Dulness, which, after I am dead and gone, will be printed with a large commentary, and lettered on the back, Pope's Dulness." [13] Evidence that he was committed to a pretentious edition by early May is more conclusive. Swift, in a letter to Pope, June 1, 1728, reported that Patrick Delany had informed him verbally

---

[10] On December 28, 1727, Swift wrote to Benjamin Motte, the publisher of the *Miscellanies,* and told of a letter he had received from Pope: "He writ to me, that he intended a pleasant discourse on the subject of poetry should be printed before the volume, and says that discourse is ready . . ." (Ball, III, 440).

[11] Pope to Swift: E-C, VII, 110.

[12] See p. 9n.

[13] Pope to Swift: E-C, VII, 110.

of a change of plans: "The doctor told me your secret about the Dunciad, which does not please me, because it defers gratifying my vanity in the most tender point, and perhaps may wholly disappoint it." [14] Since Dr. Delany was Swift's informant, the "secret" must have been settled well before the middle of May, when Delany, who had been in England since early March, returned to Ireland.[15] The *Dunciad* of 1728 itself provides quite conclusive proof that the "secret" involved plans for embellishing it. The prefatory publisher's note implies that the author would produce a "more perfect" edition: "How I became possest of it, is of no concern to the Reader; but it would have been a wrong to him, had I detain'd this publication: since those *Names* which are its chief ornaments, die off daily so fast, as must render it too soon unintelligible. If it provoke the Author to give us a more perfect edition, I have my end." [16] The text of the poem is presented in a way that would solicit public requests for the "key" which Pope was planning to publish. It contains veiled allusions to intimate events that would stimulate curiosity; the objects of the satire are generally identified only by ambiguous initial letters followed by dashes— often asterisks are used in place of initials. Such ambiguity, in an age which was curious about personalities, could only create a call for a more complete edition; and it is impossible to believe that Pope would have introduced quite so much tantalizing obscurity into his poem if he had not already formulated plans for the *Dunciad Variorum*.

The reason for publishing a preliminary effort is not clear. Waiting until the complete *Dunciad* was prepared would have been the simple and obvious course; but Pope was rarely simple and obvious in ushering poems into the world. He may have believed that the severity and personal character of the notes to be included in the projected variorum edition required him to stimulate an artificial demand by the reading public for explanatory material, a demand to which he could decently yield. One may also conjecture that he may have needed more dunces for his poem and more materials for the notes; an easy way to secure both dunces and notes was to publish a text of the poem and wait for Grub-street to reply.

Definite evidence that Pope was making progress on the *Dunciad Variorum* appears in his letters of June, 1728. On the thirteenth he reminded Lord Oxford of an earlier request for the "extract out of Caxton's preface, how he came by Virgil"; [17] and on the seventeenth he wrote Oxford telling of his preoccupation with his venture.[18] He sent Oxford on July 1 a request that an amanuensis transcribe "this preface written by a friend of mine"; [19] and before the end of the month he dispatched "the remainder of the notes on the second" book to be transcribed

---

[14] E-C, VII, 132.

[15] Gay to Swift, May 16, 1728: Ball, IV, 33.

[16] Sutherland, pp. 203–204.

[17] E-C, VIII, 236.

[18] E-C, VIII, 236–37.

[19] E-C, VIII, 238. The "preface" is obviously the "Letter to the Publisher" which appears in the *Dunciad Variorum* over the signature of William Cleland. The contribution was probably written by Pope, or at least under Pope's direct supervision. One ought also to remember that prefaces are ordinarily written late in the preparation of a book.

by Oxford's amanuensis.[20] Proof was beginning to come from the printer in October or November; for Pope, in a letter dated November 12 but perhaps written October 12, reassured Swift that "the inscription to the Dunciad is now printed, and inserted in the poem." [21]

During this period Pope sought the assistance of friends who could contribute to his notes. He was, after all, relatively remote from the Grub-street scene and could not himself easily acquire the needed information; and since variety was a principal source of interest, contributions by other hands would help.[22] Richard Savage, better acquainted with the personalities and ways of contemporary hacks than was Pope, undoubtedly furnished much particular intelligence.[23] Pope also asked Swift for contributions: "As to the latter [the Notes Variorum], I desire you to read over the text, and make a few in any way you like best, whether dry raillery, upon the style and way of commenting of trivial critics; or humorous, upon the authors in the poem; or historical, of persons, places, times; or explanatory; or collecting the parallel passages of the ancients." [24]

Writing to Thomas Sheridan, October 12, 1728, he invited contributions from the wits of Dublin: "If your university or town have produced any on this subject [epigrams on the gentlemen of the Dunciad], pray send them me, or keep them at least together; for another day they may all meet." [25] Pope approached even Sir Robert Walpole in his search for material. He wrote William Fortescue: "I have a particular reason to desire to know a thing, which I believe he [Walpole] will tell me if you ask it.—Who was author of a book called An Essay on the Taste and Writings of this Age, dedicated to him, as a libel upon me. I formerly sent it to Sir R. by you (as I think)." [26]

We do not know how generous the response to such requests was. Much of the annotation called for an interest in Pope's enemies that even his closest friends would hardly have experienced. Nevertheless, he frequently insisted that he had received help. The "Advertisement" and the "Letter to the Publisher" in the Dunciad Variorum acknowledge aid; but in public Pope may have found such an

---

[20] E-C, VIII, 239.

[21] E-C, VII, 139.

[22] One demonstration of Pope's remoteness is to be seen in his failure to identify William Warburton's attacks upon him in the Daily Journal. Had Pope known much about the hack-writers of his time, he would have known of Warburton's association with his enemies and would almost certainly have put him in the Dunciad.

[23] In the revised edition of Thomas Cooke's Battel of the Poets (1729) Savage was portrayed as a spy active in Pope's service. A similar description of Savage is to be found in Pope Alexander's Supremacy and Infallibility Examin'd (London, 1729).

[24] June 28, 1728: E-C, VII, 134.

[25] E-C, VII, 137.

[26] Pope to William Fortescue: E-C, IX, 124. The pamphlet referred to was published June 29, 1728, according to the Monthly Chronicle. Pope's letter to Fortescue was probably written either in late December, 1728, or in the following month. Pope sought this information because he wanted to include the author's name among the "Books, Papers, and Verses, in which our Author was abused . . . With the true Names of the Authors." Since the name of the author is not given in the Dunciad Variorum, one must suppose that Walpole either did not furnish the information or would not allow Pope to use it.

evasion of responsibility expedient. His letters, where distortion of the facts was not so necessary, insist, however, that others did make contributions. Writing to John Caryll, April 8, 1729, he declared: "The other book is written, all but the poem, by two or three of my friends, and a droll book it is. They have the art to make trifles agreeable; and you will not be at a loss to guess the authors." [27] He declared to Thomas Sheridan: "Some very good epigrams on the gentlemen of the Dunciad have been sent me from Oxford, and others of the London authors." [28] Some years later, November 27, 1742, he told William Warburton that Cleland and Dr. Arbuthnot had contributed to the notes.[29] Such iteration makes it hard to believe that friends did not contribute to the undertaking; but if they did so, this assistance must have been largely confined to the more purely Scriblerian material in the volume. A number of notes are explicitly assigned to "Martinus Scriblerus"; and they burlesque pedantic annotation rather than attack specific dunces. The tone and style of these notes differ from the tone and style of the unsigned notes, which concentrate on subjects of special interest to the poet himself. The *Dunciad Variorum* also includes several Scriblerian essays—"Martinus Scriblerus, Of the Poem," "M. Scriblerus Lectori," and "Virgilius Restauratus"—and the essays do not show the personal interest in Grub-street and its ways that Pope may reasonably be supposed to have had. Some, or even all of these notes, may well have been supplied by friends.[30]

As we have pointed out, the *Dunciad Variorum* was being printed early in November, 1728; but it was not published until April 10, 1729, for the course of printing did not go smoothly. Pope, as was his habit, made considerable alterations in the proofs, which delayed publication. Such at least was an explanation offered by John Dennis: "Does not half the Town know, that honest *J.W*[*right*] was the only Dunce that was persecuted and plagu'd by this Impression? that Twenty times the Rhapsodist alter'd every thing that he gave the Printer? and that Twenty times, *W.* in Rage and in Fury, threaten'd to turn the *Rhapsody* back upon the Rhapsodist's Hands?" [31]

Difficulty with the proofs was intensified by the fact that in December and January Pope was not well, and his mother extremely ill. Preoccupied with these troubles he asked a friend, possibly William Cleland or Richard Savage, to read proof, a task that was not performed to the satirist's satisfaction: "The book I

---

[27] E-C, VI, 304.

[28] [October 12, 1728]: E-C, VII, 137.

[29] E-C, IX, 225.

[30] There is fairly common agreement that the "Virgilius Restauratus" was the work of Dr. Arbuthnot (Lester M. Beattie, *John Arbuthnot: Mathematician and Satirist* [Cambridge, Mass., 1935], p. 284).

[31] *Remarks upon Several Passages in the Preliminaries to the Dunciad* (London, 1729), pp. 7–8. Because Pope was presumably paying the printer, Dennis has surely exaggerated the extent of Wright's annoyance. Pope, it might be added, habitually treated his printers in this fashion. Dr. Johnson, in his life of Pope, gives an account of Pope's somewhat similar handling of a manuscript submitted by him to Robert Dodsley (*Lives of the English Poets, ed.* G. Birkbeck Hill [Oxford, 1905], III, 221).

can't attend & have beggd a Friend to correct yᵉ press for me, who has made some mistakes." [32] Another cause for delay may have existed in Pope's concern for the possible consequences of publishing a work in which he named names, gave detailed information about the private affairs of his dunces, and made specific accusations. Although the courts had been inclined to regard literary lampoons as privileged, laws existed on the basis of which libel actions could be brought; and Pope felt the necessity for caution. [33] Early in 1729 he wrote to the Earl of Burlington requesting that sheets of the poem be shown to the lawyer Nicholas Fazakerley:

> After many unforeseen delays the Printers have got within two sheets of yᵉ book, & I chuse rather to send the papers thus, than defer too long yᵉ material point in which yʳ Lordship's friendship is to procure me Mr. Fazakerley's opinion. The whole question is only this: If there be any thing in these sheets (for yᵉ other two can have nothing of that sort) which an Action may be grounded upon? and if there be, which those things are? that Mʳ. F. wᵈ mark or alter them in this Copy. The time of publication pressing, I cᵈ wish he read them as soon as possible. Yʳ Lᵈship needs not even name *me* as any way concern'd in yᵗ publication, wᶜʰ Mʳ F. will observe is guarded agˢᵗ by yᵉ manner in wᶜʰ it is publish'd. but yᵉ apprehension is only lest if yᵉ Printer & Publisher be found, any such Action could be brought; for we wᵈ be safe even agˢᵗ this. [34]

Subsequently he requested the Earl of Burlington to consult again with Nicholas Fazakerley about arrangements for distributing the work: "Indeed I could be glad of yᵉ Decisive opinion of Mr. Fazakerly it will otherwise be impracticable to publish the thing before Mr. G's [Gay's *Polly* or Gilliver's edition of the *Dunciad*]. and I am grown more Prudent than ever, the less I think others so." [35]

We do not know what suggestions Fazakerley made in response to these queries; but if changes were recommended, publication may have been further delayed. We do know that Pope did contrive a complex arrangement for publishing his poem that would protect himself and the bookseller. First of all he assigned— or pretended to assign [36]—the poem to three of his noble friends, Lord Oxford, Lord Burlington, and Lord Bathurst, whom the dunces would not dare to prosecute. In addition, he made an apparently verbal and extralegal arrangement with the bookseller, Lawton Gilliver, who was to distribute the work in public sale for the

---

[32] Pope to the Earl of Burlington, December 23, 1728: an unpublished letter in the possession of the Chatsworth Estates Company.

[33] Matthew Concanen, in the *London* (or *British*) *Journal*, September 4, 1725, portrays a satirist who, offended by attacks, pretends to discover that the law permits even authors to defend themselves: "I have discovered a Method of defending my Reputation against such *Insolent Attacks*, unknown to all Authors who have lived before me. I can call in the Law to my Assistance; and I do hereby assure all People that read my Works for the future, that it will not be safe to dislike them in the least, or Question *my Capacity for such Undertakings*" (Matthew Concanen, *The Speculatist* [London, 1730], p. 30).

[34] An unpublished letter in the possession of the Chatsworth Estates Company. The last two "sheets," about which Pope was not concerned, contained the noncontroversial "Index . . . [to] . . . the Notes . . . ."

[35] Pope to the Earl of Burlington: from an unpublished letter in the possession of the Chatsworth Estates Company.

[36] Pope was unable, or he was unwilling, to produce a formal assignment by himself in court during suits over the property in the poem which arose in 1743.

three lords and who was probably promised a legal assignment of the property as soon as the danger of an action had passed.[37] Having made these arrangements, Pope next undertook to circulate the work privately.[38] Since he was anxious to have the good will of the Court, he procured the formal presentation of a copy to the King and Queen as a first step in bringing his poem before the public; and on March 13 he wrote Lord Oxford that "the king and queen had the book yesterday by the hands of Sir R[obert] W[alpole], so that your lordship may let me fly." [39] On the twenty-seventh of March he was ready to sell the book privately in Cambridge; and he wrote Lord Oxford again, directing that "about twenty books" be sent there, "but by no means to be given to any bookseller, but disposed of as by your own order at six shillings by any honest gentleman or head of a house." [40] He next resolved on a public sale; and on the eighth of April he wrote John Caryll that the booksellers were even then obtaining copies by the consent of Lord Bathurst.[41] Two days later, April 10, the publication notice appeared in the *Daily Post.*

II

Although the *Dunciad* was Pope's first major effort at verse satire portraying the evils of existing society, the anonymous publication of the poem fooled no one when it first appeared. The work was immediately attributed to its proper author because it illustrated so many of the qualities familiar to readers of his earlier work. Traditional enemies such as John Dennis, Edmund Curll, and Ambrose Philips, whom he had attacked before, were principal targets of the satire; the sacramental view of authorship underlying the charges against the dunces had been a distinctive feature of his own early devotion to letters. In the poem critics were satirized for pride, prejudice, imperfect learning, and lack of settled principles, conditions which had been described in the *Essay on Criticism* as the chief obstacles to good criticism. And the attack upon pedantry, an important aspect of the poem, reiterates ideas that had been the concern of the Scriblerus Club.[42]

---

[37] The formal assignment to Gilliver by the noble lords was made in a document dated October 16, 1729; see Appendix A.

[38] On February 6, 1729, Pope wrote John Caryll that he would "soon have a small parcel to send you, if I know where to leave it to be conveyed safe" (E-C, VI, 304).

[39] E-C, VIII, 250.

[40] E-C, VIII, 252.

[41] E-C, VI, 304–305.

[42] This group, which had undertaken to ridicule abuses in learning, had been formed in consequence of a suggestion that Pope himself had made in the *Spectator* (No. 457, August 14, 1712):

"Now, Sir, it is my Design to Publish every Month, *An Account of the Works of the Unlearned.* Several late Productions of my own Country-men, who many of them make a very Eminent Figure in the Illiterate World, Encourage me in this Undertaking. I may, in this Work, possibly make a Review of several Pieces which have appeared in the Foreign *Accounts* above-mentioned, tho' they ought not to have been taken Notice of in Works which bear such a Title. I may, likewise, take into Consideration such Pieces as appear, from time to time, under the Names of those Gentlemen who Compliment one another in Publick Assemblies, by the Title of the *Learned Gentlemen.* Our Party-Authors will also afford me a great Variety of Subjects, not to mention Editors, Commentators, and others, who are often Men of no Learning, or what is as bad, of no Knowledge. I shall

The *Dunciad* also reflected Pope's early love of fanciful invention. A play of fancy was everywhere to be met with—in the development of the figure of Dullness, in Theobald's propitiatory sacrifice, in the account of the games, and in the trip to the underworld. Pope's fancy, to be sure, shows a mordant quality; but the creator of the sylphs and the Cave of Spleen, of the metamorphosis of the River Loddon, had obviously lost none of his delight in contriving ingenious situations. And the grotesque satiric comedy in the poem had been anticipated in such ludicrous pieces as *The Narrative of Dr. Robert Norris, A Full and True Account of a Horrid and Barbarous Revenge by Poison on the Body of Mr. Edmund Curll,* and the double-mistress episode in the *Memoirs of Martinus Scriblerus.* Furthermore, Pope had always searched for variety in his art; and in the *Dunciad* he made every effort to secure diversity in presentation. How well he succeeded may be judged from the fact that the poem, though its subject is not one that is inherently exciting, sustains interest for over a thousand lines. Each of the three books has different subjects requiring different treatment and achieving different effects. The first book is essentially a ludicrous fancy in which only two figures, Dullness and Theobald in his symbolic capacity as a bad poet, critic, and journalist, play the leading roles. There is much description, for Pope wished to develop detailed and complementary portraits of his personified abstraction and his symbolic hero. The narration is, however, comparatively limited, although the book includes a propitiatory sacrifice and the selection of Theobald as city-poet. Theobald's long speech, in which he addresses himself to his patron goddess, is intended to be absurd, a reflection of the crazy dream-world of Dullness in which all values are distorted. By ingeniously adapting to the preposterous situation a number of details drawn from actual Grub-street practices and Theobald's career, Pope graphically reproduced the grotesque quality of dullness.

The second book approaches sordid reality more closely: the action takes place in readily identifiable locales, and the games are more credible than Theobald's sacrifice. The comedy, therefore, is much more farcical. There is plenty of action, so that only broad strokes and general characterizations are possible. Scatological

---

not enlarge upon this Hint; but if you think any thing can be made of it, I shall set about it with all the Pains and Application that so useful a Work deserves."

In his efforts to push his scheme Pope approached Addison, Swift, Parnell, and Gay; but it was not until early in 1714 that the Scriblerus Club was organized. The membership included Swift, Arbuthnot, Gay, Parnell, Lord Oxford, and Pope: their aim was to ridicule abuses in Learning in a series of prose satires. Because of his particular interests and special qualifications Pope was to concentrate upon the "fine arts" (*The Works of Alexander Pope* [1751], VI, 112 n.). Before 1720 he had drafted a number of pieces in the Scriblerean vein. Late in 1714 he published *A Key to the Lock; or, A Treatise Proving, beyond all Contradiction, the Dangerous Tendency of a late Poem Entituled, The Rape of the Lock, to Government and Religion. By Esdras Barnivelt.* Subsequently Gay, in collaboration with Pope and Arbuthnot, composed a full-length farce, *Three Hours after Marriage,* in which foolish virtuosi and blundering critics were severely ridiculed. Several minor prose pieces, generally attributed to Pope, were also sketched during these years: *Stradling versus Stiles,* a parody of legal jargon and legalistic quibbling, written in collaboration with William Fortescue; and *Memoirs of P. P., Clerk of this Parish,* a burlesque of the egotism and loquaciousness of memoir writers.

wit is employed; for the chief business of this section is to make merely odious the participants in the games, the peripheral figures in literature. Because there is an obvious similarity among the games, Pope varied circumstances and characters and introduced surprise into the episodes.

The third book, which deals with Theobald's visionary trip to the underworld, is, like the first book, a fantasy; and, as in the first, narrative is not important. The larger share of this concluding book is given over to a long speech by Settle, matching Theobald's speech in the first. To achieve the desired variation, however, this speech differs from Theobald's; the satire is that of direct invective and abuse, the words making explicit what in the first book of the poem had been largely implicit. Furthermore, Settle's speech is not dramatic, for it does not characterize the speaker in the way that Theobald's speech is intended to characterize Theobald. Indeed, Settle serves primarily as a mouthpiece for Pope, delivering the latter's judgments upon Grub-street personalities and institutions. There was nothing new to readers of Pope in such diversity; but its presence in the *Dunciad* indicates that inventive excellence remained a goal of his art.

If there is much in the *Dunciad* indicating the persistence of ideas and artistic goals that had given distinction to his early work, there is also much that reveals Pope's growth as a satirist. It reflects a greater range of interests and a more mature understanding of men. Few of the weaknesses that can plague authors are passed over. Moreover, Pope, possibly because he employed verse, exercised more control over satiric episodes than he had done in his early prose satires. Underlying the poem is the concept to which Pope in the *Essay on Man* was to give memorable expression. Man is placed on an "isthmus of a middle state," a "Chaos of Thought and Passion, all confus'd." Existing between beast and angel, he may prefer his mind or body; but his ethical duty is to realize his moral potentialities in the face of ever-present temptations to revert to the beast. His pursuit of perfection is, furthermore, complicated by human pride, so that the faster he retrogresses, the more he may convince himself that he is achieving progress. This theme is dramatically illustrated by the role assigned to the goddess of dullness in the poem. To the dunces she is a positive force, a queen, a goddess, a mother to be worshipped and obeyed; yet in reality she is a negative thing, a void or vacuum, the spirit of intellectual and moral negation. Worship of her is thus a denial of all that distinguishes man from the brute creation; and in the animal imagery applied to the dunces persistently throughout the poem Pope illustrates his thesis that they, by living for the times rather than redeeming them, by disregarding moral values and the forms through which these values may be communicated, have identified themselves with brutes rather than with the angels. And they threaten the very existence of the civilization that men have created by their own past efforts.[43]

Equally indicative of the growth of Pope's mind is his attempt in the *Dunciad*

---

[43] To point up this anatopism Pope utilized Milton's *Paradise Lost* as a frame of reference. For Dullness is presented as the daughter of "Chaos and Old Night"; and she is engaged in the task of restoring to Chaos those parts of his realm which have previously been lost to light.

to relate dullness to the ethos of contemporary society. More than once he insists that the mercenary spirit of the age has affected writers in Dullness's court. Vanity, jealousy, and ambition have inspired much inferior craftsmanship; but sordid venality, contracted from contemporary mores, has also helped. The opposition of gold and truth is symbolically presented in the initial description of Dullness in the Cave of Poverty and Poetry:

> Four guardian Virtues, round, support her Throne; . . .
> Poetic Justice, with her lifted scale;
> Where in nice balance, truth with gold she weighs,
> And solid pudding against empty praise.
>   (I, ll. 44, 50–52)

In subsequent passages readers are shown publishers who, in search of profits, encourage authors to prostitute all principles; journalists who indulge in calumny for hire; and "contending theatres" which compete with one another in efforts to attract large audiences by farce, pantomime, and mere spectacle. This attempt to relate literary iniquity to the venality of the day introduces into Pope's poetry a theme which, though it had previously been expressed in his private letters, was later to be conspicuous in most of his writing. The *Epistle to the Earl of Burlington* demonstrates how riches may corrupt taste; the fourth epistle of the *Essay on Man* is a vigorous defense of traditional humane virtues in opposition to external and material measures of happiness; the *Epistle to Lord Bathurst* anatomizes the personal corruptions that attend acquisitive enterprise; and the *Imitations of Horace* portray at length times that scorn "the Flesh, the Dev'l, and all but Gold." [44] In the *Dunciad Variorum* Pope did not focus, as he was later to do, so intensely upon this aspect of the follies he describes; but certainly there do emerge the major terms of a formula by which he was later to characterize his age. [45]

Pope is more independent with regard to the formal structure of his poem than readers of his earlier work would expect. Although he utilized the mock-heroic manner, he did not impose upon his materials the rigid pattern he had followed in the *Rape of the Lock*, where the episodes are disposed in a manner similar to that prevailing in the five-act structure of contemporary comedy. [46] He did not exploit rigorously a single, actual event; but he created, instead, a loose narrative frame based on the idea of a coronation and admitting diverse fantastic episodes which give increasingly comprehensive prospects of Dullness's dominion.

In the first book attention is focused upon Dullness and her votary Theobald; in the second book, through the account of the games, the perspective widens and we are shown other followers of Dullness, the peripheral figures of literature— booksellers, patrons, and critics. In the vision presented to Theobald in the third book, the perspective is further enlarged by the spectacle of all the literary arts

---

[44] *Second Satire of John Donne Versified*, l. 24.

[45] This aspect of the poem has been treated by Hugo M. Reichard, "Pope's Social Satire: Belles-Lettres and Business," *PMLA*, LXVII (1952), 420–34.

[46] James L. Jackson, "Pope's *The Rape of the Lock* Considered as a Five-Act Epic," *PMLA*, LXV (1950), 1283–87.

under Dullness's spell. This plan meant that an obviously articulated unity of action in which episodes follow one upon another with inevitable logical necessity is lacking. Readers are allowed to lose sight of the coronation, and even of the hero Theobald. There is, furthermore, no consistent or systematic exploitation of the mock-heroic idea; for Pope frequently descended from the elevated irony of the grand style to direct and forthright denigration. Admirers of *The Rape of the Lock* have deplored the lack of neatness in this structure; but one must not overlook the greater range of commentary, the larger view of the literary follies of the time, made possible by the looser and more thematic arrangement of materials. And, if Pope sacrificed something of form for the sake of content, the poem represents an interesting prelude to what follows—his use of the epistolary manner of Horatian satire. This form readily admitted the kind of freedom he was compelled to struggle for within the *Dunciad's* narrative frame.

The poem provides another measure of Pope's character as a satirist in that it was his first major verse satire to employ consistently the technique of particular as opposed to general satire. Although Pope by nature was tempted to use the concrete and specific in his poetry, the choice of living examples was in large part determined by the character of the *Dunciad*. The proposition that dullness posed a threat to letters became more cogent when supported by actual rather than by hypothetical examples. Moreover, the proliferation of the names of insignificant figures happily supported the contention that the dunces individually were negligible figures whose reputations would soon die. Posterity, not readily recognizing the personalities mentioned, could easily accept the validity of the assertion. The fact that identifications could not always be made meant, however, that Pope had to supply a subordinate interest by exploiting the artistic possibilities inherent in names. He varied the selection as much as possible; he attempted to use names in a manner appropriate to the logic of the passages in which they occur. He employed names that were strange, bizarre, or intrinsically comic; and he exploited cacophonous properties for onomatopoetic effects. Fortunately Grub-street provided him with plenty of names; and almost unlimited substitution was possible.[47]

Manuscript readings of the poem reveal how carefully he had searched for names that would be effective.[48] For example, he made at least three attempts before line 230 of Book I was ready for the press in 1728:

> Can make a Cibber, Bladen, or Ozell.
> (Marginalia, 1728, p. 13)

> Can make a Shadwell, Welstead, or Ozell
> (Marginalia, 1728, p. 13)

---

[47] The remark on the subject made in "The Publisher to the Reader" should not be taken too seriously: "And I should judge they were clapp'd in as they rose, fresh and fresh, and chang'd from day to day, in like manner as when the old boughs wither, we thrust new ones into a chimney" (Sutherland, p. 206). Pope was less casual in selecting his dunces than he pretended to admit.

[48] See Appendix B for the source of manuscript readings given in the text. In illustrations drawn from Richardson's record of manuscript variants I have given the printed form last. Unfortunately, except in isolated cases which are specifically noted, it is impossible to determine from Richardson's marginalia the order of variants.

Can make a C[ibbe]r, Jo[hnso]n, or O[ze]ll
(1728, I, l. 230)

He also made three revisions before he was satisfied with line 240 of Book I:

Where Dunton, Babor, Gildon, Howard rest!
(Marginalia, 1728, p. 13)

Where Touchin, Banks, and high-born Howard rest!
(Marginalia, 1728, p. 13)

Where G[ildo]n, B[anks], and high-born H[oward] rest!
(1728, I, l. 240)

More complicated changes and rearrangements occur in a long passage in which Pope sought to capture by sound and syntax something of the confusion and vociferation of the contest of critics he was describing (the passages are given in the order in which they were revised):

Now thousand Tongues are heard in one loud Din,
Welsted & Wicksted at each other grin;
'Twas mouthing, chattring, answring, snip-snap all,
Kelsal at Cibber, Cibber at Breval.
Now, shrugging, all was wrong, now nodding, right,
Now Friends they hug, now Enemies they bite.
Scramble o'er empty Authors, & dispute
For Shells of which a Meggot is the Fruit.
(Marginalia, 1728, verso
of title page)

Now thousand Tongues are heard in one loud Din,
Sudden ye Monkey Critics all rush in:
'Twas chattr^s, grin^s, mouth^s, jabbring all,
Welsted at Wicksted, Cibber at Breval.
Now shrugging, all was wrong; now nodding, right,
Now Friends they hug, now they writhe & bite
Enucleate empty Authors, & dispute
Those Nuts of which a Meggot is the Fruit.
(Marginalia, 1728, verso of title page)

Now thousand tongues are heard in one loud din,
The Monkey critics all rush in;
'Twas chatt'ring, grinning, mouthing, jabb'ring all,
Welsted at Wicksted, Budgel at Breval,
And loud tongu'd Dissonance; & each sustains his part.
With snip-snap short, and interruption smart.
(Marginalia, 1728, p. 26)

When the lines were finally first printed in 1728, they had been once more re-worked:

Now thousand tongues are heard in one loud din,
The Monkey-mimicks rush discordant in;

'Twas chatt'ring, grinning, mouthing, jabb'ring all,
And R———, and railing, Brangling, and B———,
D———s and Dissonance; And captious art,
And snip-snap short, and interruption smart.
(1728, II, ll. 215–20)

In these examples the demands of onomatopoeia seem largely to have dictated the alterations; but in other passages names were substituted in order to support a central or controlling idea. For example, among Richardson's marginalia we have two versions of one passage:

Concanen next, and Michel's rueful face!
One great of stomach, one of greater mind,
And thousand thousand nameless names behind.
(Marginalia, 1728, p. 44)

Concanen meek, and Michel's rueful face!
Cook great of stomach, Horneck <light> of mind,
And thousand thousand nameless names behind.
(Marginalia, 1728, p. 44)

When these lines were about to be published in 1728, they were expanded and altered:

Lo H[orne]ck's fierce and M[ichel]'s rueful face!
W[otto]n, the scourge of Scripture, mark with awe!
And mighty J[aco]b Blunderbus of Law!
Lo thousand thousand, ev'ry nameless name,
All crowd, who foremost shall be damn'd to fame; . . .
(1728, III, ll. 154–58)

And in 1729 they were revised again:

Lo Horneck's fierce, and Roome's funereal face;
Lo sneering G[oo]de, half malice and half whim,
A Fiend in glee, ridiculously grim.
Jacob, the Scourge of Grammar, mark with awe,
Nor less revere him, Blunderbuss of Law.
Lo Bond and Foxton, ev'ry nameless name,
All crowd, who foremost shall be damn'd to Fame?
(III, ll. 146–52)

Obviously, in making these changes, Pope was influenced by the need to support the idea of "nameless names" with a substantial catalogue and by the logic which called for the naming of the obscurer denizens of Grub-street in place of more widely publicized figures.

The *Dunciad* illustrates major developments in Pope's technique and yet, at the same time, a certain lack of direction in his major satirical intention. The charges leveled against the dunces—however brilliantly stated—were sometimes basically conventional, in the tradition of literary controversy. Pope failed to achieve a perfect unity of impression; for his desire to portray all the faults of writers in his day in terms of dullness attenuated the concept to a point where it lost some of its meaning. Furthermore, the poem involved an imperfect fusion of ethical idealism and purely personal animus. Pope did not subordinate his own personal antagonisms to his larger purposes, and his work does not have sufficient meaning and relevance apart from his personal quarrels. In selecting examples he most frequently chose writers who had personally offended him; and, indeed, in the "Publisher to the Reader" prefixed to the *Dunciad* of 1728, readers were told that no man living is attacked who "had not before printed or published some scandal against" Pope.[49] In the notes to lines he frequently justified the charge of dullness in terms of offenses individual dunces had given him; and some of the prose pieces annexed to the *Dunciad Variorum*—"The Testimonies of Authors," "A List of Books, Papers, and Verses in which our Author was Abused," and "A Parallel of the Characters of Mr. Dryden and Mr. Pope"—betray how much purely personal indignation went into the work.

III

Although Pope once confessed to Swift that an object of his *Dunciad* was to "rid me of these insects,"[50] his belief that severe humiliation would shame his enemies into silence was naive. The *Dunciad Variorum* created new enemies and gave new life to old ones; and their fulminations did much to shape the course of Pope's later work as well as to condition subsequent responses by readers to his satire. Although the diatribes lacked quality, they were sufficiently shrill to be persuasive. The campaign against Pope by his dunces was helped by the fact that a group of Grub-street authors had banded together to war upon him soon after the *Peri Bathous* came out; and with the publication of the *Dunciad* this group immediately began to retaliate.[51] *Mist's Weekly Journal,* June 8 and June 15, 1728, inserted notices describing the plans of the cabal, which the writer facetiously dubbed the "Knights of the Bathos":

To be publish'd Weekly in this Paper,
May 27, 1728

By Authority,

THIS Day at a GENERAL COURT of the KNIGHTS of the BATHOS, Esquires, Gentlemen, and others of the same Society, and of all the worshipful and weighty Members of this ancient and solid Body, it was *resolved,*

That our sessions, hitherto held at Mr. C [url] l's in the *Strand,* be henceforth removed to the *Blue Posts* at *Charing Cross,* in regard to the President of this Society, who is too aged to walk farther from his lodgings.

And that for the greater Tranquillity of this our Sessions, and better Security of the Members thereof, it be held for the future only on *Sundays* (as has been practised on great Emergencies.)

---

[49] Sutherland, p. 203.

[50] March 23, 1728: E-C, VII, 124.

[51] On April 14, 1728, Edward Young, reporting London gossip to Thomas Tickell in Ireland, wrote: "I have no Manner of News, but that the offended Wits, are entered into a Club to take Revenge on Swift & Pope for their late attack & that hitherto they have justified all that can be said ag^t them" (R. E. Tickell, *Thomas Tickell and the Eighteenth-Century Poets,* p. 146). See Appendix E for an attempt to list pamphlets produced in answer to the *Dunciad,* as well as to Pope's other major satires.

Resolv'd, Nemine contradicente, that a Committee of this whole Lower House, do consult on Ways and Means for reducing the *current Sense* of this Kingdom, and the exorbitant Power of the *Pope.*

Order'd, That all Papers, Pamphlets, Letters, Advertisements, &c. relating to the said *Pope,* which have past since the *First of April* last, be laid on the Table, in order to be revised and published in one Volume, not exceeding the Value of *one Shilling, one Penny, half penny.*

Order'd, that a Committee of Secrecy be appointed to draw up a Report against the said *Pope.* And that Mr. *M[ore-Smythe]*, Mr. *W[elsted]*, Mr. *D[ennis]*, and the Rev. Mr. *W[esley]* do prepare and bring in the same.

Mr. *A[aron] H[ill]* petition'd to be excus'd on Account of some Business he had to do in *Muscovy.*

The Rev. Mr. *W[esley]* did the same, on Account of an ancient Friendship between his *best Patron* and the *Pope.*

Order'd, That a *Key* to the *Dunciade* be composed; and that Mr. *C[url]l* attend next *Saturday,* to receive Instructions for the same.

A Message from Mr. *C[url]l,* by Mr. *C[oo]k,* that Mr. *C[url]l* humbly craves to be excus'd from coming to Charing-Cross, so soon after his standing in the *Pillory* there.

Order'd, that Mr. *C[oo]k* do compose the said *Key* to the *Dunciade.*

And then this House adjourn'd till after the Holidays.

I do appoint Edm. C[url]l *to print all the Votes, Resolutions Orders and Reports of this most dishonourable House,* and that no other person presume to print the same.

J[ames] M[ore] S[mythe]. Speaker

The next week *Mist's Weekly Journal* published an account of the further proceedings of the Knights:

Sir, I send you a Piece of News concerning the present unnatural War betwixt the Sons of Parnassus, which, perhaps, is not yet come to your Notice.

There have been several hot Skirmishes of late, betwixt the Parties concern'd in the political War, to which both Sides claim the Advantage. The Allies of Charing Cross, lately held a Council concerning the Operations of the Campaign, in which it was resolved to besiege the *Pope* at T[wickenha]m, and to open the Trenches without LOSS of Time; they also came to a Resolution to begin their Attack by a *Battery of Epigrams,* by which they propose to beat down a certain *Pillar of Fame,* which has been the chief Support of his *Holiness:* their Engineers having view'd the said Pillar, and found it to stand upon a very tottering Foundation. On the other Side, his *Holiness* has not been idle for having Intelligence of their Designs by his *Spies,* he is laying in a Magazine of *Satyr,* which being fill'd with *merdose* Matter, he thinks, will annoy the Enemy, and oblige them to raise the Siege.

P. S. There is a Rumour, that the Allies having discovered one *E[dmun]d C[url]l* lurking about their head Quarters, they siez'd him, and found him to be one of the *Pope's* Spies; upon which, according to the Law of Arms, they hang'd him up immediately; he died very hard, and no Body pittied him.

Both of these notices anticipate the publications that were to appear in the following weeks; and there is no reason to doubt that the dunces were collaborating closely in their revenge.

Judging from what was produced, the cabal planned to attack several clearly defined aspects of Pope and his writing. There was a conspicuous effort to blacken his moral character and thus cast doubt on the motives that had prompted the *Dunciad.* The charges which had earlier been aired against him were revived once more—his allegedly unethical practices in misrepresenting his share in the *Odyssey* translation, his composition of obscene and blasphemous verses, his supposed ingratitude and treachery with respect to Addison and Wycherley. The dunces, taking their cue from Pope's "character" of Addison, asserted that he had been ungenerous to other poets, arguing that he attacked those who received applause equal to or greater than that accorded his own work. In *Sawney,* for example, James Ralph portrayed Pope as seeking aid from Shameless (Swift) and Hounslow (Gay) against rivals who had published the truth about him. This unsavory triumvirate then plan the *Dunciad,* summoning the aid of Envy and Fraud. Fancy, Imagination, and Invention, when solicited, refuse to help the three writers, however, because the three have for so long derived their inspiration from Spleen, Pride, Revenge, and Ill-nature. The following lines from Edward Ward's *Durgen* are equally representative of the kind, and quality, of the invective directed at the poet's moral character during the campaign against his *Dunciad:*

> To ease his Spleen, at e'ery Author growls,
> And deems his wiser Brethren Frogs and Owls,
> Strikes at 'em all with an audacious Hand,
> And strives to humble those he can't command. . . .
> Pride, the sure Comrade of ill-natur'd Wit,
> Will still persist, 'tis Penance to submit;
> For Self-conceit makes weak Offenders strong,
> And buoys up proud Aggressors in the wrong;
> Supports a vile callumniating Crew,
> And prompts Lampooners to report, like you,
> Injurious Falsehoods, scandalously base,
> Too mean to gain Applause or fix Disgrace.[52]

Some critics, asserting that Pope's popularity with readers had declined, declared that his indulgence in satire was an effort to reclaim his public: "The poor Gentleman had long found himself upon the Decline, his Strength failing him, his Credit and Reputation sinking, in short, he was just setting in the poetical Hemisphere, when he resolves to make one last Push for all, and vainly endeavours to evade his Fall by levelling others with himself." [53]

Nearly all the dunces asserted that he was trying to dominate literature of the day and was making what should be a democracy into a monarchy. To emphasize this point they hit upon the pun involved in his surname and compared his attempts to rule letters with the efforts of the Pope in Rome to assert infallibility. Jonathan Smedley prepared an extended comparison between the two rulers, of which the following is characteristic:

They both usurp over greater, wiser, wittier, and better Men than themselves.

They both revile, curse and damn every one who won't admire and adore them.

They both give every one to Satan, who won't subscribe to their Rules and Directions, or who pretends to find Fault with any thing they do. . . .

---

[52] Edward Ward, *Durgen: or, A Plain Satyr upon a Pompous Satyrist* (London, 1729), pp. 4–5.
[53] *An Essay upon the Taste and Writings of the Present Times* (London, 1728), pp. 4–5.

One, as impiously, pretends to the sole *Propriety* of *Parnassus,* as t'other does to the *Keys* of *Heaven.*[54]

In order to show that Pope's assumption of authority was merely arbitrary, the dunces spent much time pointing to weaknesses and ineptitudes in his own writing:

> They meet,
> With one Consent, in *Windsor*'s Shades, and join
> Their Forces to o'erturn the Flatt'ring Pile,
> Unjustly rear'd to SAWNEY's Name.[55]

Dennis's criticisms of *Windsor Forest* and the *Temple of Fame* were re-published; and his as yet unpublished critique of the *Rape of the Lock* was brought out. Edmund Curll prepared a pamphlet entitled the *Popiad,* in which Blackmore's and Dennis's strictures on the *Iliad* were freely quoted. Some pamphlets attempted more general reviews of Pope's writings. James Ralph in *Sawney* examined the early major poems to prove that each was a poor attempt to imitate the work of earlier poets. The *Essay on Criticism* was alleged to be a series of borrowed senti-ments; the *Rape of the Lock* was declared to be nothing but a poor imitation of Garth and Boileau. Pope had failed to emulate Dryden successfully in his ode honoring St. Cecilia:

> SAWNEY attempts the like,
> And makes a div'lish Rout with Organs, Bells,
> And Bagpipes; then sends *Orpheus* down to Hell,
> With a soft Sing-song, to redeem his Spouse,
> And muzzle *Cerberus:* The forfeit Spouse
> Restor'd, again descends; an hideous moan
> Bewails her Doom, and, with a gen'ral Voice,
> The sad Musicians vote poor SAWNEY's Verse
> A victim to appease her plaintive Shade. . . .[56]

In the *Temple of Fame,* Ralph asserted, Pope had plagiarized from Chaucer to advance his own reputation; and in *Eloisa to Abelard* he had tried unsuccessfully to emulate Prior's success with *Henry and Emma.*

The *Peri Bathous* provided the dunces with hints as to another way in which Pope's writings might be attacked; and they searched for examples of bathetic expression—or for examples that could be made to appear bathetic. "An Auction of Goods at Twickenham," published in the *Daily Journal,* April 5, 1728, presented a list of awkward and incongruous epithets culled from Pope's poetry; and Mat-thew Concanen in *A Supplement to the Profund* examined the poems in the light of Pope's own standards for the bathos. Ned Ward, somewhat more ingen-iously, worked into the text of his *Durgen* a generous sampling of allegedly inept poetic phrases Pope himself had used:

> *A triple Dog,* barks noble in the line.
> *A dancing Cork* too, is extremely fine.
> The mottled Girl, his *Many colour'd Maid,*

---

[54] *Gulliveriana: or, A Fourth Volume of Miscellanies* (London, 1728), p. 284.
[55] James Ralph, *Sawney: An Heroic Poem. Occasion'd by the Dunciad* (London, 1728), p. 43.
[56] *Sawney,* p. 10.

> May pass for once upon an *oozy Bed;*
> *A branching Deer,* meet with his *feather'd Fate,*
> And *winged Wonder* stand amaz'd thereat.
> But how can any *pensive Steed* complain,
> When gently Gallup'd o'er *a velvet Plain?*
> Much better than to bear a galling Load,
> In Winter weather, thro' a *liquid Road;*
> But if he meets *brown Horror* in the way,
> Or at *blue Languish* starts and runs away,
> Should a Rouge's [*sic*] Pistol Bullet stop his Breath,
> He may be said to dye a *leaden Death,*
> And spight of all our Criticks, be allow'd
> To fall down dead beneath *a living Cloud,*
> And so become a Prodigy, I mean,
> *A quiv'ring shade* or *a sequester'd Scene.*[57]

The pamphlet war against Pope was largely over by September, 1728, possibly because the public was no longer interested and because the dunces had decided to wait until the final version of the *Dunciad Variorum,* which every one knew Pope was working on, came out. When it finally did appear in April, 1729, hostilities were renewed. All the old charges were again reiterated; for the truth seems to be that the dunces lacked ammunition, or else they were lazy. Either they were unimaginative, in which case Pope's description of them as dull was justified, or there was not much for them to say. The *Dunciad Variorum* did, however, give them a new advantage which they exploited. For the notes in which Pope attempted to make specific charges against writers appearing in the poem contained much erroneous and distorted information; and it was an easy matter for the dunces to assert that he had maliciously misrepresented the facts. Proving him a liar was the significant development in the campaign against him after the publication of the *Dunciad Variorum.* Edmund Curll devoted a large portion of the *Curliad* to an explanation of his relations with Pope, in which he principally sought to correct charges in the notes of the *Dunciad.* Dennis's *Remarks upon Several Passages in the Preliminaries to the Dunciad* and the pamphlet *Pope Alexander's Supremacy and Infallibility Examined,* sometimes attributed to Dennis, sought to prove that Pope's version of his relations with Dennis was at best inaccurate. Ned Ward's *Apollo's Maggot* concluded with a lengthy "Postscript" reviewing the "Falshoods by Alexander Pope against Edward Ward." In the summer of 1730 Matthew Concanen brought out *The Speculatist,* a collection of his essays formerly published in the *London Journal* and the *British Journal,* in order "to refute the Calumny of a rancorous and foul-mouth'd Railer who has asserted in print that the Author of them wrote *several Scurrilities* in those Papers." [58]

It is, of course, easy to exaggerate the immediate importance to Pope of this pamphlet campaign. The dunces were really insignificant; and their replies were

---

[57] *Durgen,* p. 27. The italicized phrases are from Pope's poetry.
[58] *The Speculatist* (London, 1730), p. [v].

so obviously intemperate and dull that they merely confirmed all he had said of them. Nevertheless, the *Dunciad* had been undertaken in part to silence these enemies; and it certainly did not accomplish this end. Of more consequence to Pope was the fact that his friends believed that he had committed himself to a futile and unprofitable undertaking. Bishop Atterbury, who had once declared that Pope's real genius lay in satire, was particularly distressed by the venture; and he wrote to his son-in-law, William Morice, on August 3–14, 1728, immediately after he had seen a copy of the *Dunciad* of 1728:

I find many are of my sentiment with regard to the Dunciad, and think the writer has engaged himself in a very improper and troublesome scuffle, not worthy of his pen at all, which was designed for greater purposes. Nor can all the good poetry in those three cantos make amends for the trouble and teasing they will occasion to him. Tell him so, directly, in my name; and tell him, that what I say proceeds from a tender regard I have for every thing that concerns him. I find by Mist, that Pope will be pursued with all the little spite of which that set of poor creatures is capable;—and that they will endeavour to hurt him chiefly upon the head of good-nature and probity; allowing him all manner of advantages in poetry.[59]

In November, 1729, after Pope had brought out the *Dunciad Variorum* Atterbury addressed himself in the same terms directly to Pope:

Your mind is as yet unbroken by age and ill accidents, your knowledge and judgment are at the height: use them in writing somewhat that may teach the present and future times, and if not gain equally the applause of both, may yet raise the envy of the one, and secure the admiration of the other. Employ not your precious moments and great talents on little men and little things; but choose a subject every way worthy of you, and handle it as you can, in a manner which nobody else can equal or imitate.[60]

Aaron Hill wrote a poem, *The Progress of Wit: a Caveat for the Use of an Eminent Writer,* in which he depicted Pope as one sailing across the stream of life from the shores of Oblivion to those of Fame. Blessed with every talent, he is attacked during his journey by a swarm of insects, against whom he employs energies that should have been utilized more constructively:

> Still, tho' he stagnates, he the Fight maintains,
> While Drones, applausive, with their ductile Strains,
> Homage the rising Hero's new Renown,
> And *Prince of Fly-Catchers* the Champion crown.[61]

Six months later Hill published another poem in which he reiterated the criticism in a more friendly tone:

> Let *vulgar Genii,* sowr'd by sharp Disdain,
> Piqu'd, and malignant, *Word's* low *War* maintain,
> —While every *meaner* Art exerts her Aim,
> O'er Rival Arts, to lift Her question'd Fame,
> Let half-soul'd *Poets,* still, *on Poets* fall,

---

[59] *Epistolary Correspondence, Visitation Charges, Speeches, and Miscellanies of the Right Reverend Francis Atterbury* (London, 1783–87), IV, 136–38.
[60] E-C, IX, 60–61.
[61] *Progress of Wit* (London, 1730) p. 29.

> And teach the *willing* World to scorn them *All.*
> But, let no *Muse,* pre-eminent as *Thine,*
> Of Voice melodious, and of Force divine,
> Stung by *Wit's Wasps,* all Rights of Rank forego,
> And turn, and snarl, and bite, at Every Foe.
> No—like Thy own *Ulysses,* make no *Stay:*
> Shun *Monsters*—and pursue thy streamy Way.
> Wing'd, by the Muse's *God,* to rise, sublime,
> What has thy Fame to *fear,* from peevish Rhyme? [62]

George Lyttelton, then a young man unknown to Pope, addressed a poem to him in which he asked:

> When every soft, engaging Muse is thine,
> Why court the least attractive of the Nine? [63]

Edward Young, who at the time enjoyed a reputation as a leading satirist, also condemned by implication the personal quality of the poem. In his *Two Epistles to Mr. Pope concerning the Authors of the Age* he asserted that the vices and follies of authors need correction; but he lamented the way in which authors had descended to personalities in their efforts to correct:

> If Satire charms, strike faults, but spare the man,
> 'Tis Dull to be as Witty as you can.
> Satire recoils whenever charg'd too high,
> Round your own Fame the fatal splinters fly.
> As the soft Plume gives Swiftness to the Dart,
> Good breeding sends the Satire to the Heart.
>   Painters and Surgeons may the *structure* scan,
> *Genius* and *Morals* be with you the *Man:*
> Defaults in those alone shou'd give offence;
> Who strikes the *Person,* pleads his Innocence.
> My narrow-minded Satire can't extend
> To *Codrus'* Form, I'm not so much his Friend.
> Himself shou'd publish that (the World agree)
> Before his Works, or in the Pillory.
> Let him be black, fair, tall, short, thin or fat,
> Dirty or clean, I find no Theme in That. [64]

In the eyes of most of Pope's contemporaries, the *Dunciad* had not appreciably enhanced his reputation. He introduced into it new themes, new ideas; and he gave his readers a dazzling display of satiric inventiveness. But the poem is burdened by an accumulation of personal grievances that were unworthy of true genius; and much art is squandered on what was obvious to any intelligent reader. The attempt to settle old scores also created ill feeling that was to have a lasting effect on Pope's future work. Fear of what his angry enemies might say forced him on more than one occasion to publish his work circumspectly; and much of his later

---

[62] *Advice to the Poets* (London, 1731), p. 18.
[63] *An Epistle to Mr. Pope, from a Young Gentleman at Rome* (London, 1730), p. 5.
[64] *Two Epistles to Mr. Pope* (London, 1730), p. 37.

poetry reflects his desire to correct the portrait of his moral character to which the dunces had given currency. Most important of all, his respectable critics having deplored a waste of talent upon fools whose follies were obvious, whose dullness was manifest in their decision to attack Alexander Pope, he was stimulated to strenuous efforts to create a lasting monument to his genius. Such stimulation largely made possible the *Essay on Man,* the *Ethic Epistles,* and the *Imitations of Horace.* We cannot, therefore, regret Pope's attempt to pay off his enemies.

CHAPTER THREE

The *Essay on Man* and the *Ethic Epistles*

Almost immediately after the publication of the *Dunciad Variorum,* Pope told Elijah Fenton that he had resolved to write in the future "nothing but epistles in Horace's manner"; [1] and by November, 1729, he had actually begun the work that resulted in the *Essay on Man* and four *Ethic Epistles.* For at this time Bolingbroke wrote to Swift: "Bid him [Pope] talk to you of the work he is about, I hope in good earnest. It is a fine one; and will be, in his hands, an original. His sole complaint is, that he finds it too easy in the execution." [2] Pope's plans, however, were probably not well settled. He was able to describe the project as a "system of ethics in the Horatian way"; [3] and we may guess that his conception was partly influenced by the form of Edward Young's currently popular *Universal Passion,* in which a number of generalized satirical "characters" appear in a setting of moralizing commentary. [4] But that he had more specific ideas at this early date is doubtful.

Even early in 1730 the plans which Pope had formed for his work bear little direct relationship to the poems which were actually produced. Among the unpublished items which will appear in the forthcoming edition of Spence's *Anecdotes* (being prepared by Mr. James M. Osborn of Yale University) there is a note indicating that early in 1730 Pope was contemplating a design for his moral poems in which the "several behaviours of men [were to be] flung into fables." A memorandum of one of Pope's conversations with Joseph Spence, May 1–7, 1730, indicates that plans had become somewhat more settled—and more like the plans that governed the poems which were eventually produced:

Mr. Pope How wrong y° Greatest men have been in judging of the Cause of Human Actions. Instance frō Machiavel, of concluding in y° general frō particulars (w^r Besiegd Forces ought to sally or not?) Instance frō—of judg^g of a particular frō y° General: (a person fights too soon: *bec:* he is of a Vindicative temper.) Montaigne hence concludes Pyrrhonically, That nothing can be known of the Workings of men's minds: 1 Essay, lib. 2? (The best in his whole book. There? y° Instance of Tiberius' growing an open man all at once. That Openness really y° highest piece of Dissimulation.)—New Hypothesis, That a prevailing passion in y° mind is brought wth it into y° world, & continues till death (illustrated, by y° Seeds of y° Illness y^t is at last to destroy us, being planted in y° body at our births.)

We s^d not speak agst one large Vice, without speaking agst its contrary.—As to y° General Design of Providence y° two Extremes of a Vice, serve like two opposite biasses

---

[1] Elijah Fenton to William Broome, June 24 [1729]: E-C, VIII, 155.

[2] E-C, VII, 176.

[3] Pope to Swift, November 28, 1729: E-C, VII, 175.

[4] Charlotte E. Crawford, "What was Pope's Debt to Edward Young?" *ELH,* XIII (1946), 157–67.

to keep up ye Ballance of things. Avarice, lays up (w^t w^d be hurtful;) Prodigality, scatters abroad (w^t may be useful in other hands:) The middle ye point for Virtue: M^r P has very large (prose) collections on ye Happiness of Contentment. Prodigality (in his piece) flings away all in wrong tastes. (Tis there in particular y^t some of ye Gardening Poem will be of Service.) (Ld Bolingbroke has sent M^r P a long letter on these heads; & has by him w^t w^d make 6 or 7 sheets in print toward a Second; & does not know how far it may grow; Mr Sav:)

The first Epistle? is to be to ye Whole work, w^t a Scale is to a book of Maps: in this lies ye greatest difficulty: not only in settling all ye parts, but in making them agreeable enough to be read with pleasure. Sr Balaam: The man of Ross: The Standing jest of Heaven. And sure ye Gods & We are of a mind. The Man possesd of Debts & Taxes clear, Children & Wife—Five hundred pound a year (Publ: Buildings Alms Houses, Walks, Road;) The man of Ross divides ye weekly bread: Public Table twice a week for Strangers &c.—Will give w^t we desire; Fire, Meat, & Drink—What more? Meat, Drink, & fire. No judging of a piece frō ye Scatter'd parts: ye 3 dots, & Hieroglyphic: (not as to ye Great Beauty: but we may see particular beauties in ye parts? That's very true.)[5]

Many ideas and phrases familiar to readers of the *Ethic Epistles* and the *Essay on Man* occur in these rough notes: references to the poem on avarice include phrases subsequently appearing in the epistle addressed to Lord Bathurst; and materials destined for a poem on prodigality were included in the *Epistle to the Earl of Burlington*. The "very large (prose) collections on ye Happiness of Contentment," which were originally planned for the poem treating the mean between avarice and profusion, were later used in the fourth epistle of the *Essay on Man*. Nevertheless, the poems described in Spence's note do not exactly resemble those later published. For in May, 1730, Pope was thinking of four different epistles, one of which was to serve as an introduction ("w^t a Scale is to a book of Maps") to the other three.[6] The subject of this introduction was, judging from Spence's notes, similar to the subject of the second epistle in the *Essay on Man* and of the *Epistle to Lord Cobham*. The other three epistles called for in the plans of May, 1730, were to deal respectively with avarice, profusion, and "ye point for Virtue," a neat scheme that Pope afterwards largely ignored.

Between May and October, 1730, the plans were somewhat revised. In a letter to Lord Bathurst, October 8, 1730, Bolingbroke wrote that he and Pope were then "deep in metaphysics," a statement suggesting that there had been a decision to enlarge the philosophical scope of the work.[7] Joseph Spence, in a note of November, 1730, stated more directly that plans for the introduction had been altered: "Mr. Pope's poem grows on his hands. The first four or five epistles will be on the general principles, or of "The Nature of Man"; and the rest will be on modera-

---

[5] The original MS is now among the Spence papers owned by Mr. James M. Osborn of Yale University, who has kindly allowed me to make use of it. For the possible identity of the "Gardening Poem" see R. H. Griffith, "Pope on the Art of Gardening," *The University of Texas Studies in English*, XXXI (1952), 52–56.

[6] Spence wrote another note in May, 1730—a note which has been published—in which he declared that Pope "at that time intended to have included in one epistle what he afterwards addressed to Lord Bolingbroke in four" (*Anecdotes*, p. 16).

[7] E-C, VIII, 340–41.

tion, or "The Use of Things." In the latter part each class may take up three epistles: one, for instance, against Avarice; another against Prodigality; and the third, on the moderate use of Riches; and so of the rest." [8] The introduction was now to include four or five epistles dealing with general principles; and the second part of the project was to consist of a series of epistles, in groups of three, which would advocate moderation in the use of things. It is noteworthy that the idea of the *Essay on Man,* as we know it, occurred relatively late.

On the basis of this plan Pope began to compose his poems; and in December, 1730, one month after Spence's note, he told John Caryll that he had started to put materials together:

> But the truth is, it is now in my hopes, God knows whether it may ever prove in my power, to contribute to some honest and moral purposes in writing on human life and manners, not exclusive of religious regards, and I have many fragments which I am beginning to put together, but nothing perfect or finished, nor in any condition to be shown, except to a friend at a fireside. I wish you would have so much curiosity to come and pass a few days to see them here.[9]

During the spring and summer of 1731 steady progress was made. The poem on prodigality, now addressed to the Earl of Burlington, was so nearly finished by April 4, 1731, that it was transmitted to his lordship:

> I send you the Inclosed with great pleasure to myself. It has been above ten years on my conscience to leave some Testimony of my Esteem for yʳ Lordship among my Writings. I wish it were worthier of you. As to the Thought wch. was first suggested when I saw you, of its attending yᵉ Book, I would have your Ldship think further of it; & upon a considerate perusal, If you still think so, the few Words I've added in this paper may perhaps serve two ends at once, & ease you too in another respect. In short tis all submitted to yʳ own best Judgment: Do with it, & me, as you will. Only I beg your Lds.p will not show the thing in manuscript, till yᵉ proper time: It may yet receive Improvement, & will, to the last day it's in my power. Some lines are added towd. yᵉ End on yᵉ Common Enemy, the Bad Imitators & Pretenders, wch perhaps are properer there, than in your own mouth.[10]

Much was also accomplished on the introductory epistles. Bolingbroke wrote to Swift on March 20: "Passions, says our divine Pope, as you will see one time or other, are the gales of life." [11] Since the image appears in the second epistle of the *Essay on Man,* Bolingbroke's remark suggests that this part of the poem was then being, or had been, written and that the first epistle had been completed. On July 28 Pope himself told Hugh Bethel that he had finished the third epistle and was proceeding to the fourth: "I have just finished an Epistle in Verse, upon

---

[8] *Anecdotes,* p. 48. The date of the note is supplied from the Spence papers owned by Mr. Osborn.

[9] E-C, VI, 325–26.

[10] From an unpublished letter owned by the Chatsworth Estates Company. In the letter Pope suggests that his *Epistle* be published along with the second volume of the *Fabbriche antiche designate da Andrea Palladio Vicentino,* an undertaking patronized by Burlington. The first volume of this work had appeared in 1730, at which time a second was promised. No second volume ever appeared; but uncertainties over its fate may explain why the publication of Pope's poem was delayed until December, 1731.

[11] E-C, VII, 221.

ye Nature and Extent of Good nature & Social affection; & am going upon another whose subject is The True Happiness of Man, in wch I shall prove the Best Men ye happiest, & consequently you shd pull off your hat to me for painting You as the happiest man in the Universe." [12]

Bolingbroke, writing to Swift on August 2, gave a detailed summary of the poet's progress on the work:

The first epistle, which considers man, and the habitation of man, relatively to the whole system of universal being: the second, which considers him in his own habitation, in himself, and relatively to his particular system: and the third, which shows how

a universal cause

Works to one end, but works by various laws;

how man, and beast, and vegetable, are linked in a mutual dependency, parts necessary to each other, and necessary to the whole: how human societies were formed; from what spring true religion and true policy are derived; how God has made our greatest interest and our plainest duty indivisibly the same—these three epistles, I say, are finished. The fourth he is now intent upon. It is a noble subject. He pleads the cause of God (I use Seneca's expression) against that famous charge which atheists in all ages have brought— the supposed unequal dispensations of Providence—a charge which I cannot heartily forgive your divines for admitting. . . . The epistles I have mentioned will compose a first book; the plan of the second is settled.[13]

For some reason Pope did not persevere with his work upon the fourth part of the *Essay on Man;* indeed, he probably did not seriously apply himself to this section until the summer of 1733, after the first three parts had been published.[14] Instead, in the fall of 1731 he turned to his poem dealing with avarice, the epistle addressed to Lord Bathurst. For he evidently had decided to publish his epistle to Burlington and to bring out the poem to Bathurst shortly afterwards, a decision which called for work upon the second of these compositions. He spent time checking on details for the portrait of the Man of Ross; [15] and on the seventh of November he informed Lord Oxford that he had composed for this poem some complimentary lines—that he had "taken the liberty to call at your door in my way to moral virtue, as you will see when we meet." [16]

The two epistles were ready by December, 1731; and on the fourteenth that to Burlington was published under the title *Of Taste.*[17] Unfortunately, Pope found

---

[12] British Museum, Egerton MSS. 1948, f. 17.

[13] E-C, VII, 244–45.

[14] Mack, p. xiv, notes the very rough form of Epistle IV in the only manuscript of the *Essay* preserving this last part of the poem, the manuscript in the Pierpont Morgan Library. This manuscript seems to represent a state of the poem that might have been achieved by early autumn of 1731.

[15] A letter from Pope to Hugh Bethel, which should be dated September 8, 1731, speaks of the portrait of the Man of Ross as completed (see E-C, IX, 165, for a transcription of the relevant portion of this letter). On the fourteenth of November Pope wrote to the elder Jacob Tonson requesting more information (E-C, IX, 550). Perhaps he wanted to check on the accuracy of details he had already learned or to fill out his sketch. Since he was seeking a favor in the letter, he may, of course, have been merely flattering Tonson.

[16] E-C, VIII, 291.

[17] The title was changed to the more appropriate *Of False Taste* in the second edition, published early in January. This change was suggested to Pope by Aaron Hill in a letter dated December 17, 1731 (E-C, X, 40).

himself in trouble at once. His dunces, who had been waiting for his next major publication, immediately seized upon the Timon portrait, declaring that it had been intended for the Duke of Chandos; and they noted many seeming likenesses in support of their contention.[18] For them the identification was a tempting one, because by it they could make Pope particularly uncomfortable. The Duke of Chandos was known to have subscribed liberally to the translation of the *Iliad;* and a charge that Pope had attacked his former benefactor would seem to prove the commonplace assertion that he was ungrateful and treacherous. Furthermore, the Earl of Burlington and the Duke of Chandos were close friends, as were Chandos and Dr. Arbuthnot; the report was calculated to embarrass all of them.

There can be little doubt that the "character" of Timon was intended to be a generalized one, that it had not been aimed at Chandos.[19] Nevertheless, the town greedily devoured the gossip; and Pope, to defend himself and to prevent misunderstandings among his friends, made explanations. He immediately declared his concern to the Duke of Chandos;[20] and he assured the Earl of Burlington, in a letter of December 21, that the "Character of Timon is collected from twenty different Absurditys & Improprieties: & was never yᵉ Picture of any one Human Creature."[21] He offered the public an account of the truth by publishing in the *Daily Post-Boy,* December 22, 1731, an unsigned letter to John Gay, which was assumed to have been written by Pope.[22] He also prefixed to the third edition of the poem (published January 20–27, 1732) a formal letter to Burlington in which he emphasized the general character of the Timon portrait and in which he warned critics that the Duke of Chandos was convinced "not only of my Innocence" but also of the "malignity" of those circulating the rumor.[23]

---

[18] The major likenesses alleged—not too justly—are mentioned to Pope by Aaron Hill in a letter dated December 23, 1731 (E-C, X, 44).

[19] The evidence has been carefully analyzed by George Sherburn, " 'Timon's Villa' and Cannons," *HLB*, No. 8 (October, 1935), pp. 131–52. Professor Sherburn's argument is supported by Bateson, pp. 164–68.

[20] As the Duke's letter books in the Henry E. Huntington Library reveal. See Sherburn, " 'Timon's Villa' and Cannons," pp. 137–38.

[21] Sherburn, " 'Timon's Villa' and Cannons," p. 137.

[22] The letter as published in the *Daily Post-Boy* contained obvious misprints and a long postscript. It was reprinted in the *Daily Journal*, December 23, 1731, with the explanation that the *Post-Boy* had actually run together two letters, dated December 16 and 19 respectively. The text represented as a single letter of December 16 is reprinted in E-C, VII, 444–47.

[23] Pope was attempting, among other things, to warn his enemies that they could not hope to curry favor with Chandos by circulating the story. Chandos' attitude was not essentially misrepresented, for he had written Pope on December 27:

"I am much troubled to find by Your favour of yᵉ 22ᵈ You are under any uneasiness, at yᵉ application yᵉ Town has made of Timon's Character, in Your Epistle to yᵉ Earl of Burlinton. For my own part I have recᵈ so many instances of yᵉ will they bear me, that I am as little surprized as I am affected with this further proof of it; It would indeed be a real concern to me, did I beleive One of your Judgment had designedly given grounds for their imbibing an Opinion, so disadvantageous of me. But as Your obliging Letter, is sufficient to free me from this apprehension, I can with great indifference bear yᵉ insults they bestow, and not find myself hurt by 'em: nor have I reason to be much disturb'd, when I consider how many better persons are yᵉ daily objects of their unjust censures" (Sherburn, " 'Timon's Villa' and Cannons," p. 138).

Thoroughly vexed by the treatment of his poem, Pope resorted to other measures. He permitted Richard Savage to bring out a *Collection of Pieces in Verse and Prose, which have been publish'd on occasion of the Dunciad,* a miscellany of pamphlets complimenting Pope and of lampoons attacking the dunces. He himself published a short satirical sketch, directed at Lord Hervey, in the *London Evening Post,* January 22–25, 1732:

> HORACE, *Sat. 4. Lib.* I. *paraphras'd.*
> *Inscribed to the Hon. Mr.* [Hervey].
> ——————— 1 *Absentem* qui rodit Amicum:
> 2 Qui non *defendit,* alio culpante: 3 Solutos
> Qui captat *Risus* hominum, *Famamque dicacis:*
> 4 Fingere qui *non visa* potest: 5 *Comissa tacere*
> Qui nequit.—Hic *Niger* est: Hunc, tu Romane, caveto.

> 1 That *Fop,* whose Pride affects a *Patron's* Name,
> Yet *absent,* wounds an Author's honest Fame;
> 2 That more abusive Fool, who calls me *Friend*
> Yet wants the Honour, injur'd to defend:
> 3 Who spreads a *Tale,* a *Libel* hands about,
> Enjoys the *Jest,* and copies *Scandal* out:
> 4 Who to the *Dean* and *Silver Bell* can swear,
> And sees at *C-n-ns* what was never there:
> 5 Who tells you all I *mean,* and all I *say;*
> And, if he *lies* not, must at least *betray:*
> 'Tis not the *Sober Sat'rist* you should dread,
> But such a *babling Coxcomb* in his Stead.[24]

He also drafted a more lengthy satirical response, in prose, entitled *A Master Key to Popery;* but he did not publish it, possibly because he recognized that such a retort would only give more life to a quarrel which might otherwise abate quickly.[25]

The uproar over the *Epistle to the Earl of Burlington* also affected Pope's plans for bringing out his ethic poems. He quickly determined to postpone the publication of his *Epistle to Lord Bathurst:*

The noise which malice has raised about that epistle has caused me to suppress a much better concerning the Use of Riches, in which I had paid some respect, and done some justice to the Duke of Chandos. I thought it a great proof of both, when the celebration of him was joined with one of you and of my Lord Bathurst. But, to print it now would be interpreted by malice (and I find it is malice I am to expect from the world, not thanks, for my writings) as if I had done it in atonement, or through some apprehension, or sensibility of having meant that duke an abuse, which I am sure was far from my thought.[26]

He became, in fact, temporarily indifferent to his whole moral plan. In a formal letter prefixed to the third edition of the epistle to Burlington, he muttered darkly

---

[24] These lines, somewhat altered, were later placed in the *Epistle to Dr. Arbuthnot* (ll. 291–304).
[25] The manuscript of this work is now at Chatsworth; and there is no doubt that it is Pope's composition. See John Butt, " 'A Master Key to Popery,' " in *Pope and his Contemporaries: Essays Presented to George Sherburn,* ed. James L. Clifford and Louis A. Landa (Oxford, 1949), pp. 41–57, and Bateson, pp. 168–82.
[26] Pope to Lord Oxford, January 22, 1732: E-C, VIII, 292–93.

that he might either give up his pen altogether or bring out a more vigorous satire exposing not merely follies but vices. He was still contemplating these alternatives two months later, in March, 1732:

The report was almost universal, but so very groundless and silly, that I do not yet know the effect it will have upon my conduct—whether so great a stupidity in the point of comprehending a poet's manner, being the ignorance of the very principles of that sort of writing, and so great malignity in the point of applying it in the worst sense, should give me such a pique to the world's malice as never to publish anything, or such a contempt of its judgment as to publish everything which I think right myself, without the least concern about what they think or say.[27]

This pique may have been naive and childish; but it effectively prevented him from taking up his *Ethic Epistles* and the *Essay on Man* until the following autumn. In February or March, 1732, he was composing only when he had "no other thing in the world to do, or no friend to entertain in company."[28] In April he was writing "little or nothing. You know I never had either a taste or talent for politics, and the world minds nothing else."[29] In June he told the elder Jacob Tonson: "I have no thoughts of printing the poem (which is an epistle on the 'Use of Riches') this long time, perhaps not till it is accompanied with many others, and at a time when telling truths and drawing exemplary pictures of men and manners can be of no disservice to the author, and occasion no slanderer to mistake them, and apply them falsely, as I was lately served in the character of Timon."[30]

But Pope loved his pen too much for continued self-indulgence of this sort; and by September, 1732, he was again back at work. On the twenty-second of that month he sent Lord Oxford complimentary lines destined for the epistle to Bathurst; and five days later he broadly hinted to Caryll that he would publish soon:

My work is systematical and proceeds in order. Yet that does not hinder me from finishing some of the particular parts, which may be published at any time, when I judge particular vices demand them. And I believe you will see one or two of these next winter,—one especially of the use of riches, which seems at present to be the favourite, nay, the only, mistress of mankind, to which all their endeavours are directed, through all the paths of corruption and luxury. My satire will therefore be impartial on both extremes, avarice and profusion. I shall make living examples, which enforce best, and consequently put you once more upon the defence of your friend, against the roar and calumny which I expect, and am ready to suffer in so good a cause.[31]

The following fifteen months were busy ones, in which he composed, among other things, all the poems in his ethic system which he was to publish. He completed the epistle to Bathurst during the fall; and on December 1 he wrote Lord Oxford saying that this work would be published by Christmas.[32] In January, 1733,

---

[27] Pope to John Caryll, March 29 [1732]: E-C, VI, 331.
[28] Pope to Jonathan Richardson: E-C, IX, 497.
[29] Pope to Swift: E-C, VII, 264.
[30] E-C, IX, 553.
[31] E-C, VI, 334–35.
[32] E-C, VIII, 301.

he reported to Caryll that Martha Blount had received a manuscript copy of the epistle addressed to her—the epistle on the characters of women, which was not published until 1735.[33] He told Swift on April 2 that he had finished "another of my epistles, in the order of the system," a reference, possibly, to the poem to Lord Cobham.[34] During the late spring or early summer of 1733 he turned to the fourth part of the *Essay on Man,* which had probably been left in a fragmentary state in the summer of 1731. On August 9, 1733, he wrote Hugh Bethel that he was finishing it and hoped to print it in a fortnight.[35] There were delays, however; and in October he was employing "these few days in putting the last hand to my Essay." [36] Concurrently, he was working over his epistle to Cobham. On October 23 he told Caryll that he would leave out lines in the character of the Duke of Wharton that Caryll had thought "too hard"; [37] and soon afterwards he corresponded with Lord Cobham himself regarding details in the poem to which Cobham had taken exception.[38]

While Pope composed and polished the manuscripts of his poems, he engaged in an elaborate stratagem for publishing the *Essay on Man;* for the difficulties over his epistle addressed to the Earl of Burlington had taught him the necessity of caution in bringing before the public a work that might be maliciously misconstrued. With his name appearing on the title pages, he published the *Epistle to Lord Bathurst* and the *First Satire of the Second Book of Horace, Imitated* just before the first part of the *Essay* came out anonymously, a maneuver that might lead the town to think of him as too preoccupied with other kinds of composition to write the *Essay.* The parts of the *Essay* were also not published over the imprint of Pope's current bookseller, Lawton Gilliver; the name of the printer John Wil-

---

[33] "I believe you will receive from the care of your poor god-daughter a prettier poem [than the Epistle addressed to Lord Bathurst]" (E-C, VI, 337).

[34] E-C, VII, 307.

[35] E-C, IX, 154–55.

[36] Pope to William Fortescue, November 13, 1733: E-C, IX, 125.

[37] E-C, VI, 345.

[38] Lord Cobham at first advised that the character of the lecher should be made shorter or changed (E-C, X, 133). When Pope complied with this suggestion, his friend suggested that he had failed to make an adequate distinction between the psychological human character and the affected human character, that the argument was, in effect, fatalistic:

"I like your leachour better now 'tis shorter and the Glutton is a very good Epigram but they are both appetites that from nature we indulge as well for her ends as our pleasure. A Cardinal in his way of pleasure would have been a better instance. What do you think of an old lady draping her silver locks with Pink and directing her Coffin to be lin'd with white grilled satten prin'd with gold fringe, of Councelour Vernon retiring to enjoy himself with five thousand a year which he had got and returning back to the Chancery to get a little more when he could not speak so loud as to be heard, or a judge turnd out coming again to the Bar. I mean that passion or habit that has not a natural foundation falls in better with your Subject than any of our natural wants which in some degree we cannot avoid pursuing to the last; and if a man has Spirits or appetite enough to take a bit of either kind at parting, you may condemn him but you would be proud to imitate him" (Lord Cobham to Pope, November 8, 1733: British Museum, Egerton MSS. 1949, f. 3).
A glance at the conclusion of the epistle, as it was first printed, will show that Cobham's suggestions were not ignored.

ford, who had not previously worked for Pope, was used.[39] Moreover, he eliminated from the text any direct allusion to Bolingbroke. Because everyone knew that he was then working on a series of epistles, he changed the designation of the major divisions of the poem from "epistles" to "parts." In a notice "To the Reader" prefacing the early issues of the first part of the work, he distinguished the author of the *Essay* from the author of the two poems known to have been recently published by himself: "As he *imitates* no Man, so he would be thought to vye with no Man in these Epistles, particularly with the noted Author of *TWO* lately published." [40] He deliberately introduced a bad rhyme into the second part of the poem in order to throw readers, accustomed to his usual correctness, off the track.[41] Dr. Johnson, in his *Life* of Pope, reported other interesting, but less believable stratagems: "Those friends of Pope, that were trusted with the secret went about lavishing honours on the new-born poet, and hinting that Pope was never so much in danger from any former rival. To those authors whom he had personally offended, and to those whose opinion the world considered as decisive, and whom he suspected of envy or malevolence, he sent his *Essay* as a present before publication that they might defeat their own enmity by praises, which they could not afterwards decently retract." [42]

Such arrangements to conceal the identity of the real author of the *Essay on Man* proved extraordinarily successful; Thomas Edwards of Terrick echoed the attitude of the general reader during the spring of 1733 when he wrote his friend John Clerke that the town had recently had "an Essay on Man by a New Author." [43] Pope's hand was not, indeed, publicly recognized until June 23, 1733, when the *Weekly Miscellany* published a short poem "To Mr. Pope, on his being the Author of the *Essay on Man*." By this time, however, the town was thoroughly

---

[39] Although Wilford's name appeared in the imprint, the copyright to all parts of the poem, except the first, was held for one year only by Gilliver at the time of publication. The copy of the first part of the poem was not assigned to Gilliver until March 23, a month after it had been published (see Appendix A); and Pope himself was the actual publisher of the first part. Undoubtedly Pope, and Gilliver, obtained from Wilford, for a small fee, the right to use his name in the imprint. Pope gave Gilliver the property in the first, second, and third parts of the poem on the same day; and he assigned the fourth part to him on January 10, 1734. The first part of the poem was published on February 20; the second part, on March 29. Professor Griffith dates the appearance of the third part as May 17, although this date should probably be advanced to April. The *London Evening Post,* April 17, 1733, announced the third part as published on "this day"; and the *Daily Journal,* April 19, 1733, advertised it as "being now in the press and will speedily be published." The fourth part did not come out until January 24, 1734.

[40] Mack, p. 6.

[41] "Our author told Mr. HARTE, that, in order to disguise his being the author of the second epistle of the Essay on Man, he made, in the first edition, the following bad rhyme:
  A cheat! a whore! who starts not at the *name,*
    In all the inns of court, or Drury *Lane?*
And HARTE remembered to have often heard it urged, in enquiries about the author, whilst he was unknown, that it was impossible it could be POPE's, on account of this very passage" (Joseph Warton, *Essay on the Genius and Writings of Pope* [London, 1782], II, 210–11 n.).

[42] *Lives of the English Poets,* ed. by G. Birkbeck Hill (Oxford, 1905), III, 161.

[43] V. M. Gilbert, "Unrecorded Comments on John Gay, Henry Travers, and Others," *N&Q,* CXCVIII (1953), 338.

committed to unreserved praise of the new work. On March 8 Pope wrote slyly to William Fortescue of the encomia which the first part of the *Essay* had already received: "The town, since you went, has entered much into the fashion of applauding the *Essay on Man;* and in many places it is set up as a piece far excelling any thing of mine, and commended, I think, more in opposition to me, than in their real judgment it deserves."[44]

Bezaleel Morrice and Leonard Welsted, both old hands at abusing Pope, were taken in. Morrice was so transported that he undertook a philosophical flight on a similar theme, *An Essay on the Universe,* which he dedicated to "the Author of the *Essay on Man.*" Welsted, in a letter, described the poem as an effective antidote to the kind of ribaldry which Pope had been publishing.[45]

That such enemies as Welsted and Morrice should have been tricked undoubtedly pleased the author of the *Essay on Man;* and he included in subsequent editions of the *Dunciad* selections from the praise which they unwittingly had bestowed upon him. Nevertheless, his effort at anonymity was not prompted by a desire to acquire new materials for the satire on authors. Criticism of the *Epistle to the Earl of Burlington* had shown him to what lengths his enemies would go; and he knew that the argument of the *Essay* could be distorted by determined foes. How much he feared that heterodox constructions might be placed upon his poem is revealed, for example, in his indirect efforts to obtain from his Roman Catholic friend John Caryll approval of the doctrine in the poem:

The town is now very full of a new poem entitled an Essay on Man, attributed, I think with reason, to a divine. It has merit in my opinion, but not so much as they give it. At least it is incorrect, and has some inaccuracies in the expressions,—one or two of an unhappy kind, for they may cause the author's sense to be turned, contrary to what I think his intention, a little unorthodoxically. Nothing is so plain as that he quits his proper subject, this present world, to assert his belief of a future state, and yet there is an *if* instead of a *since* that would overthrow his meaning; and at the end he uses the words "God, the soul of the world," which at the first glance may be taken for heathenism, while his whole paragraph proves him quite christian in his system, from man up to seraphim. I want to know your opinion of it after twice or thrice reading.[46]

Two weeks later he reported to Caryll, with satisfaction, that the divines of London had offered no criticism of the *Essay;* ". . . I perceive the divines have no objection to it, though now it is agreed not to be written by one,—Dr. Croxall, Dr. Secker, and some others having solemnly denied it."[47] In this concern for the possible interpretations of his poem we are to see the best explanation of his efforts to conceal his hand. Knowing that he had steered "betwixt the winds of doctrine" and that his unfriendly critics would not miss a chance to distort the tendency of his argument if they should recognize the work as his, he sought to suggest that

---

[44] E-C, IX, 122.

[45] The relevant section of the letter was published by Pope in 1735 among the "Testimonies of Authors" appended to the *Dunciad*. I have been unable to locate Pope's source.

[46] March 8, 1733: E-C, VI, 339–40.

[47] E-C, VI, 340.

the poem had been written by another poet. In this way he hoped that the critics might give it an impartial reading.

When the fourth part of the *Essay on Man* and the epistle addressed to Lord Cobham were finally published in January, 1734, only one "finished" epistle remained in his hands, the epistle addressed to Martha Blount. Nevertheless, the plans were still ambitious, although Pope had "drawn in the plan for my Ethic Epistles, much narrower than it was at first." Spence, who quotes this statement, goes on to remark:

He mentioned several of the particulars, in which he had lessened it; but as this was in the year 1734, the most exact account of his plan, (as it stood then) will best appear from a leaf which he annexed to about a dozen copies of the poem, printed in that year, and sent as presents to some of his most particular friends. Most of these were afterwards called in again; but that which was sent to Mr. Bethel was not.

The outline referred to by Spence follows:

INDEX TO THE ETHIC EPISTLES

Book I. OF THE NATURE AND STATE OF MAN.

> *Epistle* 1.—With respect to the Universe.
> 2.—As an Individual.
> 3.—With respect to Society.
> 4.—With respect to Happiness.

Book II. OF THE USE OF THINGS.

> Of the Limits of Human Reason.
> Of the Use of Learning.
> Of the Use of Wit.
> Of the Knowledge and Characters of Men.
> Of the particular Characters of Women.
> Of the Principles and Use of Civil and Ecclesiastical Polity.
> Of the Use of Education.
> A View of the Equality of Happiness in the several Conditions of Men.
> Of the Use of Riches.[48]

As far as we know, nothing of significance was done in 1734, although in this year he may have started gathering materials for epistles dealing with civil and ecclesiastical polity and with education.[49] The truth seems to be, however, that he was rapidly losing interest in the whole undertaking—that he was finding it merely burdensome. His letters to Swift in the fall of 1734 show signs of restiveness: "I have only one piece of mercy to beg of you; do not laugh at my gravity, but permit me to wear the beard of a philosopher, till I put it off, and make a jest of it myself." [50] Three months later, December 19, he declared more directly that he had exhausted his materials: "I am almost at the end of my morals, as I have been long ago of my wit. My system is a short one, and my circle narrow." [51]

---

[48] *Anecdotes*, pp. 136–37.
[49] *Anecdotes*, p. 289.
[50] September 15, 1734: E-C, VII, 325.
[51] E-C, VII, 330.

Subsequently Pope often talked of returning to the work. Writing to Swift in 1736 he contemplated a grandiose plan for continuing, though he admitted that he would probably do nothing: "But alas! the task is great, and *non sum qualis eram!* My understanding indeed, such as it is, is extended rather than diminished; I see things more in the whole, more consistent, and more clearly deduced from, and related to, each other. But what I gain on the side of philosophy, I lose on the side of poetry: the flowers are gone, when the fruits begin to ripen, and the fruits perhaps will never ripen perfectly." [52]

In 1740 William Warburton reported to Charles Yorke that Pope "is tired with imitating Horace; that he thinks he cou^d make something of the *Damasippus,* and intends to do it, but that the great scheme which he has in view is the continuation of the Essay." [53] But Pope did nothing; he merely revised and rearranged what had already been published.

This failure cannot be attributed to any lack of enthusiastic public response. Periodicals reprinted large selections from the *Essay on Man* and the *Epistles* as they appeared; and the remarks of correspondents in the periodicals were uniformly laudatory. At a time when poets were given to "enervate strains" Pope was hailed as one who had restored to poetry "her noble mien, her honours lost." [54] A sure test of the immediate success of any literary work is the number of imitations it encourages; and both the *Essay on Man* and the *Ethic Epistles* elicited a flood of attempts at emulation. Other reasons must, therefore, explain the abandonment of the ethic scheme. Pope gave one explanation to Spence in 1743–44:

I had once thoughts of completing my ethic work in four books.—The first, you know, is on the Nature of Man.—The second, would have been on Knowledge and its limits:— here would have come in an Essay on Education; part of which I have inserted in the Dunciad.—The third, was to have treated of Government; both ecclesiastical and civil— and this was what chiefly stopped my going on. I could not have said what *I would* have said, without provoking every church on the face of the earth: and I did not care for living always in boiling water.[55]

A remark to Swift in 1734 may, however, come nearer the truth:

Imagination has no limits, and that is a sphere in which you may move on to eternity; but where one is confined to truth, or, to speak more like a human creature, to the appearances of truth, we soon find the shortness of our tether. Indeed, by the help of a metaphysical chain of ideas, one may extend the circulation, go round and round for ever, without making any progress beyond the point to which Providence has pinned us: but this does not satisfy me, who would rather say a little to no purpose than a great deal.[56]

This frank admission that he was nearing the end of his resources, that he feared

---

[52] March 25, 1736: E-C, VII, 341–42.

[53] George Harris, *Life of Lord Chancellor Hardwicke* (London, 1847), I, 475.

[54] "To the Author of the *Essay on Man,*" *Poetical Works of William Somervile* (Edinburgh, 1780), II, 31.

[55] *Anecdotes,* p. 315.

[56] December 19, 1734: E-C, VII, 330.

becoming monotonous and repetitious, is probably the best explanation for his failure to go on. The *Ethic Epistles* must have represented for him the most exacting task he had ever undertaken. They called for great skill in the presentation of material and for a professional competence in philosophy and ethics. The formal satirical character, for example, was a genre that would not admit endless variety in method of treatment; yet in the *Ethic Epistles* Pope had committed himself to make extensive use of these portraits. Furthermore, though he was determined to use living examples for the characters, the supply of appropriate models was limited. As early as August, 1733, he told Hugh Bethel that he was having difficulty finding examples of virtue; and one may assume that the supply of vicious men who might be treated in formal verse characters was also limited. Furthermore, the subject matter proposed for the epistles that Pope never did complete was of a kind he could not easily deal with. He was not well equipped to say enduring things on subjects like the limits of human reason, or the principles and use of civil and ecclesiastical polity.

Private circumstances also conspired to prevent the poet from applying himself to his task. When he was most active on his project, Lord Bolingbroke lived at nearby Dawley Farm; but in 1735 Bolingbroke moved to France with the intention of residing there indefinitely. He was no longer available to give encouragement, to discuss knotty philosophical problems. If Pope was to write on such subjects, he would have to do so without a preceptor. The death of his mother in June, 1733, released him from constant attendance upon her at Twickenham; and he was free to visit the estates of his friends, a freedom of which he took full advantage. On one occasion he confessed to William Fortescue that he was spending too much time with his friends for the good of his poetry:

Those who think I live in a study, and make poetry my business, are more mistaken than if they took me for a Prince of Topinambou. I love my particular friends as much as if I knew no others, and I receive almost everybody that comes near me as a friend: this is too much; it dissipates me when I should be collected; for though I may be of some (not much) value to a few, yet, divided among so many, I must be good for nothing. Life becomes a mere pastime.[57]

Such distractions prevented the kind of concentration that work on new ethic epistles obviously required; and Pope's artistic conscience was too sensitive to permit him to perform something badly. Moreover, he had found a congenial outlet for his energies in imitating Horace, a kind of composition that could accommodate his increasingly erratic habits of writing.

II

The *Essay on Man* and the four *Ethic Epistles* represent an ambitious achievement by Pope. In them he attempted to systematize the best in the diverse speculative wisdom of his time, an aim that might well have deterred a philosopher more highly trained than he. They called for a thorough knowledge of moral

---

[57] August 23, 1735: E-C, IX, 131–32.

philosophy as well as for powers of synthesis and logic; and there was always the danger of becoming entangled in doctrinal disputes. His task might also have deterred a less versatile poet. For the plan, while it afforded opportunities for satire, did not admit many of the other things Pope liked to introduce into his poetry. There were few opportunities for natural description; and fanciful elaboration would have been inappropriate in a work with so exalted a purpose. Moreover, the subject called for powers of eloquence and expression such as Pope had never before been called upon to sustain; and the satirical character sketch, which he previously had seldom attempted, was a form which at its best is one of the most difficult in which to excel. The artistic commitments that Pope made in his grandest assault upon Parnassus were audacious and for him novel.

Although he was partially prompted to the effort by criticism of his *Dunciad*, the man largely responsible for the undertaking was Henry St. John, Viscount Bolingbroke, who had urged such a project upon Pope as early as 1724. Bolingbroke often took credit for bringing his friend to the work, and Pope freely acknowledged his indebtedness to this "guide, philosopher, and friend." Bolingbroke wrote Swift on August 2, 1731, of the noble work which Pope "at my instigation" had undertaken; [58] and in a letter to Pope prefacing his philosophical writings, Bolingbroke referred to Pope's having "begun, at my request, the work which I have wished long that you would undertake." [59] In the concluding lines of the *Essay on Man* Pope gave credit to his titled friend for persuading him to turn "the tuneful art from sounds to things, from fancy to the heart." According to Joseph Spence, Pope "mentioned then, and at several other times, how much (or rather how wholly) he himself was obliged to him for the thoughts and reasonings in his moral work; and once in particular said, that beside their frequent talking over that subject together, he had received, I think, seven or eight sheets from Lord Bolingbroke, in relation to it, as I apprehended by way of letters; both to direct the plan in general, and to supply the matter for the particular epistles." [60]

These acknowledgments combined with the unusual character of the whole undertaking have led to speculation over the contributions Bolingbroke must have made. Some have assumed that he presided over the whole work and that he even dictated the entire substance of the *Essay on Man*. Such a view has been encouraged through the story reported by Hugh Blair to James Boswell in a letter dated September 21, 1779:

In the year 1763, being at London, I was carried by Dr. John Blair, Prebendary of Westminster, to dine at old Lord Bathurst's. . . . The conversation turning on Mr. Pope, Lord Bathurst told us, that "The Essay on Man" was originally composed by Lord Bolingbroke in prose, and that Mr. Pope did no more than put it into verse: that he had read Lord Bolingbroke's manuscript in his own hand-writing; and remembered

---

[58] E-C, VII, 244.

[59] *Works of the late Right Honourable Henry St. John, Lord Viscount Bolingbroke* (London, 1754), III, 311. References to Bolingbroke's *Works* (1754) are to the quarto edition of this year.

[60] *Anecdotes*, p. 144.

well, that he was at a loss whether most to admire the elegance of Lord Bolingbroke's prose, or the beauty of Mr. Pope's verse.[61]

That Lord Bathurst *was* circulating this story cannot be doubted; for he repeated it in a letter to the Reverend Joshua Parry, April 3, 1769:

As to the extracts from Ruffhead, I believe I have told you before, that Lord Bolingbroke put into my hand a dissertation in prose, which gave Pope the scheme he pursued, and turned into that fine poem. As soon as I had read his [Pope's] essay, I said to Lord Bolingbroke that I was sure our friend was not capable of forming such a system. Upon which, knowing what I meant, he said, "I did give some hints. Read that, and return it to me again."

He left it with Pope, and I believe gave him leave to burn it. It has never appeared since, and perhaps I am the only man now alive who has read it.[62]

The testimony of Spence and Lord Bathurst is impressive, although the outline which they declare Bolingbroke gave to Pope has not been found; but one can hardly accept literally the assertion that Pope versified Bolingbroke. Dr. Johnson was more nearly right when he commented on the Blair story:

"Depend upon it, Sir, this is too strongly stated. Pope may have had from Bolingbroke the philosophick *stamina* of his Essay; and admitting this to be true, Lord Bathurst did not intentionally falsify. But the thing is not true in the latitude that Blair seems to imagine; we are sure that the poetical imagery, which makes a great part of the poem, was Pope's own. It is amazing, Sir, what deviations there are from precise truth, in the account which is given of almost every thing." [63]

Even Johnson, however, did not see that acceptance of the Spence and Bathurst stories forces one to accept untenable hypotheses about the character of Pope's thought in the poem. It compels one to see a close equivalence between Bolingbroke's philosophy and the ideas in the *Essay on Man;* but while important parallels may be found, they are often merely commonplaces of the day—and there are basic differences in the views of the two men as expressed in their philosophical writings.[64] Pope, for example, ignored his friend's insistence that God's moral attributes are unknown, and must remain unknown, to man; he shuns the anticlerical thundering that reverberates through the pages of Bolingbroke; and he

[61] *Boswell's Life of Johnson,* ed. G. B. Hill and L. F. Powell (Oxford, 1934–50), III, 402. The story was also mentioned by the Rev. Dr. Edmund Law in his edition of Archbishop William King's *Essay on the Origin of Evil* (London, 1781), p. xvii, and by Joseph Warton in the second volume of his *Essay on the Genius and Writings of Pope* (London, 1782), p. 123.

[62] Charles Henry Parry, *A Memoir of the Revd. Joshua Parry* (London, 1872). I have not seen the *Memoir;* but the relevant portion of the letter has been reprinted by Professor George Sherburn, "Two Notes on the *Essay on Man*," *PQ,* XII (1933), 402.

[63] *Boswell's Life of Johnson,* III, 403–404.

[64] Pope urged Bolingbroke to write out his philosophical ideas at the same time he himself was composing the *Ethic Epistles.* In 1734 Bolingbroke reported to Swift that he had written "six letters and a half to" Pope (E-C, VII, 325). Bolingbroke did not publish any of these compositions during his lifetime; but David Mallet, in editing Bolingbroke's *Works* (1754), included them under the title "Letters, or Essays, Addressed to Alexander Pope." Bolingbroke also compiled a record of conversations on philosophical subjects which he had had with Pope; and Mallet included these in the *Works* under the title "Fragments, or Minutes, of Essays." These two collections are the principal sources of our knowledge of Bolingbroke's philosophy.

establishes God in the chain of being, although Bolingbroke repeatedly argued that the deity could occupy no place in it. The ruling passion is not to be found in Bolingbroke's ethics; and Pope's treatment of happiness, in the fourth epistle of the *Essay on Man,* emphasizes the traditional thesis that happiness is independent of externals, that happiness is of the mind. This argument is not colored by Bolingbroke's distinctive aversion to ethical systems based on rewards and punishments in a future life. Indeed, Pope asserts that the prospect of a happy futurity is one of the strongest motives to virtue:

> He sees, why Nature plants in Man alone
> Hope of known bliss, and Faith in bliss unknown:
> (Nature, whose dictates to no other kind
> Are giv'n in vain, but what they seek they find)
> Wise is her present; she connects in this
> His greatest Virtue with his greatest Bliss,
> At once his own bright prospect to be blest,
> And strongest motive to assist the rest.
>
> (*Essay on Man,* IV, ll. 345–52)

Such differences are not superficial, they are basic; and they do not prove that the poet was making poetry from a prose treatise prepared by his friend.

Belief that Pope merely versified Bolingbroke in the *Essay on Man* also rests on an assumption that the poet was completely beyond the normal range of his interests when he undertook the work. He had, however, read widely in the philosophers and moralists; and he had in his own works revealed philosophic interests. He once told Bishop Atterbury that he had read the "best controversies between the churches" when he was fourteen years old.[65] He certainly had read Locke's *Essay* and Shaftesbury's *Characteristicks.* His library contained volumes of polemic divinity as well as the works of the philosophers who set the intellectual climate of the age, Bacon, Hobbes, and Montaigne. He had read Cudworth's *Eternal and Immutable Morality;* for he sent it to Bolingbroke to read.[66] If one could, as Norman Ault has done, attribute Spectator No. 408 to Pope, he was articulating central ideas of his poem as early as 1712.[67] The poet's letters written before 1728 are studded with moralizing observations restated with force and vigor in the *Essay on Man.*[68] Reflections upon happiness and retirement, for example, are commonplace in the letters—perhaps the retirement of his father and of his early mentor, Sir William Trumbull, had stimulated him to meditations upon the subject.[69] Pope's early work also shows his free-thinking attitudes in religious matters. He had boldly

---

[65] E-C, IX, 11.

[66] *Works of Henry St. John,* V, 3.

[67] *Prose Works of Alexander Pope,* ed. Norman Ault (Oxford, 1936), I, xlv–xlvi.

[68] Appendix C of this book contains a number of quotations from Pope's early letters that parallel ideas later included in the *Essay.* One should remember that Pope was going over his letters with a view towards publishing them at the time he was working on the poem; and this review may have brought to mind many of the ideas expressed earlier.

[69] Such sentiments find expression in poems like the *Ode on Solitude, Windsor Forest,* and the first of the *Pastorals.* Professor Sherburn, *Early Career of Alexander Pope* (Oxford, 1934), pp. 297–302, has traced Pope's concern with the subject through his early letters.

written in the *Essay on Criticism* in 1711 (quoted from E–C, II, 58–59):

> Some foreign writers, some our own despise;
> The ancients only, or the moderns prize.
> Thus wit, like faith, by each man is applied
> To one small sect, and all are damned beside.
> Meanly they seek the blessing to confine,
> And force that sun but on a part to shine,
> Which not alone the southern wit sublimes,
> But ripens spirits in cold northern climes;
> Which, from the first has shone on ages past,
> Enlights the present, and shall warm the last;
> Though each may feel increases and decays,
> And see now clearer and now darker days:
> Regard not then if wit be old or new,
> But blame the false, and value still the true.
>
> (ll. 394–407)

When the implications of this position were pointed out to him, he was prepared to defend it:

I have ever thought the best piece of service one could do to our religion was openly to expose our detestation and scorn of all those artifices and *piæ fraudes* which it stands so little in need of, and which have laid it under so great a scandal among the enemies. Nothing has been so much a scarecrow to them as the too peremptory and seemingly uncharitable assertion of an utter impossibility of salvation to all but ourselves, invincible ignorance excepted, which indeed some people define under so great limitations and with such exclusions, that it seems as if that word were rather invented as a salvo or expedient, not to be thought too bold with the thunderbolts of God (which are hurled about so freely almost on all mankind by the hands of the ecclesiastics) than as a real exceptive to almost universal damnation. For besides the small number of the truly faithful in our church, we must again subdivide, and the Jansenist is damned by the Jesuit, the Jesuit by the Jansenist, the strict Scotist by the Thomist, &c. There may be errors, I grant, but I cannot think them of such consequence as to destroy utterly the charity of mankind—the very greatest bond in which we are engaged by God to one another as christians.[70]

In subsequent years Pope frequently reaffirmed this view. About 1716 he may have composed the first draft of the deistic hymn finally published in 1738 as the *Universal Prayer*.[71] He told Lady Mary in 1716 that a man may be "ignorant, or at best doubtful, of the merits of differing religions and governments: but private virtue one can be sure of"; [72] and in 1717 he wrote Bishop Atterbury, who was attempting to convert him to the Church of England: "And after all, I verily believe

---

[70] Pope to John Caryll, July 19, 1711: E-C, VI, 150.

[71] Pope wrote to Ralph Allen, September 8 [1736], that the poem had been drafted twenty years before: ". . . I've sent you the Hymn, a little alterd, & enlargd in one necessary point of doctrine, viz: yᵉ third Stanza, which I think reconciles Freedom & Necessity; & is at least a Comment on some verses in my Essay on Man, which have been mis-construed. Mʳ Hooke transcribed this copy, without having one himself; as I believe no man has, since I gave it twenty years ago, in its first State, to the Duke of Shrewsbury" (from the letter now in the University of Chicago Library).

[72] E-C, IX, 346–47.

your Lordship and I are both of the same religion, if we were thoroughly under-stood by one another; and that all honest and reasonable Christians would be so, if they did but talk enough together every day, and had nothing to do together, but to serve God, and live in peace with their neighbour." [73]

Evidence of this kind makes it impossible for one to accept the legend that Pope was merely "poetizing" Bolingbroke's philosophy; but it would be an equally great mistake to underestimate the role of the statesman-philosopher. Bolingbroke may well have furnished a general outline; for certain main tendencies in Pope's argument and specific concepts, such as the idea of the patriot-king in the third epistle of the *Essay on Man,* may be traced directly to him. Bolingbroke may also have been responsible for something of the grandiose spirit with which Pope went about his work; for more than once Bolingbroke impressed upon the poet the messianic importance of the task he was performing. Furthermore, Boling-broke, by his presence and conversation, must have helped to strengthen Pope's own ideas. There were frequent conversations on philosophical subjects between the two: "All I dare promise you is, that my thoughts, in what order soever they flow, shall be communicated to you just as they pass thro my mind, just as they use to be when we converse together on those, or any other subjects; when we saunter alone, or as we have often done with good ARBUTHNOT, and the jocose dean of St. Patrick's, among the multiplied scenes of your little garden." [74]

The record of Bolingbroke's contributions to these conversations is preserved in his "Fragments, or Minutes, of Essays," which purport to be nothing more than "repetitions of conversations often interrupted, often renewed, and often carried on a little confusedly." [75] These conversations confirm what has already been declared, that Pope was not completely indebted to Bolingbroke's distinctive philosophical ideas, as some have supposed; they also show that Bolingbroke's was by far the more vigorous and richer speculative intelligence. They suggest that what he chiefly contributed to his friend by his conversation was an ability to think more justly than Pope otherwise would have done. Bolingbroke, more ex-perienced in systematic philosophy than the poet, undoubtedly made the synthesis Pope attempted more coherent and articulate than it otherwise would have been. He was helpful in establishing "the strong connexions, nice dependencies, grada-tions just" that a "short yet not imperfect system of ethics" required.

III

In a formal statement of the design of his *Essay on Man* Pope attempted to dis-tinguish between it and the *Ethic Epistles* in terms of general subject matter and purpose:

---

[73] E-C, IX, 11.

[74] *Works of Henry St. John,* III, 318.

[75] *Works of Henry St. John,* V, 2. It should be noted that all evidence points to the fact that Bolingbroke's record of conversations was made after the *Essay on Man* had been composed (see Mack, p. 169) and that the phrasing in the conversations seems on occasion to reflect Pope's in-fluence on Bolingbroke rather than Bolingbroke's influence on Pope.

Having proposed to write some pieces on Human Life and Manners, such as (to use my lord Bacon's expression) *come home to Men's Business and Bosoms,* I thought it more satisfactory to begin with considering *Man* in the abstract, his *Nature* and his *State:* since, to prove any moral duty, to enforce any moral precept, or to examine the perfection or imperfection of any creature whatsoever, it is necessary first to know what *condition* and *relation* it is placed in, and what is the proper *end* and *purpose* of its *being.* . . .

What is now published, is only to be considered as a *general Map* of MAN, marking out no more than the *greater parts,* their *extent,* their *limits,* and their *connection,* but leaving the particular to be more fully delineated in the charts which are to follow. Consequently, these Epistles in their progress (if I have health and leisure to make any progress) will be less dry, and more susceptible of poetical ornament. I am here only opening the *fountains,* and clearing the passage. To deduce the *rivers,* to follow them in their course, and to observe their effects, may be a task more agreeable.

The *Essay on Man* was, then, to provide a general view of man, his nature and his state, in an ideal and rational condition; the *Ethic Epistles* were to develop the ideas in more detail and to examine reality in the light of this abstract system. The poems as a group were to have a common purpose and related subjects, although the manner of each was to be different. The *Essay on Man* was to be philosophical poetry in the "same grave march with Lucretius"; the *Ethic Epistles* were to be satires "descending to the gayeties of Horace."

The achievement of the *Essay on Man* does not lie in the originality of the ideas. Many of the major propositions of the *Essay on Man* were a heritage from classical antiquity and the Middle Ages; others were taken directly from the formal philosophers who most immediately influenced the age, Thomas Hobbes, Isaac Newton, John Locke, Bernard Mandeville, and the Earl of Shaftesbury; still others came from the French moralists whom Pope knew, Montaigne, Fénelon, La Rochefoucauld, and Pascal. Pope himself did not prefer claims for his originality; he chose to pride himself on the skill with which he had woven diverse speculative materials into a coherent pattern: "If I could flatter myself that this Essay has any merit, it is in steering betwixt the extremes of doctrines seemingly opposite, in passing over terms utterly unintelligible, and in forming a *temperate* yet not *inconsistent,* and a *short* yet not *imperfect* system of Ethics." [76] In a sense Pope did for ethics what he had earlier done for criticism—he codified the best in contemporary ethical theory: and into his poem went combinations of medieval theology and scientific materialism, of Hobbesian egoism and Shaftesburean benevolence, of Epicurean hedonism and Stoic imperturbability, of Whig and Tory political theory. From these diverse materials came an eclectic system that is both vigorous and lucid.

Pope, to be sure, advanced more claims for the systematic nature of his argument than he should have. The nice division of the parts, the often pretentious formality of the argument suggest an effort at greater cohesiveness than was actually achieved. The argument suffers from important weaknesses. Attempts at resolving paradoxes are often not cogent; key terms like nature, the passions, and

---

[76] In his statement of the design of his poem: Mack, p. 7.

reason are used in shifting senses. A persistent effort at epigrammatic terseness often results in obscurity; and inversions of phrase are sometimes confusing. But even if the poem lacks philosophic sophistication, one may question that the *Essay on Man* would have been a better poem if Pope had made it more acceptable to philosophic minds. His undertaking was essentially literary rather than professionally philosophic. As Bolingbroke reminded him, he was not writing as a philosopher but as a poet:

Should the poet make syllogisms in verse, or pursue a long process of reasoning in the didactic style, he would be sure to tire his reader on the whole, like Lucretius, tho he reasoned better than the roman, and put into some parts of his work the same poetical fire. He may write, as you have begun to do, on philosophical subjects, but he must write in his own character. He must contract, he may shadow, he has a right to omit whatever will not be cast in the poetic mold, and when he cannot instruct, he may hope to please. But the philosopher has no such privileges. He may contract sometimes, he must never shadow. He must be limited by his matter, lest he should grow whimsical; and by the parts of it which he understands best, lest he should grow obscure. But these parts he must develope fully, and he has no right to omit any thing that may serve the purpose of truth, whether it please, or not. As it would be disingenuous to sacrifice truth to popularity, so it is trifling to appeal to the reason and experience of mankind, as every philosophical writer does, or must be understood to do, and then to talk, like Plato, and his antient and modern disciples, to the imagination only. There is no need however to banish eloquence out of philosophy; and truth and reason are no enemies to the purity, nor to the ornaments of language. But as the want of an exact determination of ideas, and of an exact precision in the use of words, is inexcusable in a philosopher, he must preserve them, even at the expence of style. In short, it seems to me, that the business of the philosopher is to dilate, if I may borrow this word from Tully, to press, to prove, to convince; and that of the poet to hint, to touch his subject with short and spirited strokes, to warm the affections, and to speak to the heart.[77]

The *Essay on Man* must be judged as an example of rhetoric designed to assure men that the universe is perfectly planned; and to this purpose the necessities of logic are often subordinated. It is doubtful that Pope would have accomplished his purpose so well if his argument had been directed more to the head than to the heart.

The didactic manner of the poem involved a sacrifice of action and of dramatic interest, by which Pope could warm the affections; the desire for clarity forced him to use common words—there could be no sonorous Latinisms, no exotic place names which might insure magnificence. The task was a challenge to his genius—as he confessed to Joseph Spence. His greatest difficulty, he said, lay "not only in settling and ranging the parts of it aright, but in making them agreeable enough to be read with pleasure." [78] He relied chiefly upon his verbal dexterity, upon the grandeur of the thoughts, and upon the range and variety of moods. As he himself declared in the coda of the *Essay on Man,* he moved "from grave to gay, from lively to severe." Argumentative passages of low intensity are interspersed

[77] *Works of Henry St. John,* III, 317–18.
[78] *Anecdotes,* p. 16.

with hortatory passages in the grand style; passages of polite badinage are mingled with paragraphs of high seriousness; some passages are serenely humble, while others burn with honest scorn. Throughout there is a kind of lucid compression of statement intended to give strength to the sentiments. Pope himself declared that such conciseness had been one of his principal aims: "I found I could express them [ideas] more *shortly* this way [in poetry] than in prose itself; and nothing is more certain, than that much of the *force* as well as *grace* of arguments or instructions, depends on their *conciseness*." [79] Another distinctive feature of the rhetoric of the poem is the number of grandiose figures that stream through it. Disorders in human affairs are reinforced with images of disorder drawn from the cosmic sphere; and harmony, on the other hand, is described by images of astronomical regularity:

The lawless man may

> meteor-like, flame lawless through the void,
> Destroying others, by himself destroy'd.

Pope shudders at the thought of cosmic confusion:

> Let Earth unbalanc'd from her orbit fly,
> Planets and Suns run lawless through the sky. . . .

Divine reason apparently has no such qualms. It sees

> with equal eye, as God of all,
> A hero perish, or a sparrow fall,
> Atoms or systems into ruin hurl'd,
> And now a bubble burst, and now a world. . . . [80]

The *Essay on Man* stands apart from the satires Pope composed during his later career; for it is essentially a philosophical poem. But it does have an obvious satiric flavor. Contempt and indignation are directed at the intellectual pride of "presumptuous man" which prompts the vain speculations of refining theologians, the perverseness of "subtle schoolmen" who "Grace and Virtue, Sense and Reason, split," and the impertinence of natural philosophers who would "correct old Time and regulate the Sun." Throughout the poem there occur satiric comments upon public and private vices, the "Tyrant mad with pride," the Christian "thirst for gold," the "impudence of wealth," and the "trim of Pride." Epithets of this kind do not let a reader forget that the *Essay on Man* was written by a poet in whom the satiric impulse was strong. In a more important respect, however, the *Essay on Man* occupies a central position among the major satires; for it offers a group of ethical ideas in a context of which the *Ethic Epistles* and, to some extent, the *Imitations of Horace* should be read.

Pope's views in the *Essay on Man*, and in his satires, rest on the assumption that man is a part of a comprehensive system—a chain of being—in which created things are subordinated with respect to one another by varying but prescribed

---

[79] In his statement of the design of his poem: Mack, pp. 7–8.
[80] George Sherburn, "Pope and 'The Great Shew of Nature,'" in *The Seventeenth Century: Studies in the History of English Thought and Literature from Bacon to Pope by Richard Foster Jones and Others Writing in his Honor* (Stanford, 1951), pp. 314–15.

> Wit, Spirit, Faculties, but make it worse;
> Reason itself but gives it edge and pow'r;
> As Heav'n's blest beam turns vinegar more sowr;
> We, wretched subjects tho' to lawful sway,
> In this weak queen, some fav'rite still obey.
>
> (II, ll. 128–50)

Having found that the passions are all "modes of self-love" and hence by nature selfish, Pope must show the terms in which moral distinctions can be made. This he does by assuming that there is in every man an agent—reason—by which the fundamentally egoistic promptings of the passions may be transmuted into ethically right action:

> Most strength the moving principle requires;
> Active its task, it prompts, impels, inspires.
> Sedate and quiet the comparing lies,
> Form'd but to check, delib'rate, and advise.
> Self-love still stronger, as its objects nigh;
> Reason's at distance, and in prospect lie:
> That sees immediate good by present sense;
> Reason, the future and the consequence.
> Thicker than arguments, temptations throng,
> At best more watchful this, but that more strong.
> The action of the stronger to suspend
> Reason still use, to Reason still attend:
> Attention, habit, and experience gains,
> Each strengthens Reason, and Self-love restrains.
>
> (II, ll. 67–80)

Reason is in part an appetitive faculty, which, like the other passions, seeks pleasure and avoids pain. It is also in part a ratiocinative faculty capable of apprehending the best interests of the individual, although, unlike the promptings of instinct in lower orders of being, its distinctions are not intuitively and necessarily correct:

> Reason, however able, cool at best,
> Cares not for service, or but serves when prest,
> Stays 'till we call, and then not often near;
> But honest Instinct comes a volunteer;
> Sure never to o'er-shoot, but just to hit,
> While still too wide or short is human Wit;
> Sure by quick Nature happiness to gain,
> Which heavier Reason labours at in vain.
> This too serves always, Reason never long;
> One must go right, the other may go wrong.
>
> (III, ll. 85–94)

Reason may mistake good and evil; but, properly comprehending them, it operates to "rectify, not overthrow" the passions. It is the "bias which turns to good from ill," directing the energies of the passions towards actions that serve the best interests of self, which are also the best interests of the whole:

> As fruits ungrateful to the planter's care
> On savage stocks inserted learn to bear;

> The surest Virtues thus from Passions shoot,
> Wild Nature's vigor working at the root.
> What crops of wit and honesty appear
> From spleen, from obstinacy, hate, or fear!
> See anger, zeal and fortitude supply;
> Ev'n av'rice, prudence; sloth, philosophy;
> Lust, thro' some certain strainers well refin'd,
> Is gentle love, and charms all womankind:
> Envy, to which th'ignoble mind's a slave,
> Is emulation in the learn'd or brave:
> Nor Virtue, male or female, can we name,
> But what will grow on Pride, or grow on Shame.
>
> (II, ll. 181–94)

These basic assumptions force Pope to reject extreme Stoicism as too exacting and Epicureanism as too mean for man. He also cannot accept in his ethics, as Milton had done, the comfortable solution of complete freedom of will, which places man's destiny entirely in his own hands. To Pope human character is a dual achievement, an achievement of the deity and man. The deity fixes the capacities of the individual, prescribing the limits within which he may act; and the deity insures the good of the whole, no matter what man makes of man. But if man is partly determined, there is a large area within which he is capable of acts of will by which ethical measurements become possible. These distinctions exist in the proper or improper use of reason and the passions:

> Nor this a good, nor that a bad we call,
> Each works its end, to move or govern all:
> And to their proper operation still,
> Ascribe all Good; to their improper, Ill.
>
> (II, ll. 55–58)

These faculties well employed will result in a harmony and order within the individual that contribute to the harmony and order of the cosmos. Evil is thus an assertion of self in perverse opposition to nature and society—an indulgence of the passions and misuse of reason. Virtue, on the other hand, proceeds from a harmonious concord of man's nature, a balance of reason and passion that promotes the good of the whole:

> Passions, like Elements, tho' born to fight,
> Yet, mix'd and soften'd, in his work unite:
> These 'tis enough to temper and employ;
> But what composes Man, can Man destroy?
> Suffice that Reason keep to Nature's road,
> Subject, compound them, follow her and God.
> Love, Hope, and Joy, fair pleasure's smiling train,
> Hate, Fear, and Grief, the family of pain;
> These mix'd with art, and to due bounds confin'd,
> Make and maintain the balance of the mind:
> The lights and shades, whose well accorded strife
> Gives all the strength and colour of our life.
>
> (II, ll. 111–22)

The attitudes of mind representing such harmony are described in the third and fourth epistles, where Pope addresses himself directly to what had become the principal problem of ethics since Thomas Hobbes, how self-love and social may be the same—a problem which had briefly been touched upon in the second epistle:

> Heav'n forming each on other to depend,
> A master, or a servant, or a friend,
> Bids each on other for assistance call,
> 'Till one Man's weakness grows the strength of all.
> Wants, frailties, passions, closer still ally
> The common int'rest, or endear the tie:
> To these we owe true friendship, love sincere,
> Each home-felt joy that life inherits here.
>
> (II, ll. 249–56)

The achievement of this social point of view by man is the result of progressive refinement and self-discipline under the aegis of reason:

> God loves from Whole to Parts: but human soul
> Must rise from Individual to the Whole.
> Self-love but serves the virtuous mind to wake,
> As the small pebble stirs the peaceful lake;
> The centre mov'd, a circle strait succeeds,
> Another still, and still another spreads,
> Friend, parent, neighbour, first it will embrace,
> His country next, and next all human race,
> Wide and more wide, th'o'erflowings of the mind
> Take ev'ry creature in, of ev'ry kind;
> Earth smiles around, with boundless bounty blest,
> And Heav'n beholds its image in his breast.
>
> (IV, ll. 361–72)

In the third epistle Pope undertakes to demonstrate the first stages of this development: he reveals how man committed to seek personal advantages discovers "the private in the public good." Family ties prepare the way for social attitudes; and man is eventually led to cooperation with others because society can most effectively minister to his wants. In the fourth epistle Pope attempts to demonstrate the further refinement of self-love, the manner by which it may be transformed into a "Love of God, and Love of Man." Such a state involves higher perceptions stemming from complex ratiocinative processes; and the aim of the fourth epistle is to record the steps by which reason comes to recognize the source of true happiness, which is distinguished from the pleasure associated with pure egoism. To reason "the Universal Cause acts not by partial, but by gen'ral laws," and happiness must be such that "all states can reach it, and all heads conceive." Happiness cannot, therefore, exist in conditions or circumstances that are accidental in character; it cannot exist in such external advantages as riches, titles, or fame, which are the products of fortune or chance. It can lie only in the practice of virtue, "which who but feels can taste, but thinks can know":

Know then this truth (enough for Man to know)
"Virtue alone is Happiness below."
The only point where human bliss stands still,
And tastes the good without the fall to ill;
Where only Merit constant pay receives,
Is blest in what it takes, and what it gives;
The joy unequal'd, if its end it gain,
And if it lose, attended with no pain:
Without satiety, tho' e'er so blest,
And but more relish'd as the more distress'd:
The broadest mirth unfeeling Folly wears,
Less pleasing far than Virtue's very tears.
Good, from each object, from each place acquir'd,
For ever exercis'd, yet never tir'd;
Never elated, while one man's oppress'd;
Never dejected, while another's bless'd;
And where no wants, no wishes can remain,
Since but to wish more Virtue, is to gain.

　　　　　(IV, ll. 309-26)

Virtue is for Pope the triumph of reason, an exalted state in which self-interest has been refined into a love of all things. This state is not narrowly conceived; it is a universal benevolence or *caritas,* embracing love, kindness, natural affection. It is a disposition to judge kindly the character, aims, and destinies of others. It is large-mindedness, prizing what is noble and worthy and hating what is mean, petty, and sordid.

These ethical propositions dominate Pope's satires. Because of the close relationship existing between the *Essay on Man* and the *Ethic Epistles,* similarities in these poems are most obvious; but even the *Imitations of Horace* reflect the values affirmed in the *Essay on Man.* What Pope sought in all his great satires was to inculcate the attitudes which he associated with virtue and which he believed made for harmony and order in society. The lesson of the philosophical poem is that men who would live according to nature will refine their conceptions of the sources of pleasure; the satires are attempts to encourage this refinement, to inculcate nobler conceptions of satisfaction than those prevailing in his day. What is recommended in them stems from the principle that "Faith, Law, Morals, all began, all end in LOVE of GOD, and LOVE of MAN." In castigating parochialism in letters, factionalism in government, prejudice in one's private affairs and in recommending versatility of taste, charity, justice, and moderation Pope has not forgotten that benevolence is the highest state to which man can aspire.

Throughout the *Essay on Man* as well as the satires there is the assumption that the state of the passions is the important concern in ethics. Vice follows from mean indulgence of the appetitive instincts; and virtue follows when these passions seek rationally acceptable gratifications. The aim of the satires is to furnish assistance to reason by posing the threat of exposure and ridicule and by making virtue appealing. The method of the satires is to state eloquently moral propositions and to present examples of vice in all its grossness and of virtue in all its grandeur.

Through these poems moves a parade of men whose indulgence of self, complicated by a perversion of reason, has resulted in the extremes of avarice, lechery, prodigality, and venality; and there moves a considerably smaller parade of those who have tempered passion with reason and have sought happiness in moderation, patriotism, and benevolence—the three principal stages of ethical development outlined in the *Essay on Man*. Because Pope believed that vice and virtue may proceed from the same passion—the difference existing in reason—his satires frequently demonstrate how the same passion may manifest itself in contrary ways. The possession of wealth leads to the avarice of Cotta and the charities of the Man of Ross. The love of pleasure and the love of sway that encourage the excesses of Philomedé and Atossa become good nature in Martha Blount. The vanity that leads Atticus, Bufo, and Sporus to mean efforts at patronizing men of letters becomes in the dramatic character of Alexander Pope an unselfish concern to forward merit. The love of power that prompted so many important figures of both political parties in the 1730's to sacrifice the interests of England has been refined in contemporary patriots like Lord Cobham and Lord Bolingbroke into a generous love of country.

Pope's discussion of man and society in the third epistle of the *Essay on Man* led naturally to a consideration of the role of government; and what he has to say provides a theoretical background for his later attacks upon the rulers of England. Governments are designed to supplement reason in individuals and to direct the interests of individuals toward service to the whole. In the most primitive societies the unit of government is the eldest of a family; in slightly more complex social groups governments are patriarchal in form, an extension of family organization. In larger societies where the conflicting interests of the group multiply, more complex organizations are required. The obligation of rule at any level, however, is to work for the best interests of the whole. These interests are not served by particular forms; excellence in government depends upon the moral character of those who administer it. A government is bad when it is presided over by corrupt leaders who have failed to master their own passions by reason and who prize power for its own sake or identify private with public good. Self-indulgence by the rulers results in conquest and tyranny; they prostitute religion to their own private ends; and they enslave their subjects. On the other hand, a government is good when it is directed by virtuous men, whose self-love is transmuted by reason into genuine patriotism. Such rulers have a high regard for the whole state; and they bring peace, prosperity, and happiness to those over whom they govern. Pope's satires reflect this primarily personal rather than legalistic view of government: they are for the most part concerned not with forms but with the moral character of those who rule.

IV

The *Ethic Epistles* are less sustained and exalted than the *Essay on Man;* they are primarily satires, the inspirations for which were ultimately Horatian. In consequence the style is less lofty, more informal. Perhaps the most interesting characteristic of these poems, from the point of view of Pope's development, is the number and quality of the formal satirical portraits they contain. The *Ethic Epistles,* combining moralized discourse and formal satirical characters of a Theophrastian kind, were in the general pattern of such moral discourses of the day as William Law's *Treatise on Christian Perfection* and *A Serious Call to a Devout and Holy Life.* More specifically they follow the pattern of Edward Young's *Universal Passion,* a series of seven satires published between 1725 and 1728.[81] Young's plan accommodated contemporary interests in morality and satire; and the poems proved popular. Pope, always sensitive to such trends in the taste of his own times, adopted the scheme in his own *Ethic Epistles;* but, recognizing the bland quality of Young's characters and the prolixity of his discourse, he sought to say more interesting things in a more incisive way.

The character was a genre which Pope came very slowly to utilize in his own practice. He had first drafted the portrait of Addison in 1715; and at this time or later he may have composed others, Macer and Umbra, directed at members of Addison's little senate, and Artimesia and Phryne, written in imitation of characters composed by the Earl of Dorset. Before 1729 these pieces were, however, incidental compositions, in which Pope took little interest, even though he had the practice of Dryden before him and Bishop Atterbury had declared that his "real strength" lay in this sort of writing.[82] The plan of the *Ethic Epistles* involved a series of characters offering illustrations, satirical in intent, for the moralizing commentary and providing concrete and picturesque appeal. The portraits give depth and richness to the epistles; but they remain subordinate to the argument. Most of them were written to support the proposition that in the ruling passion "the Wild are constant, and the Cunning known."

Pope once told Jacob Tonson, the elder, how important arrangement was to his characters in the *Ethic Epistles:* "To send you any of the particular verses will be much to the prejudice of the whole; which if it has any beauty, derives it from the manner in which it is *placed,* and the *contrast* (as the painters call it) in which it stands, with the pompous figures of famous, or rich, or high-born men." [83] Certainly the actual disposition of characters demonstrates the care he lavished upon design in the effort to secure compelling effects. Subordination and contrast were two principles he scrupulously observed. The plan of each epistle called for emphasis upon one or two fully developed characters, around which were grouped other less detailed sketches that pick up and emphasize suggestions in the major pieces. The *Epistle to Lord Bathurst,* for example, has many characters; but two, those of the Man of Ross and Sir Balaam, are detailed portraits, illustrating themes which serve as the basis of subordinate profiles—Cotta, Cotta's son, and Buckingham. The *Epistle to the Earl of Burlington* includes one long character, that of Timon; but prefacing it are two vignettes—of Villario and Sabinus—which to-

---

[81] Charlotte E. Crawford, "What was Pope's Debt to Edward Young?" *ELH,* XIII (1946), 157–67.

[82] Atterbury to Pope, February 26, 1722: E-C, IX, 39.

[83] June 7, 1732: E-C, IX, 552. Pope is speaking specifically of the character of the Man of Ross.

gether help to emphasize the vanity of Timon's vast landscape undertakings. Contrast often dictates the arrangement of characters. In its simplest form figures are directly balanced in pairs: Cotta, the miser, and his son, the prodigal; Atossa, with her uncontrolled vehemence, and Chloe, with her lack of spirit. The contrasting figures of Cotta and his son are in turn set against the sequent picture of the Man of Ross, who wisely employs his modest riches for the benefit of his village. Contrast of a more complex kind appears in the arrangement of several portraits leading to a final and quite dissimilar figure. The *Epistle to a Lady* is made up of increasingly complex characters, and the group ends with a courtly and complimentary character of Martha Blount. The *Epistle to Lord Cobham* concludes with a series of tableaux, posing seven figures in the grip of a ruling passion at the moment of death. This suite is followed by an eighth, which abruptly concludes the poem, an imaginary view of Cobham who in his last utterance gives expression to a noble passion, a love of country.

Nearly all of Pope's characters reflect the influence of the analogy between poetry and painting. The *Epistle to a Lady,* indeed, contains a discussion of the relationship between graphic techniques and the art of composing verse characters. Many of the sketches in this poem, and in the others, have marked picturesque qualities. The eight figures described in the conclusion to the *Epistle to Lord Cobham* are each caught and exposed at a significant moment; the character of Timon is essentially a landscape painting of the garden and villa; the description of Cotta concludes with a picturesque prospect of Cotta's gloomy and forbidding mansion. Pope's treatment of his models was analogous to the treatment painters tried to give their subjects. After his unhappy experience with the generalized character of Timon, he more commonly utilized a specific and concrete personality as the basis of a sketch. The satirical function of the characters meant, however, that the specific model should be raised to the power of a type, an artful heightening which involved shading, shifting of emphasis, and altering of detail—processes that made neat identification of his models difficult. No portrait painter of the eighteenth century sought an exact, one-to-one correspondence between his picture and his model; and Pope likewise avoided photographic accuracy. He idealized some of his subjects—as the Man of Ross—by showing them engaged in actions which they did not perform but which they ideally were capable of performing. He admitted to Jacob Tonson that he had altered, for instructive purposes, the strictest truth regarding the Man of Ross:

A small exaggeration you must allow me as a poet; yet I was determined the groundwork at least should be *truth,* which made me so scrupulous in my enquiries, and sure, considering that the world is bad enough to be always extenuating and lessening what virtue is among us, it is but reasonable to pay it sometimes a little over measure, to balance that injustice, especially when it is done for example and encouragement to others. If any man shall ever happen to endeavour to emulate the Man of Ross, it will be no manner of harm if I make him think he was something more charitable and more beneficent than really he was, for so much more good it would put the imitator upon doing. And farther, I am satisfied in my conscience (from the strokes in two or three accounts I have of his character) that it was in his will, and in his heart, to have done every good a poet can imagine.[84]

The necessity of presenting figures in a way that might strike the imagination prompted other changes in literal fact. The actual relationship of Sir John Cutler and his son-in-law, the second Earl of Radnor, was altered in the *Epistle to Lord Bathurst* to one of father and son, in order to make the contrast more pointed; legend rather than truth was employed in setting the scene of Buckingham's death in a "worst inn's worst room." The fact that the characters appeared in specific contexts frequently required simplification. In a manuscript state of the character of old Cotta, for example, the description concludes with an account of Cutler's elaborate funeral contrasting with the squalor of his life:

> He dies, & lo! a thousand Lights attend
> On him who, living, sav'd the Taper's End:
> High on his Tomb a wicked Statue stands,
> Belies his Features, & extends his Hands
> The very Wig that Gorgon's self m^{ht} own,
> Eternal Buckle takes in Parian Stone.[85]

This conclusion represents an intrusion upon the specific theme that the whole portrait was designed to illustrate—the anti-social nature of avarice; and before first printing the poem Pope wisely transferred these lines to another section of the work, in which he considers more directly the vanity of avarice.[86]

Poetry is, of course, an artistic medium fundamentally different from painting. As Sir Joshua Reynolds remarked in his Eighth Discourse: "Poetry operates by raising our curiosity, engaging the mind by degrees to take an interest in the event, keeping that event suspended, and surprising at last with an unexpected catastrophe." Although Pope's characters must necessarily develop through a succession of details, the parts are closely interrelated; and each character seems to produce, as in the graphic arts, a simultaneous rather than a sequential consciousness of meaning. Pope's most distinctive method of achieving this effect is by withholding the full intent of a character until the end, where a marked reversal in tone, or the addition of an illuminating detail, brings the whole into an unexpected but satirically inevitable focus. The portrait of the Duke of Wharton in the *Epistle to Lord Cobham* begins with dispassionate objectivity; it concludes with a series of scornful epithets describing Wharton as "Fool," "Tyrant," and "Rebel." The character of old Cotta opens with pleasantly astringent raillery; it ends with sardonic irony:

> While the gaunt mastiff growling at the gate,
> Affrights the beggar whom he longs to eat.
>
> (*Epistle to Bathurst*, ll. 197–98)

Philomedé, in the *Epistle to a Lady*, embodies lust on an almost heroic scale—until

---

[84] June 7, 1732: E-C, IX, 552.

[85] From Richardson's marginalia in *Epistle to Lord Bathurst* in a copy of Pope's *Works* (London, 1735) in the Henry E. Huntington Library.

[86] They appear, somewhat altered, after the Man of Ross passage in the first printed version, where they are applied to John Hopkins.

the conclusion of her portrait where the tendency of the description is brilliantly
revealed:

> So Philomedé, lect'ring all mankind
> On the soft Passion, and the Taste refin'd,
> Th'Address, the Delicacy—stoops at once,
> And makes her hearty meal upon a Dunce.
>
> (ll. 83–86)

The vice, which at first appears voluptuous and seductive, suddenly is made mean
and contemptible, especially when one recalls, as one is intended to do, the *Dunciad*.
The sketch of Villario opens with a description of a garden of which Pope might
have approved; there is little suggestion of the satiric intent until the concluding
couplet, which emphasizes the capriciousness of Villario's taste:

> Tir'd of the scene Parterres and Fountains yield,
> He finds at last he better likes a Field.
>
> (*Epistle to Burlington*, ll. 87–88)

Generalizing about the characters in the *Ethic Epistles* may suggest that they are
more stereotyped than they actually are. The immediate context frequently dictated different methods of treatment; and Pope was master of many techniques.
Furthermore, the characters were written over a period of years; and the later ones,
Philomedé, Atossa, and even the Duke of Wharton, are more conversational in
tone, less obviously posed, than the earlier Timon, Buckingham, and Sir Balaam.
"Flying strokes" and "wand'ring touches" that "give form and spirit to all the
composition" distinguish the art of the later characters. An analysis of three different but representative portraits will indicate something of Pope's versatility in
this kind of painting.

The first is a justly famous one, that of George Villiers, Duke of Buckingham, in
the *Epistle to Lord Bathurst*. It is in Pope's grander style, its solemnity supported
by the slow-paced resonance of the diction and by Pope's use of the pyrrhic foot,
which imparts a stately lyrical movement to the lines. It opens with an extended
portrait of Buckingham on his death bed, a picture that emphasizes the absence
of each of the four advantages possessed by the earlier Buckingham—health, fortune,
fame, and friends. In this picture a long periodic construction is skillfully employed
to bring the central figure into high relief:

> In the worst inn's worst room, with mat half-hung,
> The floors of plaister, and the walls of dung,
> On once a flock-bed, but repair'd with straw,
> With tape-ty'd curtains, never meant to draw,
> The George and Garter dangling from that bed
> Where tawdry yellow strove with dirty red,
> Great Villiers lies . . . .
>
> (ll. 299–305)

The second part of the character is given over to reflections stimulated by this
scene. The meditations focus upon Buckingham's happier days; and they include

two brief glimpses of him at the zenith of his luminous career, adorning "Cliveden's proud alcove" and performing his merry role in the royal councils—general views contrasting with the more detailed death-bed picture. An echo of *Paradise Lost* is introduced to relate the metamorphosis of Buckingham to that of Satan. The full meaning of the picture is, however, withheld until the concluding couplet; it is conveyed by the ironically applied honorific term "Victor" which sets Buckingham's personal character in perverse opposition to the external advantages that had been his.

The delineation of Buckingham recalls another famous portrayal of the same figure, the Zimri of Dryden's *Absalom and Achitophel*. Pope's characterization is somewhat briefer than Dryden's; but it is more inclusive than the latter's detailed and more narrowly focused analysis—its application to the world of men is larger. For Pope, writing after Buckingham's death and after the Restoration when a juster perspective was possible, indicts a whole society through his subject. Buckingham is a symbol of a social order, the "fat age of pleasure, wealth, and ease" which was, for Pope, the Restoration. Buckingham possessed, as did his circle, every aid to success; yet, as with the other court wits, his love of pleasure and his moral instability prevented a socially useful employment of his health, his friends, his fame, and his fortune. He set too high a premium upon his ephemeral pleasures, as did "wanton Shrewsbury," "mimick'd Statesmen," and a "merry King." Gallant, gay, and irresponsible, the whole group could, as did Buckingham, conclude its hour wretchedly, still colorful but bankrupt.

The character of Sir Balaam, which follows closely upon that of Buckingham in the *Epistle to Lord Bathurst,* is also in the highly finished style of Pope's earlier contributions to the *Ethic Epistles*. Like the portrait of Buckingham, it is an indictment of a segment of society; but to achieve the desired representation Pope did not use a specific personality as a model, a personality capable of epitomizing the tendencies of a social class in his own career. Instead, he created a highly typical figure who embraced the dominant traits of the merchant class of Augustan England. To enrich the meaning of the picture Pope utilized, as Dryden had done in *Absalom and Achitophel,* the suggestions inherent in Biblical allusions. The account of Balaam is cast in the form of a parable, an adaptation of the story of Job, with whom the devil succeeds in the eighteenth century by making rich, not poor. The name of the hero is drawn from a second Biblical narrative, the story of Balaam, whose ass was more perceptive than he in detecting the angel of the Lord. That Balaam should be knighted is Pope's comment on the kind of virtue rewarded at Court.

Pope's Balaam illustrates the corrupting power of wealth in the hands of those morally unequipped to use it wisely. The account opens with a description of Balaam in his early days, pious by his own standards but confused. He lives under a sign of bullying "enthusiasm," the monument built in memory of the fire of London with its inscription charging that the city had been burned by a Popish plot. To emphasize the blend of piety and worldliness that distinguishes the early

Balaam, Pope enters into his point of view and skillfully exploits the language of the merchants. Zeugma is used for satirical effects: Balaam is described as one "religious, punctual, frugal, and so forth"; he is "constant at Church, and Change." Terms traditionally reserved for religious mysteries of the more elevated kind are ironically applied to the worldly activities and interests of Balaam: his penuriousness is termed "saintship"; in his household an "added pudding solemniz'd the Lord's" day; and he thinks that two shipwrecks, with all their tragic implications, "bless the lucky shore." Balaam's scheme of values is unsatisfactory; but riches corrupt even it; for Balaam, when he becomes wealthy, gives up his pious canting. "Things change their titles, as our manners turn"; and Balaam's interpretation of his success becomes frankly self-indulgent. He now ascribes his

> gettings to his parts and merit,
> What late he call'd a Blessing, now was Wit,
> And God's good Providence, a lucky Hit.
>
> (ll. 376–78)

Balaam's demoralization is not yet complete, however; for he still duly sends his wife and family to Church, and he has yet to learn the vices of fashion. When he is at length condemned to die, he makes the final gesture of allying himself with the devil; for "sad Sir Balaam curses God and dies." The force of this climax is intensified by the fact that in it Pope returns his readers abruptly to the Bible, to the story of Job who remained steadfast and to the story of Balaam, of whom Moab said, "He whom thou blessest is blest; and he whom thou cursest is curst."

The character of Atossa in the *Epistle to a Lady* is in Pope's later, more informal manner. It is less obtrusively posed and more directly analytic; the style is seemingly less finished. Sentence elements are clipped; the diction is colloquial; and repetition of words and sentiments is marked. But the ease comes from art, not chance. In spite of the appearance of informality, the materials fall naturally into three different sections: the first treats Atossa's whirling mind; the second illustrates her capricious and violent turns of passion; and the third provides moralizing comment on Atossa's career. The looseness of the style reinforces basic ideas in the composition. The brevity of the syntactic elements suggests something of the breath-taking abruptness of Atossa's manner; the diction, marked by vigorous and indiscriminate pejorative words like "Knaves," "Fools," "hate," and "Cheat," echoes Atossa's vehement and unreasoned judgments. And the repetitions, which are of an incremental sort permitting new details to enter into the picture, imitate, by suggestion, the giddy turns of Atossa's thought.

The portrait is not without depth and power. Atossa is much more than Pope's appraisal of the Duchess of Buckinghamshire.[87] Concrete details associating the

---

[87] Vinton A. Dearing, "The Prince of Wales's Set of Pope's *Works*," *Harvard Library Bulletin*, IV (1950), 329–36, points to an earlier version of the Atossa portrait than that supposedly printed for the first time in the edition of *Ethic Epistles* which Pope prepared with Warburton in 1743–1744. A copy of Pope's *Works* (now in the Harvard College Library), prepared for the Prince of Wales in 1738, contains a cancelled leaf with the Atossa portrait. A few lines in this version might apply to the Duchess of Marlborough, although Pope subsequently removed them.

subject with only one model are eliminated; and Atossa is treated as the type of noblewoman who, intoxicated by wealth and power, cannot control an enormous vitality and thereby fails to attain the ends she seeks. As the portrait emerges, we find that Pope is interested not only in the ethical but also in the social implications of the type Atossa represents. The world in which she moves is one embracing husbands and children, superiors, equals, and dependents. Such a social order can exist only when these groups are bound together by ties of respect, obligation, loyalty, and affection. Atossa, in her violent pursuit of ends, ignores these natural means; and her world, in consequence, is one of disorder.

In composing these characters Pope was exercising himself in a well-established poetic genre, one that represented England's most significant contribution to formal verse satire. He was trying for perfection in this, as he had in so many other modes of composition; and he challenged comparison with other masters well known to his age, Young and Dryden. His success is distinctive. His own habits of mind, as well as the context in which he placed his characters, prevented him from achieving the boldness to be found in the work of Dryden. Nevertheless, his work is remarkable for its compactness and fertility, its technical virtuosity and allusiveness.

The *Essay on Man* and the *Ethic Epistles* are magnificent undertakings. Changes in sensibility that the poet could not have anticipated have partially obscured the merits of the poems; but they do not prevent readers from appreciating the grandeur of the conception or the subtlety with which moral corruption, its "mean compromises, sullen vanities, and secret brutalities," is detected and interpreted. And in the eyes of Pope's contemporaries he had fashioned a fitting crown for a distinguished career; he had shown that moving poetry could be created out of the most highly prized speculative materials of his day. After this display of intellectual energy, Pope was not again tempted to a comparable effort; and the *Imitations of Horace,* and even the fourth book of the *Dunciad,* were, for all their merits, produced in twilight.

CHAPTER FOUR

The *Imitations of Horace*

Pope began composing major Horatian imitations even when he was most actively at work on his *Ethic Epistles*. His earliest, the *First Satire of the Second Book,* was published on February 15, 1733; and it had probably been written in December (or January), prompted by a chance suggestion of Lord Bolingbroke:

> When I had a fever, one winter in town, that confined me to my room for five or six days, Lord Bolingbroke, who came to see me, happened to take up a Horace that lay on the table; and in turning it over, dipped on the first satire of the second book, which begins *Sunt quibus in satirâ, &c.* He observed, how well that would hit my case, if I were to imitate it in English. After he was gone, I read it over; translated it in a morning or two, and sent it to the press in a week or fortnight after. And this was the occasion of my imitating some other of the satires and epistles afterwards.[1]

The imitation was written in anticipation of criticism of the ethic epistle Pope published early in 1733. The reception of his *Epistle to the Earl of Burlington* had demonstrated how even his serious efforts might be wilfully misconstrued; and the *Epistle to Lord Bathurst,* in which he wrote boldly of the prevailing mercenary spirit and in which he named a number of particular contemporaries by way of example, promised to provoke a still more intense storm of abusive criticism. To such censure an answer from Horace would, he hoped, serve as a quick and effective response;[2] and even if the expected clamor failed to occur, publication of the imitation could be useful. The first part of the *Essay on Man* was ready; and, anxious to conceal his hand in this poem, Pope could help to preserve its anonymity by bringing out the Horatian imitation just before the first part of the *Essay* appeared. For the town, knowing that he had written both the *Epistle to Lord Bathurst* and the *First Satire of the Second Book,* might assume that he had been too preoccupied with such poems to be concerned in the philosophical work.

When Pope published this first imitation, he apparently had no plans for writing a series of such compositions. During the next five years, however, he imitated almost a third of Horace's satires and wrote several poems in the Horatian spirit, not based on specific Horatian satires. Most of these compositions were oc-

---

[1] *Anecdotes,* p. 297. There is no reason to doubt that the imitation was written quickly. Pope told John Caryll that it was "the work of two days" (E-C, VI, 338); and he declared to both Swift and Jonathan Richardson that it was "writ in two mornings" (E-C, VII, 297; IX, 501).

[2] In the "Advertisement" prefacing the *Imitations* in the second volume of Pope's *Works* (1735) Pope declared: "*The Occasion of publishing these* Imitations *was the Clamour raised on some of my* Epistles. *An Answer from* Horace *was both more full, and of more Dignity, than any I cou'd have made in my own person* . . ." (Butt, p. 3).

casional pieces; one or two of them were written quickly. Some were the casual products of idle hours; while others were mosaics of fragments composed earlier and now worked into a coherent pattern. Unlike the parts of the *Dunciad* or the various epistles in his moral plan, each imitation of Horace was not composed as part of a preconceived, cohesive design, but written as circumstances and inspiration dictated. Pope, as we have seen, imitated the *First Satire of the Second Book* in the winter of 1732–33 because he thought the *Epistle to Lord Bathurst* might need a defense; but satirical allusions to both Lady Mary Wortley Montagu and Lord Hervey in this poem led to more imitation.[3] In an effort at retaliation upon Pope, Lady Mary, with the help of Lord Hervey, published *Verses Addressed to the Imitator of the First Satire of the Second Book of Horace,* in which they charged him with ribaldry, scandal, malice, envy, and indiscriminate raillery. There was nothing really distinguished about the *Verses;* Pope had often endured such vituperative tirades. Nevertheless, the prestige of the authors and the wide circulation of the lampoon encouraged him to respond. Although he promised Sir Robert Walpole he would "never reply to such a libel as Lady Mary's," [4] he contrived in 1733 and 1734 means of delivering effective counterblows.

The quarrel with Lady Mary and Lord Hervey directed Pope's attention to the Court as an object of satirical portrayal; and he published in 1733–34 two imitations in which he attacked the manners of courtiers and in which Lady Mary and Lord Hervey were pointedly referred to. The first of these imitations, the *Second Satire of the Second Book,* which had been composed before the end of March, 1733, but was not published until September, 1734, indicted intemperance prevailing among people of quality.[5] It contained a brief satirical thrust at Lord Hervey:

> For 'faith Lord Fanny! you are in the wrong,
> The World's good word is better than a Song.
>
> (ll. 101–102)

It also included a longer and more venomous passage on Lady Mary and her husband:

> *Avidien* or his Wife (no matter which,
> For him you'll call a dog, and her a bitch)
> Sell their presented Partridges, and Fruits,
> And humbly live on rabbits and on roots:
> One half-pint bottle serves them both to dine,
> And is at once their vinegar and wine.
> But on some lucky day (as when they found
> A lost Bank-bill, or heard their Son was drown'd)

---

[3] See Appendix D for an account of Pope's relations with Lady Mary and Lord Hervey.

[4] Pope to Fortescue, March 18, 1733: E-C, IX, 119.

[5] Pope reported to John Caryll on March 20, 1733: "I have made noise enough for one winter, though I have done another of Horace's satires since I wrote to you last, and much in the same space of time as I did the former, though you do not believe when I speak truth. The next time I will compliment my own work better, and pretend it cost me more pains" (E-C, VI, 340). He declared to Swift on April 2: ". . . this week, *exercitandi gratiâ,* I have translated, or rather parodied, another of Horace's, in which I introduce you advising me about my expenses, housekeeping, &c." (E-C, VII, 307).

At such a feast old vinegar to spare,
Is what two souls so gen'rous cannot bear;
Oyl, tho' it stink, they drop by drop impart,
But sowse the Cabbidge with a bounteous heart.

(ll. 49–60)

On November 5, 1733, Pope published his imitation of John Donne's fourth satire under the title *The Impertinent*.[6] This work exposed the affectation and mean vanities of courtiers; and Hervey was directly mentioned:

Not *Fannius* self more impudently near,
When half his Nose is in his Patron's Ear.

(ll. 178–79)

Pope also alluded to his current private quarrel with his titled adversaries:

Shall I, the Terror of this sinful Town,
Care, if a livery'd Lord or smile or frown?

(ll. 196–97)

Courts are too much for Wits so weak as mine;
Charge them with Heav'n's Artill'ry, bold *Divine!*
From such alone the Great Rebukes endure,
Whose *Satyr's sacred,* and whose Rage *secure.*
'Tis mine to wash a few slight Stains; but theirs
To deluge Sin, and drown a Court in Tears.
Howe'er, what's now *Apocrypha,* my Wit,
In time to come, may pass for *Holy Writ.*

(ll. 280–87)

Meanwhile Lord Hervey made a contribution to the quarrel. In August, 1733, he penned *An Epistle from a Nobleman to a Doctor of Divinity,* inept verses in which he reiterated in prosaic fashion a number of commonplace charges against Pope. The publication of this lampoon early in November stimulated the poet to attempt a vindication of himself in the face of charges that Lord Hervey had repeated and that Lady Mary and others had preferred earlier. The task was not, however, easy; and Pope had to search for a proper means of making his response. He first attempted a prose vindication in which he sought to justify his treatment of Broome in the *Odyssey* affair and to give a full account of his relations with Lord Hervey; but he did not bring himself to publish this reply, which was too directly personal

---

[6] Pope declared that he had imitated both the fourth and second satires of Dr. Donne—the imitation of the second was not published until 1735—at the *"Desire of the Earl of* Oxford *while he was Lord Treasurer, and of the Duke of* Shrewsbury *who had been Secretary of State; neither of whom look'd upon a Satire on Vicious Courts as any Reflection on those they serv'd in"* (Butt, p. 3). No early manuscript of Pope's imitation of Donne's fourth satire is now known to exist, though a manuscript of the second satire is preserved in the British Museum (Lansdowne MSS. 852). The manuscript of the second satire, presumably, is mentioned in a letter of Lord Oxford to Pope, March 10, 1726 (E-C, VIII, 220). If the imitation of the fourth satire had been, as Pope declared, written at an early date, it was certainly much revised in 1733; for the poem has a number of allusions to events topical in 1733 but not earlier.

to be effective.[7] A more satisfactory plan occurred to him in the summer of 1734.

At this time he had determined to bring out a second volume of his *Works,* a collection of all the major original poems written or published since the first volume had appeared in 1717.[8] Because the compositions which were to go into this second collection differed significantly in subject matter, design, and tone from those in the earlier volume, a prefatory vindication describing the author's personal character and explaining the shift that had taken place in his poetic interests would hardly seem out of place in it. At the same time Dr. Arbuthnot, aware that he had not long to live and distressed by Pope's involvement in a purely personal controversy with Lord Hervey and Lady Mary, offered advice to Pope that seemed to call for some sort of apologia from the poet: "And I make it my last request, that you continue that noble disdain and abhorrence of vice, which you seem naturally endued with, but still with a due regard to your own safety; and study more to reform than chastise, though the one often cannot be effected without the other." [9]

Pope, at Bevis Mount with Lord Peterborough, replied on August 2, defending his use of particular satire on the grounds that "general satire in times of general vice has no force and is no punishment." [10] This exchange furnished Pope with the idea of casting an apology in the form of a verse epistle to his friend; and he wrote to Arbuthnot of his plan on August 25, 1734:

I took very kindly your advice concerning avoiding ill will from writing satire, and it has worked so much upon me, considering the time and state you gave it in, that I determine to address to you one of my epistles, written by piecemeal many years, and which I have now made haste to put together; wherein the question is stated, what were, and are my motives of writing, the objections to them, and my answers. It pleases me much to take this occasion of testifying, to the public at least, if not to posterity, my obligation and friendship for, and from you, for so many years; that is all that is in it; for compliments are fulsome and go for nothing.[11]

[7] Pope told Swift, January 6, 1734, that he had suppressed the work because it involved his descending to the level of purely personal controversy with Hervey: "There is a woman's war declared against me by a certain lord. His weapons are the same which women and children use, a pin to scratch, and a squirt to bespatter. I writ a sort of answer, but was ashamed to enter the lists with him, and, after showing it to some people, suppressed it,—otherwise it was such as was worthy of him and worthy of me" (E-C, VII, 318). Horace Walpole declared that Pope had suppressed the work at the request of Robert Walpole's brother Horatio: "Warburton publishes his edition of Pope next week, with the famous piece of prose on Lord Hervey, which he formerly suppressed at my uncle's desire, who had got an abbey from Cardinal Fleury for one Southcote, a friend of Pope's: my Lord Hervey pretended not to thank him" (*Horace Walpole's Correspondence,* ed. W. S. Lewis [New Haven, 1937–   ], IX, 116). The composition was first published by William Warburton in his edition of Pope's *Works* (1751), VIII, 253–80.

[8] On September 15, 1734, Pope wrote Swift, "I shall collect all the past in one fair quarto this winter . . . " (E-C, VII, 325).

[9] July 17, 1734: E-C, VII, 479.

[10] E-C, VII, 480. When Pope published his *Letters* in 1737, he included another and more formal reply to Arbuthnot, a letter dated July 26, 1734. This letter is a fabrication; Pope's only actual answer to Arbuthnot's advice of July 17 is the note dated August 2 and quoted above. The general import of the remarks in both letters is, however, the same.

[11] E-C, VII, 484–85.

Composition of the *Epistle to Dr. Arbuthnot* seemingly proceeded with what was for Pope incredible speed, especially since the poem was an original one not drawing its substance from an Horatian satire. Indeed, on September 3, some nine days after he had first announced that he was putting it together, he told Arbuthnot that he had had time to "finish" it.[12] This rapid progress is, however, less remarkable when one remembers that Pope had been contemplating such a work for a long time—as he told Arbuthnot, it had been "written by piecemeal many years." There is, in fact, an interesting manuscript in the Henry E. Huntington Library which contains about a hundred verses, in Pope's hand, with copious additions and corrections in the margins. These verses are a part of an early sketch of what became the *Epistle to Dr. Arbuthnot*. The sketch is not complete—another part of it may exist among manuscript fragments of the *Epistle* now in the Pierpont Morgan Library.[13] Nevertheless, there is enough to demonstrate that the poem is addressed, not to Arbuthnot, but to William Cleland, a friend of Pope who signed the "Letter to the Publisher" prefacing the *Dunciad Variorum* of 1729. In the sketch represented by these manuscripts, personalities who were on Pope's mind in 1732 rather than in 1734 are mentioned; and there is the notable absence of the lines alluding to Sappho, Arbuthnot, Sporus, and the Duchess of Queensberry weeping over the urn of John Gay. These facts lead to Professor Butt's reasonable conjecture that a sketch of what was eventually to be the *Epistle to Dr. Arbuthnot* was prepared in 1732, perhaps when Pope was most concerned over current interpretations of his character of Timon.

Furthermore, the *Epistle to Dr. Arbuthnot* includes several short sketches that can definitely be dated long before the summer of 1734. The sketch of Bufo, for example, was perhaps drafted by 1730–31.[14] The passage of the *Epistle* containing the Atticus lines (ll. 151–214) was already in print. A section of the conclusion to the poem (ll. 406–19), in which Pope described his care of his mother, had been included in a letter he sent Aaron Hill, September 3, 1731; and some of the Sporus lines (ll. 291–304) had been printed in the *London Evening Post*, January 22–25, 1732, as a paraphrase of a passage in the *Fourth Satire of the First Book of Horace*.[15] Such evidence proves that the *Epistle to Dr. Arbuthnot* was not conceived in great haste but had in fact been germinating in Pope's mind for almost four years, perhaps ever since the uproar over the *Dunciad Variorum*.

---

[12] E-C, VII, 485.

[13] Professor Butt, in the Warton lecture delivered before the British Academy on January 20, 1954, has ingeniously attempted to reconstruct the sketch by comparing manuscripts at the Henry E. Huntington Library and at the Pierpont Morgan Library. The lecture will presently be published in the *Proceedings of the British Academy*.

[14] Daniel A. Fineman, *Leonard Welsted* (Philadelphia, 1950), p. 197. The manuscript variants indicate that the sketch had at one time portrayed Doddington with Theobald and Welsted as satellite poetasters. This relationship was more relevant to circumstances of 1730–31 than to those of 1734–35.

[15] For Pope's lines on his mother, see E-C, X, 30–31; for the lines imitated from Horace, see above, p. 37. Dr. Johnson in his *Life of Thomson* relates that Pope had expressed his regard for Thomson in a "poetical Epistle" sent to Italy, and that some lines of this epistle were subsequently transferred to the *Epistle to Dr. Arbuthnot* (*Lives of the Poets*, ed. G. Birkbeck Hill [Oxford, 1905], III, 291). Nothing is now known of this "poetical Epistle."

Although the original plans called for the first publication of the new satire in the second volume of *Works*, Arbuthnot's failing health and the slow progress of the collection made early and hence separate publication of the poem desirable if Arbuthnot were ever to see it in print. New arrangements that would appear to justify the publication of such a defense were improvised. They involved the almost simultaneous appearance of the *Epistle* and the somewhat libidinous *Sober Advice from Horace,* an imitation of the *Second Satire of the First Book* which Pope had completed by June 27, 1734.[16] Various features of this work as published were calculated to suggest that it was not Pope's composition but a parody of his style. The title page told readers that the poem had imitated Horace "in the Manner of Mr. Pope"; the imprint, "Printed for T. Boreman, at the Cock on Ludgate-Hill; and sold by the Booksellers of London and Westminster," implied that the poem was the work of a Grub-street author. The general impression that such details create is that *Sober Advice* is an attack upon the satirist, an obscene parody of his manner in the *Imitations of Horace.* Pope evidently hoped that if readers could be made to think that *Sober Advice* was an abusive lampoon, they would be prepared to accept his apologia without question.

The publication of the *Epistle to Dr. Arbuthnot* marks the end of one period in Pope's concern with Horace, a period in which an important aim was to attack Lady Mary and Lord Hervey by exposing the Court and to defend his character as a man and satirist against the charges which his adversaries had made. Pope did not again return to Horace until the spring of 1736; and when he did, he utilized the Latin poet for different purposes. For by this time he had become entangled in the cause of the Opposition to Sir Robert Walpole. After 1733 his more or less friendly relations with Walpole had deteriorated. Although he may not earlier have been entirely sympathetic with the government, he was on friendly terms, through William Fortescue, who began his career as Walpole's secretary, and the Burlingtons, with England's political leader; and he was often in Walpole's company. On February 17, 1726, he told Fortescue that he had "dined the other day at Sir Robert Walpole's";[17] on August 5, 1727, he "waited on Sᵣ. R.W." after a ramble to Cambridge;[18] and on May 10 [year?], he wrote, possibly with reference to Walpole's help in securing a position for the Abbé Southcott, "How kind Sir R. Walpole has been to me."[19] In 1732 he was determined to remain free from political parties:

---

[16] Bolingbroke wrote Swift on June 27: "The demon of verse sticks close to him [Pope]. He has been imitating the satire of Horace, which begins *Ambubaiarum collegia pharmacopolæ,* &c., and has chosen rather to weaken the images, than to hurt chaste ears over much. He has sent it me; but I shall keep his secret as he desires, and shall not, I think, return him the copy; for the rogue has fixed a ridicule upon me, which some events of my life would seem, perhaps, to justify him in doing" (E-C, VII, 322).

[17] E-C, IX, 107.

[18] An unpublished letter now preserved in the Harvard College Library.

[19] E-C, IX, 109. Elwin conjectured that the kindness referred to was Walpole's help in securing the abbey of St. André at Villeneuve-les-Avignon for Thomas Southcott. G. D. Henderson, *Chevalier Ramsay* (London, Thomas Nelson and Sons, 1952), p. 90, says that "though negotiations [for the post] were definitely on foot early in 1723, as the *Stuart Papers* bear witness, Southcott

"You know I never had either a taste or talent for politics, and the world minds nothing else. I have personal obligations, which I will ever preserve, to men of different sides, and I wish nothing so much as public quiet, except it be my own quiet. I think it a merit, if I can take off any man from grating or satirical subjects, merely on the score of party: and it is the greatest vanity of my life that I have contributed to turn my Lord Bolingbroke to subjects moral, useful, and more worthy his pen." [20]

Although Pope did not engage in partisan strife before 1733, efforts had been made by his dunces to link him with the Opposition, just as earlier critics had once attempted to label him a Jacobite. "Orator" Henley, for example, wrote in the *Hyp-Doctor,* November, 1731: "We are told that Mr. P—e wrote the Poem call'd *The Dawley Farm* and the *Norfolk Steward* besides several Letters in *Fog* and *Crafts-man."* Both *Dawley Farm, by an Admirer of Lord Bolingbroke,* which had appeared in *Fog's Weekly Journal,* June, 1731, and the *History of the Norfolk Steward,* first printed in the *Craftsman,* September 2, 1727, had venomously attacked Walpole; but it is most unlikely, in spite of Henley's hostile testimony, that Pope had had anything to do with either.[21] In 1727, when the *Norfolk Steward* first appeared, he was often at Walpole's dinner table; and in 1731, when *Dawley Farm* was first published, he still hoped to secure a place for John Gay. He could hardly have obtained his end if he had in fact composed this mordant satire. Another effort was made to link him with the Opposition when he published his *Epistle to the Earl of Burlington;* for Matthew Concanen, in *A Miscellany on Taste,* alleged not only that Timon was the Duke of Chandos but also that the lines on Sir Shylock were intended for Walpole:

> What brought Sir *Shylock*'s ill-got Wealth to waste?
> Some Dæmon whisper'd, *"Knights* shou'd have a *Taste."*
> Heav'n visits with a *Taste* the wealthy Fool,
> And needs no Rod, but *S——d* with a Rule.
>
> (ll. 15–18)

---

did not in fact obtain his abbey until after the death of the afflicted de Roure [Southcott's predecessor who had become insane] in 1728." But in the letter of May 10 Pope is thanking Walpole for some kindness done instantly and with dispatch; and it seems unlikely that the letter refers to the affair of the abbey. Pope was indebted to Walpole from time to time for a number of kindnesses. In 1725 Walpole got for Pope a treasury grant of £200 for his *Odyssey;* and Walpole also helped to get Mrs. Howard the title to additional land she wanted at Marble Hill, a business in which Pope interested himself. In 1729 Walpole presented a copy of the *Dunciad Variorum* to the King and Queen on behalf of Pope, and it may well be this favor to which Pope alluded in his letter to Fortescue.

[20] [April, 1732]: E-C, VII, 264.

[21] Pope did utilize a line from *Dawley Farm* in his imitation of the *First Satire of the Second Book of Horace:* "The Feast of Reason, and the Flow of Soul" (l. 128). Pope sometimes "stole" good lines from his contemporaries, however. Edward Young told Joseph Spence in January, 1743: "Pope was so superior, to all the Poets his Contemporaries in Versifⁿ, that if he met with a good line (evⁿ in a work inferior) he wᵈ take it (like a Lᵈ of yᵉ Manʳ) for his own. This evⁿ frō Ambrose Philips. Nor shall his promise to his people fail in his Iliad" (from the Spence manuscripts [p. 433] now in the Henry E. Huntington Library).

Shylock, however, was hardly an appropriate name for the leader of the government; and at no time in his career was Pope prepared to describe him as a "fool." This description, as other descriptions in this satire, was undoubtedly intended to designate no particular person but a typical city merchant indulging in fashionable folly.

In 1733 Pope began to give up his carefully preserved detachment from the political strife of his day. The quarrel over the proposed excise bill in the spring of 1733 created circumstances that indirectly impelled him towards the Opposition. For after the defeat of his bill Walpole, anxious to assert his authority, sought the resignations of men in government and in the Court who had opposed him: Lord Marchmont, Lord Stair, and the Duke of Montrose were dismissed from their places; the Duke of Bolton and Lord Cobham were forced to surrender their regiments; and Lord Chesterfield and Lord Clinton were asked to resign from the cabinet. This high-handed action forced these figures, many of whom were friends of the poet, into the Opposition and alienated one of Pope's closest friends, the Earl of Burlington. Since John Gay was dead and there was no further need to placate those who might give him a place, Pope was more ready to condemn abuses in the Court and government. Indirect reflections upon the government were allowed to appear in ethic epistles, which professed to concern less journalistic affairs. The third epistle of the *Essay on Man* concluded with an account of the remedies for a tyranny that postulates "th'enormous faith of many made for one"; and the proposal followed closely political remedies currently being advocated by Bolingbroke. Pope also published his epistle to Cobham in January, 1734, just when the Opposition was on the point of bringing out a bill aimed to prevent the King from dismissing without a court-martial officers in the army not above the rank of colonel. The timing of Pope's epistle and the tribute to Cobham's "patriotism" in it were designed to support the proposed bill. Such partisan gestures combined with Pope's unflattering remarks upon the royal family and the Court in the imitation of the *First Satire of the Second Book* as well as references in his subsequent imitations—references to the influence of the Queen over the King, to corruption in Parliament, to the excise scheme, to the Walpole party's policy of peace at any price, and to the virtue of patriotism—all indicate the direction in which his sympathies were moving.

During the summer of 1735 Pope was introduced into the inner councils of a vigorous and idealistic segment of the Opposition. At this time he visited Lord Cobham at Stowe, where he found a number of interesting people, William Pitt, Gilbert West, and George Lyttelton, who was secretary to Prince Frederick. These men all had political aspirations; all of them were disciples of Bolingbroke's "patriotism." Even while Pope was with them, they drew up plans for continuing the program of Bolingbroke, who had retired to France. In the absence of many of his earlier friends, Pope was delighted with the company of these young and eager men. He wrote Swift late in 1736:

Thus I have acquired, without my seeking, a few chance acquaintance of young men, who look rather to the past age than the present, and therefore the future may have some hopes of them. If I love them, it is because they honour some of those whom I, and the world, have lost, or are losing. Two or three of them have distinguished themselves in parliament, and you will own in a very uncommon manner, when I tell you it is by their asserting of independency, and contempt of corruption. One or two are linked to me by their love of the same studies and the same authors: but I will own to you, my moral capacity has got so much the better of my poetical, that I have few acquaintance on the latter score, and none without a casting weight on the former. But I find my heart hardened and blunt to new impressions: it will scarce receive or retain affections of yesterday; and those friends who have been dead these twenty years, are more present to me now, than those I see daily.[22]

In consequence of these friendships described to Swift he became interested in their political hopes. To encourage this interest Prince Frederick, the hero of the Opposition group, did "Mr. Pope the honour of a visit at his house in Twickenham" in October, 1735, shortly after the poet had returned there from his visit with Cobham.[23]

In the following months, Pope, more than has generally been recognized, played an active role in the effort to unseat the government. His grotto was frequented by Opposition leaders; and he wrote a poem in late 1739 describing its political importance:

VERSES *on a* GROTTO *by the River* Thames
at Twickenham,
composed of Marbles, Spars, and Minerals.

Thou who shalt stop, where *Thames'* translucent Wave
Shines a broad Mirrour thro' the shadowy Cave;
Where lingering Drops from Mineral Roofs distill,
And pointed Crystals break the sparkling Rill,
Unpolish'd Gemms no Ray on Pride bestow,
And latent Metals innocently glow:
Approach! Great NATURE studiously behold!
And eye the Mine without a Wish for Gold.
Approach: but aweful! Lo the Ægerian Grot,
Where, nobly-pensive, St. JOHN sate and thought;
Where *British* Sighs from dying WYNDHAM stole,
And the bright Flame was shot thro' MARCHMONT's Soul,
Let such, such only, tread this sacred Floor,
Who dare to love their Country, and be poor.[24]

His part in the councils of the Opposition is difficult to determine. His personal and intellectual attachments were to the more altruistic members of the group, to Sir William Wyndham, to Bolingbroke, and to George Lyttelton; and he was opposed to those members of the heterogeneous group whose selfish interests were quite obvious, William Pulteney and Lord Carteret. Pope's correspondence with Lyttelton suggests that one of his functions was to state the cause of the idealists

[22] December 30, 1736: E-C, VII, 351–52.
[23] *London Evening Post,* October 4–7, 1735.
[24] The verses were enclosed in a letter from Pope to Bolingbroke, September 3, 1740 (E-C, VII, 404–407).

to the others whose self-interest threatened the cause of the whole coalition.[25] In such an undertaking he had at least the advantage of impartiality; for no one could suspect him of seeking political office for himself. He also assisted in various ways writers whose work gave expression to the best ideals of the Tory cause. He may have had a hand in Richard Glover's *Leonidas* (1737), the epic poem of the Opposition; and possibly because he saw an effective attack upon the government in Samuel Johnson's *London* (1738), he tried to help Johnson obtain a master's degree from Trinity College, Dublin. Although Pope may have wished to forward genius, he probably wanted to encourage the then obscure satirist to write more attacks upon the Walpole administration. In the latter part of 1738 he also interested himself in four plays, all of them designed to advance the cause of "patriotism": Aaron Hill's *Caesar,* James Thomson's *Edward and Eleanora,* David Mallet's *Mustapha,* and Henry Brooke's *Gustavus Vasa.*

The Horatian satires Pope produced between 1736 and 1738 are partly colored by his interest in politics; for in most of them he seized opportunities to castigate conditions that were in part, so he alleged, fostered by the Court and the government.[26] To trace the story of the composition of these poems is difficult because Pope was unusually reticent about his work on them; but brief allusions help to fix the times when he composed four of them. He began working on the *First Epistle of the Second Book* in the spring of 1736, when he was visiting at Bevis Mount; and in September he was proposing to finish it during the fall:

> I am as you guess'd, returned from one Journey, & now I must add I am going on another: But to the quietest place I can go to, where I never yet pass'd a fortnight, but by a fatality, I think, I fall to writing verses. I wrote here my last Epistle [that to Dr. Arbuthnot]; & began an Imitation of the finest in Horace this spring; wch I propose to finish there this autumn. I mean Ld Peterborow's at Southampton, where I am to put ye last hand too to the Garden he begun, & lived not to finish. It is a place that always made me Contemplative, & now Melancholy; but tis a Melancholy of that sort wch becomes a Rational Creature, & an Immortal Soul. I propose to go next week & stay till ye middle or tow^d ye End of October, when I hope to find you in London, as well or better than you set out.[27]

By February 9, 1737, Swift had seen a manuscript of at least a part of this poem

---

[25] See especially Pope's letter to Lyttelton [1739]: E-C, IX, 178–81.

[26] The major imitations published in 1737–38 appeared in the following order (the dates are supplied from Griffith):

March 9, 1737	*Horace his Ode to Venus*
April 28	*Second Epistle of the Second Book*
May 25	*First Epistle of the Second Book*
January 23, 1738	*Sixth Epistle of the First Book*
March 1	*Sixth Satire of the Second Book*
March 7	*First Epistle of the First Book*
May 16	*One Thousand Seven Hundred and Thirty-Eight. A Dialogue Something like Horace*
July 18	*One Thousand Seven Hundred and Thirty-Eight. Dialogue II*

[27] Pope to Fortescue, September 21 [1736]. An unpublished letter in the possession of Mr. Arthur A. Houghton, Jr.

as well as lines from the *Second Epistle of the Second Book,* an imitation that had presumably been completed by this time:

I heartily thank you for those lines translated, *Singula de nobis anni, &c.* You have put them in a strong and admirable light; but however I am so partial, as to be more delighted with those which are to do me the greatest honour I shall ever receive from posterity, and will outweigh the malignity of ten thousand enemies. I never saw them before, by which it is plain that the letter you sent me miscarried.[28]

By the spring of 1738 Pope had hit upon a scheme for a series of poems imitating more or less the Horatian spirit and employing dialogue. One of these was to be published each year; and each was to contain his reflections upon current affairs, a plan which was perhaps suggested by Fielding's *Historical Register of 1736.* In April he was working on the first, which was to have the title *One Thousand Seven Hundred and Thirty Eight;* and he solicited Ralph Allen's approval of a compliment he intended to pay him (ll. 135 ff. in the printed poem): "Pray tell me if you have any objection to my putting your name into a poem of mine, (incidentally, not at all going out of the way for it,) provided I say something of you, which most people will take ill, for example, that you are no man of high birth or quality? You must be perfectly free with me on this, as on any, nay, on every other occasion." [29] This poem was published the middle of May; but as soon as it appeared Pope changed his original plans for a series of satires to be produced annually, proposing instead a group of dialogues, each to appear as rapidly as he could complete it. A second dialogue was published in accordance with this scheme on July 18, 1738. At the beginning of it Pope offered a public explanation of this shift in plans; for he stated that he was led to publish at once lest the government would soon suppress hostile poets as it had already suppressed hostile dramatists:

> Fr. Tis all a Libel—*Paxton* (Sir) will say.
> P. Not yet, my Friend! to-morrow 'faith it may;
>   And for that very cause I print to day.
>
> (ll. 1–3)

Probably a better reason for the modification of the original plan is that he had been assailed by the demon of verse and had produced a poem ready for publication.

Soon after bringing out his second dialogue, Pope contemplated a third. He wrote William Fortescue on July 31, 1738:

Your friend Sir Robert has but one of these helps [quiet and hunting]; but I remember when I saw him last, which was the last time he sent to desire me, he told me he owed his strength to it. You see I have made him a second compliment in print in my second Dialogue, and he ought to take it for no small one, since in it I couple him with Lord Bol——. As he shows a right sense of this, I may make him a third, in my third Dialogue.[30]

He did not, however, produce a third dialogue; and he did not again publish an

---

[28] E-C, VII, 340. The letter is misdated by E-C, February 9, 1735/36. See Ball, V, 415 n.
[29] E-C, IX, 194.
[30] E-C, IX, 142.

imitation of Horace.[31] This failure to continue has been attributed to political pressure. Dr. Johnson stated that the government indirectly warned Pope against further writing of this sort by hailing Robert Dodsley and Paul Whitehead before the House of Lords when they published a satire entitled *Manners* early in 1739. Johnson, assuming that both Whitehead and Dodsley were allies of Pope in the paper war upon the government, conjectured that the "whole process was probably intended rather to intimidate Pope than to punish Whitehead." [32] In a note which he appended to the second dialogue late in his life, Pope himself hinted that he had reason to fear retaliation from the government.

This was the last poem of the kind printed by our author, with a resolution to publish no more; but to enter thus, in the most plain and solemn manner he could, a sort of PROTEST against that insuperable corruption and depravity of manners, which he had been so unhappy as to live to see. Could he have hoped to have amended any, he had continued those attacks; but bad men were grown so shameless and so powerful, that Ridicule was become as unsafe as it was ineffectual. The Poem raised him, as he knew it would, some enemies; but he had reason to be satisfied with the approbation of good men, and the testimony of his own conscience.[33]

Although there is no evidence that he was actually threatened in any overt way, there is a consistency in these explanations from different sources that is impressive in spite of the melodramatic overtones. But it is not necessary to assume that official pressure accounts for the abandonment of his work. Though he wrote vaguely of a third dialogue, the valedictory tone in the two published dialogues suggests that he had reached the end of his journey with Horace. He may have seen that such poems could not really do much towards altering existing conditions; they could only perpetuate ill will and slander at a time when he was anxious for peace. He confessed to William Fortescue in September, 1738, that he had grown tired of involvement in controversy: "I am as content to quit the clamorous Part of a Poet, Satire, as you c^d be to quit that of a Pleading Lawyer, Et in Otia tuta concedere.... Quiet is the Life of Innocence & Good Nature." [34] Furthermore by this time Pope was in real trouble over the *Essay on Man,* trouble that could well have distracted him from politics and from any plans he may have formed for more imitations of Horace.

---

[31] *The Seventh Epistle of the First Book of Horace: Imitated in the Manner of Dr. Swift* was first published in 1739 in Vol. II, Pt. 2, of Pope's *Works* in octavo (Griffith 507); but it had probably been written earlier. Joseph Warton, in his edition of Pope, first printed a fragment of a dialogue under the title *One Thousand Seven Hundred and Forty,* which may represent a part of the third dialogue Pope was contemplating in late July, 1738; or it may represent an effort to comply with George Lyttelton's request that he write once more on behalf of the Opposition, a request made to Pope on October 25, 1739 (E-C, IX, 176–78).

[32] *Lives of the Poets,* ed. G. Birkbeck Hill, III, 181.

[33] These words were appended as a note to the last line of the second dialogue when it was printed by Warburton in the *Works* (1751), IV, 338.

[34] From an unpublished letter in the Pierpont Morgan Library. It is to be noted that this confession of lassitude was made some months before Dodsley and Whitehead were hailed before the House of Lords.

II

Pope's *Imitations of Horace* belong to a well-recognized and popular genre, the business of which was to adapt materials from classical satires to the times in which the imitator wrote. Boileau had made it a fashionable form; and since the late seventeenth century few writers in England had left unattempted an imitation of a classical ode, satire, epistle, epigram, or pastoral. In the actual practice of these imitators the concept of imitation was loosely conceived: occasionally imitations approximated translations; at other times they differed from translation in demanding a knowledge of the original work from a reader. Some imitations preserved a consecutive correspondence with the original; others employed a quite different framework in which different passages from the original were embedded; still others were not based on specific classical works but attempted to capture the spirit of a classical writer. At its best, however, this kind of imitation approached original composition.

Imitation had long been one of the most readily identifiable characteristics of Pope's own poetry. Early in his career he had resorted to it for purposes of rhetorical discipline: "My first taking to imitating was not out of vanity, but humility: I saw how defective my own things were; and endeavoured to mend my manner, by copying good strokes from others." [35] Later, when the need of such discipline had passed, he continued to resort to it. He translated Homer for his age; and imitation was a form of translation. In his original poems he persistently adapted good passages from earlier writers, in order to enrich the effects of his poetry. He offered his readers the aesthetic pleasure of recognizing a good thing in an earlier work made more brilliant and incisive in his own; and he found that use of passages from other contexts was an efficient means of introducing into his own work complicated overtones and suggestions. That readers might not miss these meanings he included in official editions of his poems texts of many passages he had imitated.

The *Imitations of Horace* involved, however, adaptation on a larger scale than Pope had previously attempted. Such sustained imitation recommended itself to him in his later career for a number of reasons. He was entirely confident of his own distinctive satirical powers; and imitation invited comparison between his own genius and Horace's, comparison that Pope was willing to solicit. Imitation also permitted him to say more daring things about personalities and institutions than he might otherwise have ventured to assert in times when authority was not inclined to tolerate severe criticism: it offered a convenient evasion in the event of trouble. Moreover, Horatian satires, or *sermones,* provided basic thematic patterns and situations for his poems. To Pope a most difficult part of composition was that of arrangement and organization; and this persistent difficulty was intensified after 1733 by diversions that prevented intense application to composition and by the very character of the satire he wished to write. Formal satire did not involve a narrative frame; and Pope's desire to comment diversely in his writings made it

---

[35] *Anecdotes,* p. 278.

difficult to build his satires upon formal and sustained arguments of the kind utilized in the *Ethic Epistles*. Horatian satires, however, solved the difficulty; for the Horatian original gave the poet a pattern of discourse which also allowed him considerable freedom to drift about a theme or situation.

Pope's interest in Horace was persistent, even though in his youth he most highly admired Virgil and Ovid among the Latin poets. Of course, no cultivated man of the day, particularly a poet who had dedicated himself to the ideal of "correctness," could overlook Horace; and there are numerous signs of Pope's early acquaintance with him. Horace was a favorite source of quotations in his correspondence; echoes of Horace are to be met with in the earliest poems, and the *Essay on Criticism* had obviously been helped by the *Ars Poetica*. The *Temple of Fame* placed Horace among the immortals in the lyric—not satire— and its tribute is filled with echoes demonstrating Pope's knowledge of Horace's songs:

> Here happy *Horace* tun'd th'*Ausonian* Lyre
> To sweeter Sounds, and temper'd *Pindar*'s Fire:
> Pleas'd with *Alcæus'* manly Rage t'infuse
> The softer Spirit of the *Sapphick* Muse.
> The polish'd Pillar diff'rent Sculptures grace;
> A Work outlasting Monumental Brass.
> Here smiling *Loves* and *Bacchanals* appear,
> The *Julian* Star and Great *Augustus* here.
> The Doves that round the Infant Poet spread
> Myrtles and Bays, hung hov'ring o'er his Head.
>
> (ll. 222–31)

In view of this familiarity and the interest in imitation it is not surprising that Pope early attempted an adaptation of an Horatian poem, the *Ode on Solitude*, which may have been first written when Pope was under twelve and which is clearly drawn from the second epode.[36] Nevertheless, Horace's really significant influence began when Pope was definitely committed to a career as a satirist.

After the publication of the *Dunciad Variorum* in 1729 Pope's work reflects an increased interest in Horace. He learned from him something of the techniques of formal satire; and he undoubtedly acquired from him concepts of what is worthy. But, even so, it is easy to exaggerate Horace's influence at this period. Pope was, after all, an artist in his own right, anxious to reveal his own powers; and in his *Imitations* he felt no pedantic sense of obligation to the work he imitated. In most of the *Imitations,* to be sure, he attempted to preserve some correspondence between the materials in the original and those in his imitation; but he freely deleted passages and often added materials.[37] Three of the so-called *Imitations,* the

---

[36] Pope to Cromwell, July 17, 1709: E-C, VI, 82–83. Butt, p. xxvi, notes that in 1716 the anonymous author of *A True Character of Mr. Pope and his Writings* rated Pope's "present Imitation of HORACE" as the most execrable of all his undertakings. This imitation has not been identified; but Pope did tell Spence that he had translated the "First Satire of Horace a good while before any of the rest; & closer than the rest" (from the Spence manuscripts now in the Henry E. Huntington Library).

[37] Undoubtedly Pope worked into these imitations many fragments of verse which he had composed earlier and which he hoped would be better preserved in the larger context.

Epistle to Dr. Arbuthnot and the two dialogues making up the *Epilogue to the Satires,* are not based on specific Horatian satires but attempt only in a very general way to emulate the spirit of Horace's work. Some of the *Imitations* —the *First Epistle of the Second Book,* for example—preserve a consecutive correspondence with the poems on which they are based; but they drastically alter the original intention. Generally speaking, Pope was most effective when dealing freely with his originals, when the poems take on the character of original creations. These are the poems that best reveal the qualities that constitute Pope's satiric genius, which was essentially different from Horace's. Pope is much less given to raillery; but good-humored jesting is not a necessary qualification of good satire. Pope is more definite, personal, and concrete than his model; and his satire is therefore more pungent. And Pope had a more energetic moral idealism, a greater contempt for spiritual meanness, and an awareness of moral corruption in its subtle and insidious forms that in more than one poem enabled him to leave Horace far behind.

III

Because the *Imitations of Horace* were composed, not as parts of a predetermined and cohesive plan, but as individual poems written in response to circumstances, there is a good deal of repetition in them. There is also more variation in quality than readers of Pope's earlier poetry might expect. Nevertheless, as a group they reveal many of the best properties of his satire. Artifice is everywhere present. Heightening, exaggeration, and shading are employed to secure more direct and pointed effects. Imitation involved a display of ingenuity in the contrivance of parallel situations; and Pope's ability to find clever parallels seems never to flag. His virtuosity is everywhere evident. The style varies from the colloquial to the eloquent; and the moods vary from the brutal vigor of the Sporus passage, or the gay contempt directed at fools, to the elevated grandeur of the hortatory paragraphs. Irony also is used, though sparingly. It appears in epithets involving an inversion of blame and praise: "wise Peter," "the City's best good men," "Budgell's Fire and Force," "modest Cibber;" and there is a brilliant effort at sustained irony in the *Epistle to Augustus,* in which the poet mockingly eulogizes his monarch as he instructs him in the elementary principles of literary appreciation and good taste.

Pope consistently preserved the distinctive vigor of his satire by using the concrete and specific. The satiric epithets on which he impaled his victims ("slashing Bentley," "piddling Theobald") are sharp and vivid; the metaphors are graphic:

> I ne'r with Wits or Witlings past my days,
> To spread about the Itch of Verse and Praise.
> (*Epistle to Dr. Arbuthnot,* ll. 223–24)

In search of compelling visual effects, Pope seldom resorted to scatological wit of a Swiftean character; but one incisive instance occurs in the *Epilogue to the Satires:*

> Let Courtly Wits to Wits afford supply,
> As Hog to Hog in Huts of *Westphaly;*
> If one, thro' Nature's Bounty or his Lord's,

Has what the frugal, dirty soil affords,
From him the next receives it, thick or thin,
As pure a Mess almost as it came in;
The blessed Benefit, not there confin'd,
Drops to the third who nuzzles close behind;
From tail to mouth, they feed, and they carouse;
The last, full fairly gives it to the *House.*

(*Epilogue,* II, ll. 171–80)

A more distinctive means of securing concrete effects, however, was to present the objects of his satire in brief scenes involving a characteristic gesture or remark:

Oldfield, with more than Harpy throat endu'd,
Cries, "Send me, Gods! a whole Hog *barbecu'd!"*

(*Sat.,* II, ii, ll. 25–26)

Shou'd such a man, too fond to rule alone,
Bear, like the *Turk,* no brother near the throne,
View him with scornful, yet with jealous eyes,
And hate for Arts that caus'd himself to rise;
Damn with faint praise, assent with civil leer,
And without sneering, teach the rest to sneer; . . .

(*Epistle to Dr. Arbuthnot,* ll. 197–202)

The *Temple* late two Brother Sergeants saw,
Who deem'd each other Oracles of Law;
With equal Talents, these congenial Souls
One lull'd th'*Exchequer,* and one stunn'd the *Rolls;*
Each had a Gravity wou'd make you split,
And shook his head at *Murray,* as a Wit.
'Twas, "Sir your Law"—and "Sir, your Eloquence"—
"Yours *Cowper's* Manner—and yours *Talbot's* Sense."

(*Epistle,* II, ii, ll. 127–34)

Although the formal satirical character which had distinguished the *Ethic Epistles* is not a conspicuous feature of the *Imitations,* some characters are inserted for the sake of variety and to remind readers of Pope's excellence in this satiric form. Pope more commonly illustrates general assertions by brief satirical references to specific contemporaries, references which support his indictment of his times. He explained:

To attack vices in the abstract, without touching persons, may be safe fighting indeed, but it is fighting with shadows. General propositions are obscure, misty, and uncertain, compared with plain, full, and home examples. Precepts only apply to our reason, which in most men is but weak: examples are pictures, and strike the senses, nay, raise the passions, and call in those, the strongest and most general of all motives, to the aid of reformation. Every vicious man makes the case his own; and that is the only way by which such men can be affected, much less deterred. So that to chastise is to reform. The only sign by which I found my writings ever did any good, or had any weight, has been that they raised the anger of bad men. And my greatest comfort, and encouragement to proceed, has been to see, that those who have no shame, and no fear of anything else, have appeared touched by my satires.[38]

Unfortunately the decision to use actual examples meant that Pope had to utilize a number of journalistic personalities whose names no longer have the force they once had. In the interests of strict truth, moreover, Pope denied himself opportunities to use names to secure comic effect, as in the *Dunciad*. The poems have consequently lost something of their original color. Nevertheless, readers may still admire the noble concepts in the poems; especially since Pope's primary interest lay in the ideas rather than in the personalities who are incidentally introduced.

The satire of the *Imitations* is also marked by the variety of ways in which Pope undertook to present the positive aspect of his work, to recommend the virtues that the times demanded; for satire must heal "with Morals what it hurts with Wit." Often he describes explicitly the attributes of the good life, as in the following passage on temperance in diet:

> Hear Bethel's Sermon, one not vers'd in schools,
> But strong in sense, and wise without the rules.
> Go work, hunt, exercise! (he thus began)
> Then scorn a homely dinner, if you can.
> Your wine lock'd up, your Butler stroll'd abroad,
> Or fish deny'd, (the River yet un-thaw'd)
> If then plain Bread and milk will do the feat,
> The pleasure lies in *you*, and not the meat.
>
>   (*Sat.*, II, ii, ll. 9–16)

Frequently he cited examples of virtuous men to contrast with the weak or foolish persons described in his work:

> God knows, I praise a Courtier where I can.
> When I confess, there *is* who feels for Fame,
> And melts to Goodness, need I Scarbrow name?
> Pleas'd let me own, in *Esher's* peaceful Grove
> (Where *Kent* and Nature vye for Pelham's Love)
> The scene, the Master, opening to my view,
> I sit and dream I see my Crags anew!
>   Ev'n in a Bishop I can spy Desert;
> *Secker* is decent, *Rundel* has a Heart,
> Manners with Candour are to *Benson* giv'n,
> To *Berkley*, ev'ry Virtue under Heav'n.
>
>   (*Epilogue*, II, ll. 63–73)

---

[38] Pope to Arbuthnot, July 26, 1734: E-C, VII, 481–82. This letter is a fabrication first published by Pope in his edition of his letters (1737). It was designed as a public explanation of his satirical aims. Pope's actual answer to Arbuthnot's criticism (dated August 2 [1734]) represents, however, no significant alteration in the argument: "But general satire in times of general vice has no force and is no punishment: people have ceased to be ashamed of it when so many are joined with them; and it is only by hunting one or two from the herd that any examples can be made. If a man writ all his life against the collective body of the banditti, or against lawyers, would it do the least good, or lessen the body? But if some are hung up, or pilloried, it may prevent others. And in my low station, with no other power than this, I hope to deter, if not to reform" (E-C, VII, 480).

Pope occasionally contrasted England of the present with England of an earlier, simpler, and more virtuous day:

> Time was, a sober Englishman wou'd knock
> His servants up, and rise by five a clock,
> Instruct his Family in ev'ry rule,
> And send his Wife to Church, his Son to school.
> To worship like his Fathers was his care;
> To teach their frugal Virtues to his Heir;
> To prove, that Luxury could never hold;
> And place, on good Security, his Gold.
> Now Times are chang'd, and one Poetick Itch
> Has seiz'd the Court and City, Poor and Rich:
> Sons, Sires, and Grandsires, all will wear the Bays,
> Our Wives read Milton, and our Daughters Plays,
> To Theatres, and to Rehearsals throng,
> And all our Grace at Table is a Song.
>
> *(Epistle,* II, i, ll. 161–74)

Perhaps the most distinctive method by which Pope makes clear the virtues he seeks to recommend is through the development of a well-rounded picture of the personality and character of the satirist.[39] This implied character may vary from poem to poem, depending upon the theme of each *Imitation;* and, indeed, the characterization may not be consistent within any one poem. Nevertheless, the attributes ascribed to the satirist always help to define Pope's idea of what is worthy. In the *Epistle to Dr. Arbuthnot* there is a carefully evolved portrait of Pope as a man of letters—modest, unassuming, hostile to vice and friendly to virtue. One important purpose of this self-portrait is to develop a picture of an ideal and successful man of letters. The implied character of the satirist is similarly important to the positive argument of the *Epilogue to the Satires,* in which Pope appears as the outspoken citizen incensed by corruption in high places. He is no flatterer or time-server; he is incomparably patriotic, honest, uncompromising, and fearless. In every way he is an admirable citizen, representative of that civic virtue which the times so badly needed.

In emphasizing the satiric virtuosity of the *Imitations,* we should not ignore the fact that these poems also include a fund of invigorating commentary on social morality in Pope's day. Taken together the poems "publish the present age." Pope does in a more inclusive way what he had done in the *Dunciad,* although more varied aspects of contemporary society become his province. The *Imitations* are principally concerned with the spread of venality and the mercenary spirit:

> 'Tis Av'rice all, Ambition is no more!
> See, all our Nobles begging to be Slaves!
> See, all our Fools aspiring to be Knaves!
> The Wit of Cheats, the Courage of a Whore,
> Are what ten thousand envy and adore.
> All, all look up, with reverential Awe,

---

[39] Maynard Mack, "The Muse of Satire," *Yale Review,* XLI (1951–52), 80–92.

> On Crimes that scape, or triumph o'er the Law:
> While Truth, Worth, Wisdom, daily they decry—
> "Nothing is Sacred now but Villany."
> (*Epilogue,* I, ll. 162–70)

In such an ethos "a Man of wealth is dubb'd a Man of worth" (*Epistle,* I, vi, l. 81); and everywhere one is advised, "Get Place and Wealth, if possible, with Grace; if not, by any means get Wealth and Place" (*Epistle,* I, i, ll. 103–104). England had become a "Land of Hectors, Thieves, Supercargoes, Sharpers, and Directors" (*Sat.,* II, i, ll. 71–72). For the spread of this corruption Pope held the traditional buttresses of order and morality guilty. Irresponsible men were "safe from the Bar, the Pulpit, and the Throne" (*Epilogue,* II, ll. 210); indeed, though conscience told the people to prize virtue, Court and Church encouraged them to esteem wealth:

> Here, Wisdom calls: "Seek Virtue first! be bold!
> "As Gold to Silver, Virtue is to Gold."
> There, London's voice: "Get Mony, Mony still!
> "And then let Virtue follow, if she will."
> This, this the saving doctrine, preach'd to all,
> From low St. James's up to high St. Paul;
> From him whose quills stand quiver'd at his ear,
> To him who notches Sticks at Westminster.
> (*Epistle,* I, i, ll. 77–84)

Public honors were given to those whose only achievement was the possession of wealth and to those who distinguished themselves by mediocrity and subservience. The government shamelessly resorted to bribery and corruption in order to win elections and to control parliament. In the churches thrift, cunning, and ambition were raised to heavenly virtues; and preferment was reserved for the clergy who endorsed the new morality.

Some of the *Imitations* are concerned with the state of letters. Ideas that had already been expressed in the *Dunciad* were reiterated, especially in the *Epistle to Dr. Arbuthnot;* but Pope's social view of his times resulted in some significant developments in his conception of current follies in literature—developments that prepared the way for the fourth book of the *Dunciad.* In the *Dunciad Variorum* the principal ingredients of dullness were ignorance, pedantry, and venality; but in the *Imitations* the vacuity and inanity of letters as practised and patronized by members of the court are emphasized:

> The Honey dropping from *Favonio's* tongue,
> The Flow'rs of *Bubo,* and the Flow of *Y - - ng!*
> The gracious Dew of Pulpit Eloquence;
> And all the well-whipt Cream of Courtly Sense.
> That first was *H - - vy's, F - -'s* next, and then
> The *S - - te's,* and then *H - - vy's* once agen.
> O come, that easy *Ciceronian* stile,
> So *Latin,* yet so *English* all the while,
> As, tho' the Pride of *Middleton* and *Bland,*
> All Boys may read, and Girls may understand!

> Then might I sing without the least Offence,
> And all I sung should be the *Nation*'s *Sense*:
> Or teach the melancholy Muse to mourn,
> Hang the sad Verse on CAROLINA's Urn,
> And hail her passage to the Realms of Rest,
> All Parts perform'd, and *all* her Children blest!
>
> (*Epilogue*, I, ll. 67–82)

For this saccharine verse Pope blamed the King and Queen, who had no ear but for the "Panegyric strains." The monarch encouraged glib poetasters who "spin a thousand" weak verses every day; and he had appointed Colley Cibber as poet laureate. Meanwhile the genius of Gay had been neglected; and Swift had been allowed to languish in Ireland.

Although an important function of the *Imitations of Horace* was the exposure of the corrupt state of morality in his day, Pope was no mere railer, delighting in exposure for its own sake. His ultimate end was the improvement of public morals; and he made a consistent effort to insure that his conception of the good life should be clear. The qualities of character recommended are essentially traditional and humane. Naturally, the Horatian virtues of moderation, restraint, and good sense have central roles; but Pope's immediate purposes involved some shifting of emphasis. At a time when men were willing to submit to "golden chains," he stressed the dignity of independence and self-reliance, the state of being "un-plac'd, un-pension'd, no Man's Heir, or Slave." At a time when profit, power, and advantage were the principal motives behind friendship, he advanced strongly the claims of merit, respect, and affection:

> Content with little, I can piddle here
> On Broccoli and mutton, round the year;
> But ancient friends, (tho' poor, or out of play)
> That touch my Bell, I cannot turn away.
>
> (*Sat.*, II, ii, ll. 137–40)

His conviction that the end of individual effort should be the achievement of order, stability, and harmony in one's own life as well as in the society of which he is a part made Pope emphasize those virtues involving self-discipline and self-restraint— benevolence, patriotism, and responsibility. It also made him condemn most strongly the unsocial and self-indulgent passions—avarice, prodigality, ambition— that set the claims of the individual above those of society.

In developing these ideas Pope did not deliberately attempt to work within the framework of moral concepts in the *Essay on Man* and *Ethic Epistles;* but major propositions in these poems do underlie tendencies in the *Imitations*. The conceptual interest in vice and virtue manifested in the earlier undertaking persists in the later work, although there is a more extensive effort to apply to the society of the 1730's concepts already formulated. At the root of the *Imitations* lies the proposition implicit in the *Essay on Man* that man's destiny lies in his own hands: he alone is responsible for his society and can improve it only by his efforts to develop his potentialities as a social being. The key to moral character is the state

of his passions. Vice is irrational self-indulgence proceeding from narrowly conceived ideas about the means of pleasure; virtue proceeds from the awareness
that self-love and social are the same, an awareness that prompts men to benevolence or socially useful action. The conception of the well-conducted state explicitly developed in the third epistle of the *Essay on Man* fashions the attacks upon
government in his own time. Pope asserts more than once that the state leaders
pursuing mean notions of public interest have ignored the fact that the health
of a society depends upon the moral state of the people. They have accepted the
"enormous faith of many made for one"; they have deprived citizens of their
liberty; they have confused private advantage with civic virtue; and they have
neglected the arts that offer the most efficient means by which worthy social attitudes may be propagated. Meanwhile citizens, lacking enlightenment, have
accepted base ideas of happiness, vainly pursuing the external, uncertain, and
private advantages of fame, fortune, titles, and power; and they have neglected the
benevolent attitudes of mind that can alone lead men to direct their energies towards virtuous action. Exposure of man's pursuit of material gods and reaffirma-
tion of the happiness attendant upon virtue are the business of the *Imitations of
Horace,* just as they had been the business of the speculative poems that preceded
them.

IV

Although the *Imitations* are among Pope's best poems, only a few of them are
now read; and these have not always been fully appreciated. The *Epistle to Dr.
Arbuthnot,* which is Horatian in spirit but not based on any specific Horatian
satire, has been the most enduringly popular—and deservedly so. It is quite the
most complex of the group. The self-portrait of the poet, his description of life at
Twickenham, his somewhat obvious bids for sympathy, the essential manliness
of his ideals, and his presentation of the plight of one who wills peace and retirement but who is forced by circumstances to play a different role, give the work an
enduring charm. There is also a variety of perceptive satirical commentary directed
at the more common vices and follies of writers. As a poem the *Epistle to Dr.
Arbuthnot* is also marked by different and skillfully modulated moods. It opens
with a description, humorously exaggerated, of the vexations of life at Twickenham.
Gradually the comic tone disappears, as the satirist turns to subjects requiring more
serious treatment; and the poem reaches its emotional climax in the intense scorn
of the Sporus passage, a peak of indignation from which the poet retreats to a
humble and prayerful close. This basic pattern is, however, so elaborately embroidered with passages of wry comedy, pathos, contempt, and serious expostula-
tion that the whole represents one of Pope's most ambitious and successful
symphonies.[40]

The poem is shaped by two purposes which reinforce one another. One object

---

[40] This feature of the poem has recently been discussed in some detail by Elias F. Mengel, Jr.,
"Patterns of Imagery in Pope's *Arbuthnot*," *PMLA,* LXIX (1954), 189–97.

is to justify the conduct of Alexander Pope in the face of charges leveled at him by his critics; it is a more ambitious attempt to do what he had tried to accomplish in his imitation of the *First Satire of the Second Book*. But the poem is more than an apologia: it is a study of the character and conduct proper to a successful writer. The picture in it of reasonable patience with importunity, concern for merit, scorn of patronage, and humility in private life is a lecture to the times on the principles by which a literary man should live.

To accomplish his dual purpose Pope employed three formal satirical characters—the portraits of Atticus, Bufo, and Sporus. For purposes of vindicating Pope himself these characters suggest what he might have become but did not. He might have been a member of Addison's "little senate" if he had wished to practice the kind of obsequiousness that alone pleased Addison; if he had been willing to flatter without conscience, he might have been one of a servile band surrounding Bufo; or he might have been a society-poet like Sporus, if he had indulged in the mean shifts that had won for Lord Hervey the ear of the Queen. The characters also serve Pope's desire to write on the conduct proper to a successful man of letters; for each of them demonstrates how men may face the obligations that prestige involves. Atticus, Bufo, and Sporus are all in a position to advance the interests of good writers. Atticus, by his undoubted merits and success as a writer, can forward those who excel; Bufo, by virtue of his wealth, can render financial assistance to young authors; and Sporus, who has acquired influence at Court, can secure royal favors for others. Nevertheless, the jealousy of Atticus, "too fond to rule alone," prevents him from supporting effectively those whose success might result in a diminution of his own pre-eminence; the vanity of Bufo leads him to respond only to flattery; and the sordid opportunism of Sporus prompts him to seek his own private advantage alone. In opposition to these patrons Pope projects into the poem a dramatically idealized character of himself. He too has achieved a position of influence in literary affairs; but unlike the others he has been guided by principles of integrity and modesty as well as by a sincere interest in merit. He has succeeded, where the others have failed.

The three formal verse characters in the *Epistle* are distinguished by the compactness and acuteness that had marked Pope's contributions to the *Ethic Epistles*. The Atticus sketch is a judicious and discriminating appraisal of the successful writer who tries to maintain his pre-eminence by insidious denigration of the work of others. Pope's power to detect and immortalize an unworthy gesture is at its best in the catalogue of subtle means by which Atticus attempts to ruin the fortunes of others; and his use of antithesis and balance to suggest something of the poise and deliberate calculation of Atticus's efforts is characteristic of Pope's management of rhetoric to complicate his meaning. Included in the portrayal of Atticus is an indictment of those who surround him and who, blind to the moral corruption of the man, grin approvingly at one who would not hesitate to do them an injury. To Pope the subject is remarkable for the ironies it includes and for the delicate balance of comedy and tragedy existing in it. The meanness of the group is in one sense ridiculous; but there is also something tragic in the wasted opportunities for good that the weakness of Atticus involves.

The sketch of Bufo is in a somewhat different vein; for Bufo is a more frankly contemptible figure. To set the mood of the description Pope begins with a picture of his subject posed as a toad:

> Proud, as *Apollo* on his forked hill,
> Sate full-blown *Bufo*, puffed by every quill;
> Fed with soft Dedication all day long,
> *Horace* and he went hand in hand in song.
>
> (ll. 231–34)

Such a pose is a graphic representation of the theme of the character, the distortions in human relations that pertain to the system of patronage. This central theme is reinforced by other details. Bufo's library is adorned with "Busts of Poets dead" and "a true *Pindar* without a head"; Bufo helps to bury Dryden, though he never aided him alive. The exchanges between patron and patronized are portrayed as similarly grotesque and bloated: in return for excessive adulation and prostitution of principle, the flatterers receive a dinner, a little port, and sometimes merely praise. Pope, by precept and example, had often condemned the dying system of patronage, but nowhere else had he succeeded in so effective a manner in defining the moral conditions that such a scheme fosters.

The portrait of Sporus is undoubtedly the most virulent piece of invective Pope ever wrote. It receives its primary inspiration from a personal animosity to John, Lord Hervey, no aspect of whose private or public character is left unmentioned. To regard the passage merely as an effort to determine a private quarrel is, however, to miss its more important intent. The whole is an anatomy of the kinds of moral weaknesses which may develop in a weak man whom circumstances have conspired to place in courtly circles. Undoubtedly the most notable feature of Pope's technique in the sketch is the use of graphic imagery to define the nature of the corruption that has overtaken Sporus.[41] The sketch is introduced with apparent

---

[41] That Pope succeeded in introducing order and meaning into the imagery of the passage only after some effort is apparent from one manuscript version which I reconstruct from Jonathan Richardson's marginalia in a copy of the poem preserved in the Henry E. Huntington Library:

> Who hates not Sporus when his whisp'ring Breath
> Would blast a Foe, & stinks a Friend to Death;
> When on th'Imperial Car (a shamefull Load!)
> Close at the Ear of Eve is perch'd the Toad.
> Sputt'ring low Politics, unmanly Lies,
> & Tales, & Bawdy, Puns, & Blasphemies.
> Or when that florid Impotence of Stile
> (Like his own Face, half Malice half a Smile)
> In grave Buffon'ry begins to break
> When W - - - - le blows, & bids yͤ Puppet squeak.
> His Wit all See-saw between *that* and *this,*
> Now high, now low, now Master up, now Miss,
> And he *himself* one poor *Antithesis.*
> Who sillily Imoral, pertly Dull,
> Profess'd a Knave, yet nothing but a Fool,

casualness: Pope mentions Sporus by name, and his interlocutor, dramatically yielding his previous reserve, interrupts to abuse Sporus:

> What? that Thing of silk,
> *Sporus,* that mere white Curd of Ass's milk?
> Satire, or sense, alas! can *Sporus* feel?
> Who breaks a Butterfly upon a Wheel?
>
> (ll. 305–308)

The images used here imply that Sporus, a silkworm, a butterfly, is merely a vapid creature, a suggestion to which Pope takes exception. His answer employs images that bear odious and loathsome connotations. Sporus is a bug, a fawning spaniel, a toad, a snake. The series culminates in the identification of Sporus with Satan; for Sporus in his position may be as dangerous to society as ever Satan was to man. The whole results in a calculating and deadly exposure of an individual—and also a fascinating study of a complex kind of moral corruption.

The *Epistle to Augustus* is another of Pope's deservedly famous imitations. Unlike the *Epistle to Dr. Arbuthnot,* it is based upon a specific Horatian satire, the *First Epistle of the Second Book;* but it completely alters the import of that poem. What had been quite sincere praise of the emperor's accomplishment by Horace became in Pope mockery of George II. The monarch's meanness of spirit, his lack of taste, his pusillanimous conduct of foreign affairs made him, in Pope's eyes, contemptible; and the satire upon him was severe and biting. Such an attack upon a reigning monarch had, of course, to be veiled in irony and *double entendre;* and Pope's success was such that he made it impossible for anyone to proceed against him without risking the imputation of disloyalty. As an aid to his ironical purposes Pope casts himself in a unique role. The writer is not, as in the *Epistle to Dr. Arbuthnot,* an idealized projection of Pope himself; he is rather a rhetorical contrivance, an *ingénu* approaching his king with humility and esteem. The studied quality of this pose reveals its essential artificiality, an artificiality which emphasizes the mockery that is intended.

> Tatler at Toilets, Fop at c - - - l Board,
> Now trips a Lady, and now struts a Lord.
> Eternal smiles his emptiness betray,
> As shallow streams run dimpling all the way.
> Beauty, or Wit, his Courtly Hours employs,
> This he ne'er Tastes, & That he ne'er Enjoys;
> So well bred Spaniels civilly delight
> In mumbling of the Game they dare not bite.
> Satire & Sense are things he cannot feel,
> Who breaks a Butterfly upon a *Wheel?*
> Yet let me flap this Bug with Silken [wings,]
> This glitt'ring [child of dirt, that *stinks* and *stings;*]
> This Thing Amphibious, acting either Part,
> A trifling H^d or a corrupted heart,
> A Pimp, yet Babler; Sycophant, yet Spy;
> Did ever Smock-face hide such Villany?
> *Eve's* tempter thus by Rabbins is exprest,
> A Cherub's face, a Reptile all the rest,
> Beauty that *shocks* you, Parts that none can *trust,*
> Wit that can *creep,* and Pride that *licks the dust.*

The attack upon George II is most heavily concentrated in the opening and concluding sections of the satire; the bulk of the work is given over to commentary upon literature. A primary purpose of this commentary is to defend the dignity and vitality of letters against George II, and others like him, whose indifference was a challenge to Pope's conception of the importance of letters to a society. The poet begins by reducing to absurdity the proposition that works may be prized only when they are old, a position implying that literature is an academic activity having no direct relation to the times that produce it. In the second part of the epistle he turns to those critics who more directly hold a poet is of no weight and use to the state. Granting that there exist a number of worthless poetasters, Pope cites the example of writers and literary forms that have in practice exerted a strong influence for good: Addison, "who from the taste obscene reclaims our Youth and sets the Passions on the side of Truth," Swift, who saved the rights a court attacked, the unnamed dramatist who "can make me feel each Passion that he feigns, inrage, compose, with more than magic Art, with Pity, and with Terror, tear my heart," and satire which "heals with Morals what it hurts with Wit."

Woven into this defense of the activity to which Pope had devoted his life are a number of digressions and comments upon writers and literature. Epigrammatic wit so highly prized in literary conversation is here raised to the level of great poetry; and Pope has added in this poem more phrases to the permanent storehouse of brilliant literary comment. Readers of the poem will not find in it any significant change in the principles by which the author judged literature; he will find brilliant reaffirmations of what Pope had been asserting all his life. For the writers who are praised are those whose work is distinguished by moral intent, as Addison and Swift, or by correctness which to Pope embraced vigor of thought as well as energy in expression. Dryden is praised because he

> taught to join
> The varying verse, the full-resounding line,
> The long majestic march, and energy divine.
>
> (ll. 267–69)

The cavaliers are condemned for insipidity in thought and expression, for

> One Simile, that solitary shines
> In the dry Desert of a thousand lines,
> Or lengthen'd Thought that gleams thro' many a page.
>
> (ll. 111–13)

Conformity to nature is invoked more than once as a test of art; and by this standard developments in the contemporary theatre are condemned:

> The Play stands still; damn action and discourse,
> Back fly the scenes, and enter foot and horse;
> Pageants on pageants, in long order drawn,
> Peers, Heralds, Bishops, Ermin, Gold, and Lawn;
> The Champion too! and, to complete the jest,
> Old Edward's Armour beams on Cibber's breast!
>
> (ll. 314–19)

Pope's characteristic aversions also find expression in the poem, his distrust of popular judgment, his scorn of the cant of literary criticism, and his contempt for flattery, blasphemy, and lewdness.

But if Pope's basic critical principles had not changed, they were variously and perceptively applied to a number of English writers. There is, of course, no effort to present a carefully organized and systematic treatise. The commentary, which does follow Horace, is discursive and diffuse; but what is said proceeds from a mature and consistent critical position which Pope had definitely made his own. If that position had its limitations and prevented the one who held it from recognizing certain kinds of merit, there is nothing in it inherently mean or ignoble. It is judicious and reasonable; it prizes nobility of conception as well as consummate mastery of expression; and it sets the highest standards of mind and character for the author.

The two dialogues making up the *Epilogue to the Satires* are the last imitations Pope published. They are not, however, based on any specific Horatian satire, nor are they particularly Horatian in spirit; but they do reiterate what Pope had often been saying in the earlier *Imitations,* that corruption prevailed in high places, that England was experiencing tyranny, that the Court countenanced insipid verses, and that satire offered the promise of improving the times. The techniques to be found in the two dialogues are also those that had become features of Pope's *Imitations.* There is varied satire under the guise of apologia; there is the expert use of dialogue, one purpose of which is to develop a dramatic portrait of Pope. This self-portrait is, however, different from that in the *Epistle to Dr. Arbuthnot.* Pope is here the outraged champion of virtue, who is far from humble and reserved. Absolutely uncompromising, he earnestly defends what he believes to be right. The interlocutor is also a more fully developed character than the strawmen Pope had introduced into his earlier dialogues. He has a larger part in the exchange and appears as an unfriendly critic whose expostulations are colored by spiritual timidity and mean prudence. He heightens by contrast the nobility of Pope's own attitudes.

The movement in both poems conforms to a pattern familiar to readers of the other *Imitations.* The opening is informal and colloquial; each dialogue moves toward a passage of eloquent declamation; each ends by a striking shift in key to the simple and direct, which brings the dialogue to an unexpectedly quick but forceful close. The passages occurring at the climax of each dialogue are apocalyptic in their splendor and suggestiveness. The argument of the climactic passage in the first dialogue (ll. 141–70) is that toleration of vice in high places has led to almost universal corruption. This idea is presented in what is best described as a large allegorical painting of the apotheosis of vice through the agency of Greatness. Vice occupies a central position in the canvas with her followers grouped in symbolic postures about her. No small part of the effectiveness of the presentation comes from the complicated frame of reference in which Pope invited his reader to place it. William Warburton, in his note on the passage, found the whole an allusion to the elevation of the Empress Theodora. Dr. James M. Osborn has pointed out, however, that contemporary readers would also have been tempted to refer the passage to the recent marriage of Sir Robert Walpole and his long-time mistress, Molly Skerrett.[42] It was equally important to Pope's purposes, however, that his readers should recognize in the passage the allusions to the Biblical Whore of Babylon, who served well as a symbol of the kind of mercenary corruption which, Pope believed, stemmed from the merchants of London and which he thought to be the central evil of his times.

The conclusion to the second dialogue is equally powerful: it is perhaps Pope's finest effort to justify satire as great art. Rejecting the Shaftesburean proposition that satire is a test of truth, Pope accepts satire as a species of rhetoric, a technique of persuasion. To achieve greatness it must be joined with truth; but in such a combination satire is a noble endeavor. To give this concept graphic concreteness Pope utilized a tableau comparable to that in the climactic passage of the first dialogue: Truth "diademed with rays divine" is here apotheosized, with satire serving as the "Priestess Muse." Truth is here distinguished from Vice, however, in so far as she is vested with divine qualities; and worship of her is a sacramental function as opposed to the abject servitude and slavery imposed upon those who have placed themselves in bondage to Vice.

The *Epilogue to the Satires* is not merely a triumph of Pope's satiric art. From the point of view of understanding his attitudes, especially the nature of his opposition to the government of Sir Robert Walpole, it is important. In the dialogues he attacks much that flourished under the government of Walpole; but he is not narrowly partisan in spirit. Much of what he has to say is not concerned with purely factional issues designed to attract selfish interest; the language he employs is dignified rather than inflammatory; and the treatment of Walpole himself, the principal target of opposition writers, is mildly complimentary in the second dialogue. Pope's desire in the *Epilogue,* as well as in the other *Imitations,* was to inculcate nobler conceptions of public morality than those prevailing among political leaders, Whig or Tory. As a means of accomplishing this end he undertook to expose prevailing corruption and to recommend means of improving public conduct. Because the Whigs were in power, and had been in power for over twenty years, they provided most of the evidence; but Pope nowhere suggests that Tories might have done better. In the first dialogue he included the "Patriots" among those who had been seized by the venal spirit:

> In Soldier, Churchman, Patriot, Man in Pow'r,
> 'Tis Av'rice all, Ambition is no more!
>   (ll. 161-62)

He grants that Tory leaders are as prone to corruption as Whigs:

> Good Heav'n forbid, that I shou'd blast their Glory,
> Who know how like Whig-Ministers to Tory.
>   (ll. 105-106)

---

[42] "Pope, the Byzantine Empress, and Walpole's Whore," read at a meeting of the Modern Language Association of America, December, 1954.

He bestows praise upon deserving Whigs as well as Tories. Such reservations could hardly have been made by one who wanted to unseat one political party in order that another might take its place. They are the views of one determined "to restore the Faith and Moral, Nature gave before," to teach "Power's due use to People and to Kings."

Such was Pope's aim in the *Epilogue;* and such was his aim in the other *Imitations,* which are efforts to improve his own country and particularly his own times. Undoubtedly the *Imitations* did not secure, as the author may have hoped, any pronounced and immediate change in public morality. On the other hand, they did help to enlarge the conceptions of thoughtful contemporaries at a time when men were losing sight of basic virtues. By juxtaposing corruption prevalent in the society of his day and the traditional virtues of western civilization Pope did something to shatter the complacency that the prosperity of the time tended to foster. His vigorous and incisive indictment made it impossible for his readers to accept uncritically the society in which they found themselves.

CHAPTER FIVE

Warburton and the Later Satiric Mode

Judged in terms of creativity, Pope's last years were not a period of great accomplishment; they were largely devoted to the preparation and ordering of final versions of his poems. The important achievement of these years was a recasting of the *Dunciad;* but Pope also brought out his letters to Swift and prepared the *Memoirs of Scriblerus* for publication. For the most part he polished and arranged what had already been published: the *Essay on Man* was altered in order to soften the fatalistic implications of the original argument; and some changes were made in the *Ethic Epistles.* Helping Pope in this work was the Reverend William Warburton, who after 1738 became closely associated with the poet and who to a small extent may have imposed marks of his personality upon Pope's final work. Warburton became Pope's friend almost by chance. During the war with the dunces after *Shakespeare restored* he had been friendly with Theobald and the dunces; and, although Pope probably never knew it, he contributed three abusive articles to the *Daily Journal* in March and April, 1728.[1] He may also have been critical of the *Essay on Man* when it first appeared. Thomas Tyers wrote: "What is a little singular, Warburton, amongst his earliest friends, who were Pope's enemies, had roughly and roundly asserted, that the Essay was collected 'from the worst passages of the worst authors.'"[2] James Prior, in his *Life of Edmond Malone,* reported: "The late Dr. ———— informed Dr. Warton that when Warburton resided at Newark, he and several others held a club, where Warburton used to produce and read weekly essays in refutation of Pope's *Essay on Man.*"[3] William Stukeley asserted that Warburton had written "a treatise against Mr. Popes essay on man, to prove it to be atheism, spinosaism, deism, hobbism, fatalism, materialism, & what not."[4] Undoubtedly there is exaggeration in these statements, for the writers were not sympathetic with Warburton; but taken together they suggest that he may have at first been critical of the poem. And Warburton himself declared that until Pope's "Letters were published, I had as indifferent an opinion of his morals as" the dunces pretended to have.[5]

If Warburton at first disapproved of the *Essay on Man,* his later defense of its

---

[1] Convincing evidence in support of these attributions has been presented by Arthur W. Evans, *Warburton and the Warburtonians* (Oxford, 1932), pp. 73–75.

[2] *An Historical Rhapsody on Mr. Pope,* 2nd ed. (London, 1782), p. 78.

[3] *Life of Edmond Malone* (London, 1860), p. 430.

[4] *Family Memoirs of the Reverend William Stukeley* (Durham, 1882), I, 127.

[5] Warburton to Hurd, January 12, 1757: *Letters from a Late Eminent Prelate* (London, 1809), p. 224.

orthodoxy was responsible for the friendship between him and Pope. Pope had feared at the time this poem was published that the rational tendency of the argument would be distorted and misrepresented by his enemies.[6] In the first reception, however, very little attention was paid to this aspect of it; and only slowly did the disposition to find traces of heterodoxy grow. A few brief criticisms appeared during 1734 and 1735, but nothing alarming. In 1736 a more serious critique was published under the title *Divine Wisdom and Providence: an Essay Occasion'd by the Essay on Man.*[7] Although the author of this didactic poem did not attribute any deliberate intention of heterodoxy to Pope, he objected to the suggestions in the *Essay on Man* that the omnipotence of the deity was circumscribed by an antecedent principle of fitness and that evil somehow pertained to the nature of things rather than to the abuse of free will. This poem, which ran through three editions, impressed Pope; and he included lines affirming his belief in free will in his next publication, his imitation of the *Second Epistle of the Second Book of Horace* (April, 1737):

> That God of Nature, who, within us still,
> Inclines our Action, not constrains our Will;
> Various of Temper, as of Face or Frame,
> Each Individual: His great End the same.
>
> (ll. 280–83)

He also polished, but did not publish (until 1738), his *Universal Prayer,* which he said he had first composed about 1715. He sent a draft of it to Ralph Allen in a letter dated September 8, 1736: "I've sent you the Hymn, a little alterd, & enlarged in one necessary point of doctrine, viz: yᵉ third stanza, which I think reconciles Freedom & Necessity; & is at least a Comment on some Verses in my Essay on Man, which have been mis-construed."[8]

Serious trouble for Pope was occasioned, however, by the turn criticism of the *Essay on Man* took in France. A French prose translation of the *Essay on Man* was published in 1736 by Étienne de Silhouette, an enterprising young man with literary aspirations; and a second, inaccurate verse translation by the Abbé du Resnel followed in 1737. These translations won great popular favor, which alarmed some of the more conservative theologians who were intent upon subduing heresies; and they sought to expose the dangerous propositions in the new poem. In 1737 the Swiss theologian, Jean Pierre de Crousaz, who had achieved a reputation for

---

[6] See above, pp. 39–42.

[7] The title page of the second edition declares that the poem was "by Mr. Bridges." Mr. Bridges may have been the Rev. Ralph Bridges to whom Pope had submitted some passages of his translation of Homer for criticism. Bridges was a nephew of Sir William Trumbull; he held the rectory of South Weald in Essex from 1713 until his death in 1758.

[8] The letter is in the library of the University of Chicago and is quoted here with permission. The third stanza, to which Pope refers, reads:

> Yet gav'st us in this dark Estate
> To know the Good from Ill;
> And, binding Nature fast in Fate,
> Left'st Conscience free, and Will.

the zeal with which he had attacked impiety, published his *Examen de l'Essai de M. Pope sur l'homme;* and in 1738 he published a sequel entitled *Commentaire sur la traduction en vers de Mr. l'Abbé du Resnel, de l'Essai de M. Pope sur l'homme.* In the *Examen* Crousaz assumed that Pope was indebted to the arch-heretic Leibnitz for his system; and then, in an obvious effort to discredit Leibnitz's philosophy, he proceeded to demonstrate the dilemmas, inconsistencies, and equivocations which he found in the *Essay on Man.* In the *Commentaire* Crousaz shifted the grounds of his attack, admitting that he had perhaps erred in his earlier effort to relate the moral ideas of the poem to Leibnitz's metaphysics. He therefore undertook to prove that Pope had offered a vague and uncertain ethical treatise: "Celui qui prendra pour guide Mr. Pope, & qui n'étudiera cette importante science que sous lui, se trouvera rempli de doutes, d'incertitudes, de contradictions, peu d'idées nettes, & encore moins de preuves." [9]

Both of the critiques were severe and somewhat perverse; but because of Crousaz's impressive reputation they attracted attention not only in France but also in England. Edward Cave, the publisher of the *Gentleman's Magazine,* was the first to undertake translations: he asked Samuel Johnson to translate the *Commentaire* and Elizabeth Carter to translate the *Examen.* Edmund Curll, always ready to sponsor any criticism of Pope, also set one of his writers, Charles Forman, to translating the *Commentaire,* the first part of which, hastily done, was published in November, 1738. The same month Miss Carter's translation of the *Examen* also appeared.[10] These publications gave currency in England to Crousaz's animadversions; and they seriously disturbed Pope. Bolingbroke was in France, unable to help; and the *Essay on Man* had fallen into the hands of theologians, with whom the poet himself could hardly debate.

In this crisis William Warburton wrote, without Pope's knowledge, a letter published in the *History of the Works of the Learned* (December, 1738), a letter in which he discussed a review of the *Examen* in the *Bibliothèque raisonnée.* Subsequently he contributed to the same periodical four other letters on Crousaz's critiques.[11] In view of Warburton's early hostility and the rewards he reaped for his defense of the *Essay on Man,* his motives in coming gratuitously to the rescue have always been somewhat suspect. But his action can be explained plausibly in terms other than those of selfish opportunism. Warburton offered one explanation for the undertaking when he asserted: "I make no question but another sort of those they call *great* men will hold themselves outraged by me in my vindication of Mr. Pope against M. de Crousaz in some letters which are going to be collected

---

[9] *Commentaire* (Geneva, 1738), p. 351.

[10] The publication of Johnson's translation of the *Commentaire* was considerably delayed. The Yale University Library has a copy of this work, with a title page bearing the date 1739. Because copies of this issue are extremely rare, one suspects that Cave may have withdrawn the book immediately after printing it and that he held it until 1742, when he formally published it and provided a new title page. See A. T. Hazen and E. L. McAdam, Jr., "First Editions of Samuel Johnson," *The Yale University Library Gazette,* X (1935–36), 45–51.

[11] These four letters appeared successively in the issues of the *History* for January, February, March, and May, 1739.

together and published. But I cannot forbear shewing my esteem of merit, and my contempt of their calumniators, or thinking that it is of use to Religion to prove so noble a genius a friend to it." [12] The Reverend William Clarke believed that Warburton was prompted to write his vindication because he himself had experienced misrepresentations of his own views by critics and therefore could sympathize with Pope's predicament after Crousaz had attacked him: "I thank you for Warburton's Defence of Pope. I find him an excellent Commentator: he proves, that 'self-love and social' are the same; for he could not vindicate Mr. Pope without having many glances at his own adversaries." [13]

One may add that the task of establishing the orthodoxy of Pope's poem in the face of Crousaz's criticisms must have offered Warburton the kind of challenge he was always ready to accept, an opportunity to display his dialectical skill.

If Warburton's motives were baser than these, Pope apparently did not detect them; and in a grateful mood he sought out his defender soon after the first letter of vindication had been published. He wrote Warburton for the first time on February 2, 1739:

> I cannot forbear to return you my thanks for your Animadversion on Mr Crousaz: tho' I doubt not, it was less a Regard to me, than to Candor & Truth, which made you take the pains to answer so Mistaken a Man. I fear indeed he did not Attack me on quite so good a Principle: and whenever I see such a Vein of Uncharitableness & Vanity in any Work, whether it concerns me or another, I am always ready to thank God to find it accompanyd with as much Weakness. But this is what I sh^d never have Exposed myself, because it concern'd myself: And therfore I am the more oblig'd to You for doing it.
>
> I will not give you the unnecessary Trouble of adding here to the Defence y^u have made of me (tho much might be said on ye article of the Passions in the Second Book) Only it cannot be unpleasant to y^u to know, that I never in my life read a Line of Leibnitz, nor understood there was such a Term as Præ-established Harmony, till I found it in Mons. Crousaz's book.
>
> I am, Sir, with a due Esteem for your Abilities & for y^r Candor, (both which I am no Stranger to, from your other Writings, as well as this). [14]

Soon Pope was busying himself in attempts to show his gratitude by advancing Warburton's interests. He arranged to have him meet Lord Bathurst and George Lyttelton; in 1741 he invited Warburton to journey to Lord Cobham's for a visit. On August 12, 1741, he expressed the hope that "some Great Person or other" would provide a suitable living for Warburton; and he announced his intention of refusing to accept an honorary degree from Oxford unless his new friend was also granted one. On November 12, 1741, Pope invited Warburton to visit with him at Ralph Allen's estate near Bath; and on December 28, 1742, he planned a meeting with Lord Carteret. Through these introductions Pope hoped to secure preferment for his friend; and his efforts bore fruit. In 1740 Warburton was made

---

[12] Quoted by Richard Hurd in his biographical sketch of Warburton prefacing the *Works of the Right Reverend William Warburton* (London, 1788), I, 29. Warburton's remarks were directed to Conyers Middleton, July 16, 1739.

[13] John Nichols, *Literary Anecdotes of the Eighteenth Century* (London, 1812), IV, 427.

[14] British Museum, Egerton MSS. 1946, f. 3.

chaplain to the Prince of Wales; and, in view of the poet's relations with the
Prince, Pope undoubtedly had favored the appointment.[15] In 1741 Pope told Warburton that the Earl of Chesterfield intended to serve him; and later, when Chesterfield became Lord Lieutenant of Ireland in 1745, he did offer Warburton a chance
to accompany him as his chaplain, an invitation that was declined. Pope also introduced his friend to William Murray; and Murray in 1746 persuaded the benchers
of Lincoln's Inn to make Warburton their preacher. The introduction of Warburton into the family of Ralph Allen proved even more fortunate; for Warburton
eventually married Allen's favorite niece, Gertrude Tucker—an alliance that certainly assisted the ecclesiastical rise of the town clerk's son.

II

These services to Warburton were motivated in part by genuine gratitude; but
Pope also hoped to secure help from his defender. He was at first anxious to insure
that the defense of his *Essay on Man* be as widely circulated as possible; and he
proposed that the letters, currently appearing in the *History of the Works of the
Learned,* be printed in book form and also be translated into French: "I cannot
but wish these letters were put together in one book, and intend (with your leave)
to procure a translation of part at least of them into French, but I shall not proceed
a step without your consent and opinion." [16]

Warburton's consent was readily obtained; and the letters were in the hands of
the printer in September. They were formally published, in six letters, by the
middle of November, 1739.[17] Plans for a French translation, to be prepared by

---

[15] The *DNB* erroneously says that Warburton received this honor early in 1738. The *Register of
Tradesmen's Warrants and Others of Frederick Prince of Wales, February 1728/9 to June, 1747*
in the British Museum (Add. MSS 24,399) has (folio 53) the Prince's warrant appointing Warburton as Chaplain in Ordinary to himself: "Frederick P. Whereas We have thought fit to Nom-
inate and Appoint Our Trusty & Welbeloved the Rev.^d Mr. William Warburton M. A. to be one
of Our Chaplains in ordinary during Our Pleasure. Our Will and Pleasure therefore is that upon
making out Our Establishment of Our Household You do enter him therein as such. And for so
doing This being enter'd in your office shall be to you a sufficient Warrant. Given at Norfolk
House the 14th. day of May 1740 In the 13th. year of the Reign of our Royal Father the King."
[16] April 11 [1739]: E-C, IX, 204.
[17] The published collection contained one letter that had not previously appeared, an analysis
of the second epistle of the *Essay on Man* which Pope requested Warburton to write. The order
of the letters in the collection also differs somewhat from the order in which they had appeared in
the *History of the Works of the Learned:*

Vindication	Works of the Learned
I	III (February, 1739)
II	I (December, 1738)
III	II (January, 1739)
IV	IV (March, 1739)
V	Not published in the *History*
VI	V (May, 1739)

The revised ordering was an effort to introduce more coherence into the arrangement of letters.
The texts of the letters in both sources agree in most ways; but Warburton sometimes altered
the wording to improve the style and supplied new transitional paragraphs required by the
different sequence of the letters. In the second letter of the *Vindication*—the first letter in the
History—he dropped the references to the review in the *Bibliothèque raisonnée,* possibly because
he had had an opportunity to read the *Examen* itself.

Étienne de Silhouette, were also formulated: on September 20, 1739, Pope asked Warburton to direct the printer, James Robinson, to dispatch a copy of the complete *Vindication* as soon as possible to the translator. On January 17, 1740, Pope wrote that he was planning to return to Twickenham from Bath in order to revise "what my French Gentleman has done." [18] And at the same time Warburton, presumably acting upon Pope's suggestion, had composed a seventh letter in which he treated the fourth epistle of the *Essay on Man,* a section of the poem he had earlier neglected as noncontroversial.

Having accomplished these immediate ends, Pope proposed—by September, 1741—a more formal edition of Warburton's defense as well as an edition of the disputed poem with an exegesis by Warburton, an edition that would go to posterity in a form not admitting further misconstruction.[19] Collaboration on these projects was close, as the two friends exchanged samples of their work for criticism and approval. Warburton, for example, submitted to Pope the proposed dedication of his vindication of Pope to Ralph Allen: "I can find no fault in y^r Epistle to Mr Allen: but 2 or 3 single words I w^d expunge in favor to his Modesty, or rather, his real humility; and ye last Sentence softend, or changed into something more familiar." [20] Pope solicited Warburton's judgment. On April 23, 1742, he told him that he would "make my profit of what you observe in a passage or two of the Essay on Man"; [21] and the end of December saw Pope still trying to satisfy Warburton's objections: "Pray tell me if the inclosed Alteration satisfies your Objection in ye fourth Epist. of ye Essay?" [22]

A month later he again asked Warburton to approve revisions in the fourth epistle:

Pray will ye following lines answer your Idea? or can you bring them to it with a little alteration?

> Ask of the Learn'd the way, the Learn'd are blind,
> This bids to serve, & that to shun mankind;
> Some place the Bliss in Action, some in Ease,
>   Apathy
> [1] Those call it Pleasure, and [2] Contentment these: [1] Epicur
> [1] Some sunk to Beasts, find Pleasure end in Pain;   [2] Stoics
> [2] Some swelld to Gods, confess ev'n Virtue vain;
> Or indolent, to each extreme they fall,

---

[18] Pope to Warburton: British Museum, Egerton MSS. 1946, f. 13. Silhouette did not publish the French translation until 1742, when it appeared in an edition of Silhouette's miscellaneous writings.

[19] In a letter to Warburton, September 20 [1741], Pope clearly indicates that the two projects were then in hand: "I think in ye new Edit. of y^r answer to Crousaz, you sh^d not cite those discarded Verses of mine, but rather reserve them to be made a Confirmation of y^r Opinion in ye Comentary on ye Poems themselves; and I think it will better appear there, & more naturally, than to be insisted on here, especially as you are known to have written that Vindication before y^u had any acquaintance wth me, or any Sight of those papers" (British Museum, Egerton MSS. 1946, f. 36).

[20] Pope to Warburton, June 5 [1742]: British Museum, Egerton MSS. 1946, f. 47.

[21] E-C, IX, 223.

[22] British Museum, Egerton MSS. 1946, f. 70.

dignify'd Method of declaring y^r intention of a General Commentary before That, than before This Poem." [25] Progress was delayed somewhat because a revision of the *Essay on Criticism,* which, it was hoped, would appear concurrently with the *Essay on Man,* was undertaken during the spring and early summer of 1743; and Pope's quarrel with Ralph Allen and his wife resulted in a brief period of coolness between the two collaborators that further delayed their common task.[26] But by November 19, 1743, the two were once more at the *Ethic Epistles:*

> Your Partiality to me is every way so great, that I am not surprized to find you take it for granted, that I observe more Method, & write more correctly, than I do. Indeed in one of y^r Conjectures you are right, as I see by casting my eye on ye Original Copy; but in ye other, no such matter, the Emendation is wholly y^r own. (except I find in ye margin *How-ere,* instead of *Well then,* but cross'd over.) Upon ye whole I will follow y^r Method, & therfore return ye paper that you may accordingly refer ye notes. (The mark N wch I've put upon ye margin is only to direct ye Printer to such Notes as are in ye Copies already printed.) and the beginnings of verses crost over again, only to shew you how they once did stand.) As for the other part, concerning the Extravagant Motives of Avarice, I meant to show those wch were Real were yet as mad or madder than those wch are Imaginary (vid. vers.
> > For tho' Such Motives Folly y^u may call,
> > The folly's greater to have none at all.
>
> So I w^d let that remain as it is.—I am glad you proceed upon these Epistles first, as they will best joyn with ye Essay on Man, of which & of ye Essay on Crit. I will publish a small number, however, very soon, to try ye Taste of the Town: and then give (as soon as you can conveniently) ye Notes on ye Epistles all together, in one volume with ye Essay on Man already printed off, (leaving ye Pastorals, Rape of ye Lock &c to the last, to join with ye Essay on Criticism.) [27]

Pope's letters to Warburton written during the winter and spring of 1744 indicate that he was preoccupied with the *Ethic Epistles* almost to the time of his death. On January 27, 1744, he wrote Warburton:

> I have gone over all y^r Papers on ye 2 Epistles, to my Satisfaction and I agree with you to make shorter work with those to the Lady, & to Ld Burlington (tho I have re-

---

[25] Pope to Warburton, January 8 [1743]: British Museum, Egerton MSS. 1946, f. 72. On March 3, 1743, Pope wrote the printer William Bowyer: "On second thoughts let the proofs of the Epistle to Lord Cobham I. be done in the quarto, not the octavo size. Contrive the capitals and everything exactly to correspond with that edition. The first proof send me. The number of the whole but 1,000, and the royal over and above" (E-C, IX, 521).

[26] The quarrel, which took place during the summer of 1743, was touched off by the cool treatment Martha Blount received from the Allens during a visit with them at Bath. Pope, in answering Martha's letter recounting the story, referred to Mrs. Allen as "a minx, and an impertinent one" and to Warburton as "a sneaking parson" (E-C, IX, 334–35). We do not know what occasioned the Allens' treatment of Pope's friend; but Thomas Birch writing to Charles Yorke, October 27, 1744, gave one explanation: "The Bishop of Bristol explain'd to me last Sunday at Dinner the true Origin of the Dispute between Mr. Pope & Mr. Allen, which he had from the mouth of the latter. It was simply this, that Miss Blount insisting upon going publicly in that Gentleman's Coach to the Mass-House at Bath, he desir'd to be excus'd, because, as it was the Year of his Mayoralty of that City, it might give Offence; tho' at the same time he offer'd the Coach, on condition she would go the back Way, & leave it at some little Distance" (British Museum, Add. MSS. 35396, ff. 275–76). My attention was called to this letter by Mr. Edward Ruhe of Rutgers University.

[27] British Museum, Egerton MSS. 1946, f. 68. The letter itself is undated; but Nov. 19, 1742, is a reasonable conjecture.

placed most of y⁰ omitted lines in the former) . . . I will omit the Person's name [Sir Robert Sutton in the *Epistle to Lord Bathurst,* ll. 107–108] to whom you shew favour, in this Edition: I am glad to have any occasion to do any thing that may be half so agreeable to You, as a hundᵈ things you have done have been to me.²⁸

A month later he was still working on *Ethic Epistles:*

. . . whatever very little respites I have had from y⁰ daily Care of my Malady have been employd in revising y⁰ papers on y⁰ Use of Riches, wᶜʰ I would have ready for yʳ last Revise agˢᵗ you come to Town yᵗ they may be begun with by Bowyer while you are here.—I wᵈ also defer till then y⁰ publication of y⁰ Two Essays with yʳ Notes in Quarto, that (if you thought it wᵈ be taken well) you might make the Compliment to any of yʳ Friends (& particularly of y⁰ Great ones, or of those whom I find most so) of sending them as Presents from yʳself.—For what I writ of yʳ forwarding y⁰ Satires and Imitations, wᶜʰ I agree with you to add to y⁰ Epistles; I own the late Encroachments upon my Constitution make me willing to see y⁰ End of all further Care abᵗ *Me* or my *Works.* I wᵈ rest, for y⁰ one, in a full Resignation of my Being to be disposd of by y⁰ Father of all Mercy; & for y⁰ other (tho indeed a Triffle, yet a Triffle may be some Example) I wᵈ commit them to y⁰ Candor of a sensible & reflecting Judge, rather than to y⁰ Malice of every shortsighted, & malevolent Critic or inadvertent & censorious reader; And no hand can set them in so good a Light, or so well turn their best side to y⁰ day, as your own. This obliges me to confess, I have for some months thought myself going, and that not slowly, down the hill; the rather, as every Attempt of y⁰ Physicians, & still the last Medcines more forcible in their nature, have utterly faild to serve me.²⁹

In March he was pressing forward hurriedly, as though against time:

I receivd yʳˢ just now & I write to hinder Bowyer from printing y⁰ Com̄ent on y⁰ Use of Riches too hastily, since wᵗ you write me, intending to have forwarded it otherwise, that you might revise it during yʳ stay. Indeed my present weakness will make me less & less capable of any thing.³⁰

In April he wrote:

PS. I have just run over y⁰ Second Epistle frō Bowyer, I wish you cᵈ add a Note at y⁰ very End of it, to observe y⁰ authors Tenderness in using no *living Examples* or *real Names* of any one of y⁰ softer Sex, tho so free with those of his own in all his other satyrs.

　　　　　x and a Note on
　　　　　　　—half yʳ Parents simple Prayr,
　　　　　　grave *Beauty*　　　　　　　　　but refusd *Wealth.*
if you think it worth one.³¹

III

The poems receiving all this attention finally appeared in 1744. In February an *Essay on Man: Being the First Book of Ethic Epistles to H. St. John L. Bolingbroke, with the Commentary and Notes of W. Warburton* was published; and, about May 1, *Four Ethic Epistles, by Alexander Pope, with the Commentaries and Notes of W. Warburton* was printed, but not formally published. These editions demon-

---

²⁸ British Museum, Egerton MSS. 1946, ff. 78–79.
²⁹ British Museum, Egerton MSS. 1946, f. 80.
⁰ British Museum, Egerton MSS. 1946, f. 82.
³¹ British Museum, Egerton MSS. 1946, f. 96.

strate that the collaboration between Pope and Warburton had resulted in some interesting changes in the poems. Numerous alterations were made in the text of the *Essay on Man* for the sake of clarity and precision; but several had been made in order to temper statements on which constructions antithetical to orthodox dogma could be placed.[32] A comparison of the last authorized edition of the *Essay on Man* to appear before the friendship of Pope and Warburton developed (Griffith 505) with the text of the edition on which the two collaborated (Griffith 589) reveals the following representative alterations in phrasing designed to make the poem more acceptable (in each example the earlier reading has been given first):

> a. Then, in the scale of life and sense, 'tis plain
>   There must be, *somewhere,* such a rank as Man . . . .
>   (I, ll. 47–48)

> Then, in the scale of reas'ning life, 'tis plain
>   There must be, somewhere, such a rank as Man . . . .
>   (I, ll. 47–48)

This change, which emphasizes man's place among rational creatures, was calculated to circumvent the criticism that Pope, in his efforts to stress the limitations of human reason, had failed sufficiently to differentiate man from beast.

> b. His being measur'd to his state and place,
>   His time a moment, and a point his space.
>   (I, ll. 71–72)

> His knowledge measur'd to his state and place,
>   His time a moment, and a point his space.
>   (I, ll. 71–72)

The assertion that man's "being" is measured to his state and place seemed to some to deny the possibility of a future life. The substitution of "knowledge" for "being" obviously removed this objection.

> c. The soul, uneasy, and confin'd at home,
>   Rests, and expatiates in a life to come.
>   (I, ll. 93–94)

> The soul, uneasy and confin'd from home,
>   Rests and expatiates in a life to come.
>   (I, ll. 97–98)

The earlier reading implied that because the body was the home of the soul, the soul was thus subject to decay. The change permitted Warburton to declare of Pope's intentions: "By these words, it was the poet's purpose to teach, that the present life is only a state of probation for another, more suitable to the essence of the soul, and to the free exercise of its qualities." [33]

---

[32] I have already discussed these changes in an article, "Notes on Pope's Collaboration with Warburton in Preparing a Final Edition of the *Essay on Man*," *PQ*, XXVI (1947), 358–66.

[33] *Works* (1751), III, 14 n.

Several passages were also added to the later edition in order to clarify Pope's intentions:

a. Added after II, l. 42:

> Trace Science then, with Modesty thy guide;
> First strip off all her equipage of Pride,
> Deduct what is but Vanity, or Dress,
> Or Learning's Luxury, or Idleness;
> Or tricks to shew the stretch of human brain,
> Mere curious pleasure, or ingenious pain:
> Expunge the whole, or lop th'excrescent parts
> Of all, our Vices have created Arts:
> Then see how little the remaining sum,
> Which serv'd the past, and must the times to come!

Pope's remarks on natural and moral science in the introduction to the second epistle had been variously interpreted as a description of the weakness of the human mind with respect to all knowledge, as a derogatory reference to the Newtonian achievement, and as an effort to distinguish the potentialities of natural and moral science. The passage was undoubtedly added in order to provide more textual support for Warburton's summary of the intent of the introduction: ". . . as on the one hand, we should persist in the study of Nature; so, on the other, in order to arrive at Science, we should proceed in the simplicity of Truth; and the product, tho' small, will yet be real." [34]

b. Added after II, l. 274:

> Behold the child, by Nature's kindly law,
> Pleas'd with a rattle, tickled with a straw:
> Some livelier play-thing gives his youth delight,
> A little louder, but as empty quite:
> Scarfs, garters, gold, amuse his riper stage;
> And beads and pray'r-books are the toys of age:
> Pleas'd with this bauble still, as that before;
> 'Till tir'd he sleeps, and Life's poor play is o'er!

Crousaz had asserted that the lines immediately preceding this passage implied that life was a grand illusion maliciously perpetrated by a deceitful deity. The added passage fills out the sense of the earlier lines to demonstrate, as Warburton declared, "that these Illusions are the Follies of Men, which they *wilfully* fall into, and thro' their own *Fault;* thereby depriving themselves of much Happiness, and exposing themselves to equal Misery: But that still God (according to his Universal way of Working) graciously turns these Follies, in some measure to the Advantage of his distressed and miserable Creatures." [35]

c. Added after III, l. 306:

> In Faith and Hope the world will disagree,
> But all Mankind's concern is Charity.

---

[34] *Works* (1751), III, 47–48 n.
[35] *A Vindication of Mr. Pope's* Essay on Man *from the Misrepresentations of Mr. Crousaz* (London, 1740), pp. 81–82.

The couplet preceding this addition had always read:

> For Modes of Faith let graceless zealots fight;
> His can't be wrong whose life is in the right.

To some of Pope's readers this couplet standing alone was objectionable because it seemed to declare that all religions were indifferent as to their forms and object. The additional couplet buttressed Warburton's argument that Christianity and the natural religion of Pope were not in effect antithetical because the ethical ideals of the two were the same. It should be noted that Warburton did not argue that the *Essay on Man* was a Christian poem; he merely contended that there was nothing in the natural religion of the poem incompatible with revealed religion.

d. Added after IV, l. 172:

> Weak, foolish man! will Heav'n reward us there
> With the same trash mad mortals wish for here?
> The Boy and Man an individual makes,
> Yet sigh'st thou now for apples and for cakes?
> Go, like the Indian, in another life
> Expect thy dog, thy bottle, and thy wife:
> As well as dream such trifles are assign'd,
> As toys and empires, for a god-like mind.

This addition subsumed the idea of a future life; and it helped to allay criticism of Pope's intentions in Epistle I, ll. 99 ff.

The *Ethic Epistles* were also revised, in some places at the suggestion of Warburton; but the changes were in matters of presentation rather than of substance. The *Epistle to Lord Cobham* was significantly altered by transpositions of passages and paragraphs in the first half of the poem, for which re-ordering Warburton took full credit:

> Whoever compares this with the former Editions of this poem, will observe that the order and disposition of the several parts are entirely changed and transposed, tho' with hardly the Alteration of a single Word. When the Editor, at the Author's desire, first examined this Epistle, he was surprized to find it contain a number of fine observations, without order, connexion, or dependence: but much more so, when, on an attentive review, he saw, that, if put into a different form, on an idea he then conceived, it would have all the clearness of method, and force of connected reasoning. Indeed the observations then appeared to him so jumbled and confounded in one another, as if the several parts of a regular poem had been rolled up in tickets, drawn at random, and then set down as they arose. The author appeared as much struck with the observation as the editor, and agreed to put it in the present form, which has given the poem all the justness of a true composition.[36]

A few transpositions of a similar sort were also made in the *Epistle to Lord Bathurst*, at Warburton's suggestion: "The introduction of the epistle on Riches was in the same condition, and underwent the same reform." [37]

Although it is possible to argue that improvements in logic resulted from these

---

[36] *Works* (1751), III, 163. The question of Warburton's changes in this poem and in the *Epistle to Lord Bathurst* is fully discussed in Bateson, pp. 5 ff., 74 ff.

[37] *Works* (1751), III, 163.

changes, the alterations are not entirely necessary or happy. For they obviously destroy something of the spirit of causerie that existed in the original organization of
the poems; and Pope's failure to work out carefully new transitions in the light of
the rearrangement has resulted in more obscurities than were removed. One suspects
that Warburton, having actually very little to offer to the *Ethic Epistles* by way of
suggestion, felt constrained to make some comments in an effort to be of service.
And one may conjecture that Pope, unwell and anxious to finish his work, accepted
the suggestions too uncritically.

The satirical portions of the *Ethic Epistles* were not much altered in this last
revision; and the changes which were effected cannot reasonably be traced to
Warburton. Perhaps the principal alteration was the introduction into the *Epistle
to a Lady* of three satirical characters which had not previously appeared in that
poem, the characters of Philomedé, Atossa, and Chloe (together with the lines on
Queen Caroline).[38] The first two of these characters had probably been a part of
the original poem, although Pope had not ventured to print them earlier because
they attacked "vice too high." [39] The character of Chloe, however, seems to have
been a late addition. It had appeared as a separate poem in 1738; and it does not
fit neatly into the structure of the *Epistle to a Lady*.[40] It is in a more formal
style than the others; and it seems to intrude into the exposition. Nevertheless, no
reader can be seriously troubled by its presence; and Pope, undoubtedly wishing
to place the fragment in a larger context, found the best possible position for it.

IV

The great creative achievement of Pope's years of friendship with Warburton
was the composition of the fourth book of the *Dunciad*. Writing to Warburton,
December 28, 1742, Pope confessed that "the Encouragem^t you gave me to add
the fourth book, first determind me to do so; & the Approbation you seemd to
give it, was what singly determind me to print it." [41] Warburton undoubtedly
assisted in the preparation of the fourth book; but his influence may easily be
exaggerated, for changes in the poem had probably been developing in Pope's mind
for some time. The copy of the *Dunciad* (1736) with marginalia by Jonathan
Richardson in the New York Public Library has on the flyleaf a sketch of a plan
for the "2nd Canto," a plan that is an almost complete outline of materials in the
fourth book.[42] This sketch may have been drawn up before 1740, and perhaps
even before 1736.

---

[38] The characters of Philomedé and Atossa had already been printed in the *Epistle,* in a special
version of the poem Pope included in a volume of his *Works* prepared for the Prince of Wales,
presumably in 1738. See Vinton A. Dearing, "The Prince of Wales's Set of Pope's *Works," Harvard
Library Bulletin,* IV (1950), 320–38.

[39] Pope had, however, hinted at their existence in a note to line 103 of the *Epistle to a Lady* as
printed in the second volume of the octavo *Works* of 1735 (Griffith 388–89). In this note he apol-
ogized for "a want of Connection" at this point in the argument "and also in some following
parts," owing to "the ommission of certain *Examples* and *Illustrations* of the Maxims laid down."

[40] It was first published in the *Works . . . Vol. II. Part ii,* 1738 (Griffith 507).

[41] British Museum, Egerton MSS. 1946, f. 69.

[42] See Appendix B.

Pope had definitely decided to revise the *Dunciad* by the end of January, 1741, when he wrote to the publisher and owner of the copy, Henry Lintot:

> When you purchas'd the Shares in the Dunciad, I hope Mr. Gilliver delivered you his title under y⁰ Hands of y⁰ Lords as well as mine to them, of wᶜʰ I wish you wᵈ acquaint me, for he told me he could not find it, and without it yours wᵈ be (I apprehend) insufficient. . . . I will revise the new edit. of y⁰ Dunciad or do anything yᵗ may be of service to you wᶜʰ is not very greatly to my own Injury.[43]

In September, 1741, he invited Warburton in an indirect manner to collaborate with him and provide notes:

> If I can prevail on myself to complete the Dunciad, it will be published at y⁰ Same time with a General Edition of all my Verses (for Poems I will not call them) and I hope Your Friendship to me will be then as well known, as my being an Author, & go down together to Posterity; I mean to as much of posterity as poor Moderns can reach to, where the Commentator (as usual) will lend a Crutch to y⁰ weak Poet to help him to limp a little further than he could on his own Feet.[44]

A letter he wrote to Hugh Bethel, January 1, 1742, indicates that most of the actual composition was probably done between October, 1741, and January, 1742:

> I little thought 3 months ago to have drawn the whole polite world upon me, (as I formerly did the Dunces of a lower Species) as I certainly shall whenever I publish this poem. An Army of Virtuosi, Medalists, Ciceronis, Royal Society-men, Schools, Universities, even Florists, Free thinkers, & Free masons, will incompass me with fury: It will be once more *Concurrere Bellum atque Virum*. But a Good Conscience a bold Spirit, & Zeal for Truth, at whatsoever Expence, of whatever Pretenders to Science, or of all Imposition either Literary, Moral, or Political; these animated me, & these will Support me.[45]

At this period Pope visited with Ralph Allen at Bath and asked Warburton to join him for a month or six weeks in order to "unbend to yᵉ idle Amusement of commenting upon a Poet, who has no other Merit than that of aiming by his Moral Strokes to merit some Regard from such men as advance Truth & Virtue in a more Effectual way." [46] During Warburton's visit the poem was largely finished; and it was published independently on March 20, 1742.

Pope planned to set the printer William Bowyer to work on an edition of the complete *Dunciad,* in four books, immediately after the publication of the fourth book; but Pope became preoccupied with the edition of the *Essay on Man*. He was able to turn back to the *Dunciad,* however, in the fall of 1742; for printing had begun by November 1, when he wrote Warburton:

> I wish Mʳ Bowyer wᵈ send me once more y⁰ proof of y⁰ Sheet he sent last, in wᶜʰ is y⁰ Conclusion of the first book, before it is work'd off. He may at y⁰ same time go on with y⁰ Corrections you will make in y⁰ half sheet to be cancelld at y⁰ beginning.—so that no Time will be lost.[47]

---

[43] January 31, 1741: E-C, IX, 543–44.
[44] British Museum, Egerton MSS. 1946, f. 36.
[45] British Museum, Egerton MSS. 1948, f. 52.
[46] British Museum, Egerton MSS. 1946, f. 38.
[47] British Museum, Egerton MSS. 1946, f. 60.

On November 6 Pope communicated with Warburton again:

That part of y° Note may well be omitted, w^(ch) Bowyer tells you, & w^(ch) I found was left out. But I can't tell why he has omitted the latter p^t of another Note at y° End of Book 1. w^(ch) is work'd off. It is that w^(ch) mentions y° Second Lye of y° Abbe Tallemant on Boileau, that he had been beaten by Pradon a bad poet, & w^(ch) was paralleld by w^t C. says of Philips & me. It certainly sh^d be in, & y° note as it now stands refers to it, in citing y° Notes on Boileau's 6^(th) & 7^(th) Epistles, in y° former of w^(ch) y° Story is told. I send y° leaf, & have so shortend y° thing to be added that I hope it can be cancelld, & ye rather as it will contain also y° Alteration I desired so much of one Verse. Pray let him Send y° half sheet & this leaf to me as soon as you have corrected & work'd y^m off. I like y° Note on Proteus much.[48]

A week later he wrote to the printer Bowyer: "I've sent you another leaf to cancel by all means. P. S. Just now I receive y^(rs) ab^t y^e *Brazen Image*, I w^d have it stand as it is, & no matter if ye Criticks dispute ab^t it." [49] Before the end of November he proposed to make Warburton the official editor of the poem—in order, so he argued, to give the work more prestige; and he requested Warburton to append his name to a prefatory note:

A Project has arisen in my head to make you in some measure y° Editor of this new Edit. of the Dunc. if you have no scruple of owning some of y° *Graver Notes* w^(ch) are now added to those of Mr Cleland & Dr Arb. I mean it as a kind of Prelude or Advertisem^t to y° publick of y^r Comentarys on y° *Essays on Man*, and on *Criticisme*, w^(ch) I propose to print next in another Volume, proportiond to This. I have scratched out a sort of *Avis au Lecteur*, w^(ch) I'l send you to this effect, w^(ch) if you disapprove not, you'l make your own. I have a particular reason to make you Interest y^rself in Me & My Writings. It will cause both them & me to make y° better figure to Posterity.[50]

Warburton immediately acquiesced in the proposal; and on December 4 the *Dunciad* was almost ready:

I thank you for what you so speedily have done, & shall put it to y° press with all haste, y° rest of y° book being ready. If any thing more can be done for y° Dunciad, it must be to acquaint y° public that you have thought it worth y^r Care by bestowing some Notes upon it to make it more Important & Serious. Whether the Sketch inclosed be proper for You to authorize so far, I know not; but do y^u consider or whether with any Initial Letters, at y° End, or no? I only doubt whether an Avowal of these Notes to so ludicrous a poem, be suitable to a Character so Establishd as yours for more Serious Studies? [51]

The poem was printed before December 27, 1742,[52] but not placed on the stalls of booksellers until the following October; for its author had run into difficulties over the copyright. The publisher, Bernard Lintot, had received the property of the poem from Lawton Gilliver, copyright lasting under the law of 1709 for fourteen years from the time of the original assignment. Although Pope went to Chancery and argued that the copy had been assigned to Gilliver in December,

[48] British Museum, Egerton MSS. 1946, f. 62.
[49] Pope to Bowyer, November 13 [1742]: British Museum, Egerton MSS. 1946, f. 63.
[50] November 27 [1742]: British Museum, Egerton MSS. 1946, ff. 64–65.
[51] British Museum, Egerton MSS. 1946, f. 66.
[52] British Museum, Egerton MSS. 1947, f. 121.

1728, and that Lintot's rights to the *Dunciad* therefore expired in December, 1742, he could not prove his case. The earliest instrument he could produce was the assignment of rights in the poem to Gilliver by Lord Bathurst, the Earl of Burlington, and the Earl of Oxford, an assignment dated October 16, 1729.[53] Thus Pope was forced to delay the publication of his revised *Dunciad* until after October 16, 1743.[54]

V

One significant feature of the revised *Dunciad* was the substitution of the actor-dramatist-laureate Colley Cibber for Lewis Theobald as hero of the poem. It has commonly been supposed that the substitution was made in consequence of Cibber's publication in late July or early August, 1742, of a pamphlet attacking Pope, *A Letter from Mr. Cibber to Mr. Pope*. This pamphlet, written in response to the fourth book of the *Dunciad*, undertakes to give an account of Cibber's relations with the poet. As an instance of alleged ingratitude, it includes the story of a jest played upon Pope by Lord Warwick in a "certain House of Carnal Recreation." "A Girl of the Game" was encouraged to seduce the young poet; but when her efforts were about to prove successful, Cibber intervened for "the Honour of our Nation." Undoubtedly, if Pope had not already planned to change heroes, this pamphlet would have made him do so; but it should be noted that Pope had already made the substitution in the fourth book. The hero of the poem is mentioned only once in the addition to the *Dunciad*, but he is there described as the "Laureate son," an allusion that in 1742 could point only to Colley Cibber. Cibber in his *Letter* owned the soft impeachment;[55] and if Cibber's pamphlet really did influence Pope, it could merely have determined him to substitute Cibber for Theobald in the first three books. It seems more reasonable to suppose that the possibility had probably occurred to Pope before Cibber's pamphlet appeared and that the pamphlet only gave him a public excuse for doing what he had already planned to do.

Contempt for Cibber had developed early. Pope may have been the author of an anonymous attack, *The Plot Discover'd; or, A Clue to the Comedy of the Non-Juror* (1718); and he included Cibber in the *Peri Bathous* among the parrots who "repeat another's words, in such a hoarse odd voice, as makes them seem their own."[56] Cibber was given a more than minor supporting role in the *Dunciad Variorum*, particularly in the third book. After 1730, when Cibber had been appointed poet laureate, he, along with Lady Mary and Lord Hervey, were the more frequent objects of Pope's ridicule. If a specific occasion is required to explain this persistent hostility, Cibber's *Letter* suggests one, in an account of a display of temper by Pope occurring after Cibber made a jesting allusion to *Three Hours*

---

[53] See Appendix A.

[54] Pope's petition is in the Public Record Office (Cll 549/39). See Howard P. Vincent, "Some *Dunciad* Litigation," *PQ*, XVIII (1939), 285–89.

[55] *A Letter from Mr. Cibber to Mr. Pope, Inquiring into the Motives that might induce him in his Satyrical Works, to be so frequently fond of Mr. Cibber's Name* (London, 1742), pp. 52–53.

[56] E-C, X, 361.

after Marriage in a revival of *The Rehearsal;* [57] and a letter from Montagu Bacon to James Montagu confirms Cibber's report that there had been a quarrel in February, 1717.[58] Nevertheless, Pope would undoubtedly have brought Cibber into his later satires, even had there been no incident that aroused personal animosity. For as a man and as a writer Cibber epitomized much that Pope, in his later satires, condemned. Cibber was pert and vain; he was a notorious gambler and babbler. As the manager of Drury Lane he was arbitrary and tyrannical, a shrewd promoter who held no exalted views about the purpose of the drama. After 1730, when he became poet laureate, he was associated with the Court party which Pope had come to detest; and his odes written to commemorate important occasions in the life of the royal family are among the more insipid performances in the English language. Cibber's good qualities—and he had good qualities—were of a kind that Pope was not prepared to value. His animal spirits, his natural ebullience, his spontaneity that brought so much good fun to the stage of the time could not have impressed the "swan of Twickenham"; and the temper of his morality, bourgeois and pedestrian, could hardly have won the respect of one whose moral sensibilities were as delicate as Pope's. In short, Cibber, just by being himself, was a "natural" for Pope's satire.

Moreover, when the *Dunciad* was revised, Cibber in some ways was a more suitable hero than Theobald. Theobald, in his edition of Shakespeare, had proved his real merits; and he had largely given up the kind of hack writing which had helped to qualify him for his place in the *Dunciad Variorum*. The very fact that Cibber had been made poet laureate added to the appropriateness of his being appointed king of dunces; and Cibber's publication of his amusing but vainglorious *Apology for the Life of Mr. Colley Cibber* had created such universal merriment that he was a sufficiently topical hero. Pope's attitude toward the state of letters had also changed between 1729 and 1742; and he had come to see a principal source of bad writing, not in the mean-spirited, ignorant, and mercenary figures who had been tempted to take up the pen, but in the corrupt taste of a Court that neglected the best interests of letters. Desiring to express this newer concern more pointedly in his poem, Pope utilized Cibber, a figure more capable than Theobald of dramatizing the extent to which the Court had patronized bad writing.

Because Theobald had been treated as a symbol of dullness in drama and poetry,

---

[57] *A Letter from Mr. Cibber to Mr. Pope* (London, 1742), pp. 17–20.

[58] "To touch upon the polite world before I conclude, I don't know whether you heard, before you went out of town, that *The Rehearsal* was revived, not having been acted before these ten years, and Cibber interlarded it with several things in ridicule of the last play, upon which Pope went up to him and told him he was a rascal, and if he were able he would cane him; that his friend Gay was a proper fellow, and if he went on in his sauciness he might expect such a reception from him. The next night Gay came accordingly, and, treating him as Pope had done the night before, Cibber very fairly gave him a fillip on the nose, which made them both roar. The Guards came and parted them, and carried away Gay, and so ended this poetical scuffle" (George Paston [Miss E. M. Symonds], *Mr. Pope his Life and Times* [London, 1909], I, 197). An episode of this sort may help to explain why Pope and Cibber quarreled, though it does not really explain why Pope so persistently satirized him.

the substitution of heroes was not an impossible undertaking. A few necessary changes were made in deference to the facts of Cibber's career; but these were of a superficial sort that did not involve extensive alterations. Difficulties arose, however, in making Cibber substitute for Theobald as a symbol of pedantry. Cibber, though he was many things, was hardly a pedant; yet many good lines on the pedantic interests of the hero had appeared in the earlier versions. Obviously these could not be sacrificed; and Cibber was forced to play two incompatible roles in the poem—he is presented as both a learned pedant and an empty-headed fool. Cibber may not have been exactly suited to the work; but we can hardly regard the change as one that "depraved" it.

The fourth book represents an even more important change in the *Dunciad Variorum* than the substitution of heroes. Although an effort was made to link it with the rest of the poem on the grounds that it demonstrated the fulfillment of the prophecies in Book III, it is significantly different; and one is tempted to regard it as an independent but related work. There are obvious formal differences. The central situation, involving the award of honors in the royal drawing room, had no direct parallel in epic poetry, whereas the action of each of the first three books proceeds from an easily recognized epic episode. The character of the satire is general rather than particular; and even when specific personalities are introduced, they are generalized and made to speak, not for themselves, but for a class or group. Moreover, the subject of the fourth book is quite different from that of the first three, in which dullness is associated primarily with ignorance and venality. In the last book dullness is imputed to the genteel and polite whose irresponsibility with regard to the arts has contributed to its prevalence. Although the dunces in the first three books didn't really matter much, those in the last book do; for they are the ones who by birth and fortune set the intellectual tone of the country.

The fourth book of the *Dunciad* shows, however, no diminution in Pope's powers. If the satire is, contrary to his prevailing manner, general rather than specific, it nevertheless retains the trenchancy and vigor that had become characteristic of his work. There is the same delight in grotesque fancy that had been responsible for so much of the comedy in the first three books; and the descriptions are marked by concrete and picturesque detail. The range of material compacted into the work is also remarkable; for seemingly all the polite follies in the reign of George II are there—editing, education, the Grand Tour, virtuosi collecting, rational theology, feasting in the French manner. The presentation of these materials placed a heavy strain on Pope's skill in arrangement and organization; but, taking a hint perhaps from Fielding's *Author's Farce* (1730) and *Pasquin* (1736), he adapted for his purposes the idea of a Court ceremony in which aspirants to recognition offer their pretensions. Such a situation had the additional advantage of burlesquing the academic ceremony involving the awarding of degrees, a subject that was fresh in the minds of Pope and Warburton when the fourth book was composed.[59] The plan permitted the votaries of dullness to appear before their goddess and themselves manifest their devotion to her in varied ways. The educators and rationalizing divines with studied seriousness describe the principles on which they act; the fop, presumably too inarticulate to speak for himself, must be described by his governor. Two of the virtuosi, the horticulturist and the collector of butterflies, reveal their inanity in a review of a quarrel that has arisen between them. The result of such portraiture is an elaborately embroidered tapestry that embraces a seemingly inexhaustible fund of criticism.

If there is diversity in the portrayal and in the kinds of folly described, there is a basic similarity in the follies depicted. For all who appear before dullness have neglected good sense. They are guilty of a self-indulgence that is unmindful of the moral and social responsibilities that direct all human activities. The virtuosi, pursuing private enjoyment, have spent money and energy in pursuit of useless rarities; the rationalizing divines have sought to found metaphysics in reason and refined away the only concepts by which morality is possible. Educators have evolved a discipline that ignores responsibility for the development of moral character; and if a product of their system succeeds, he does so in spite of their methods. Thus the fourth book reaffirms once again what Pope's satires had said many times, that civilization must perish if men persist in making private concerns and desires a measure of happiness, if they cease to regard social utility and reason as the proper guides for human action.

William Warburton undoubtedly made some contributions to the fourth book; but what these were it is difficult to determine. Certainly he gave moral support; and he supplied a number of notes. A few details may have been introduced into the poem at his suggestion. The attack on Sir Thomas Hanmer as Montalto (ll. 105-18) may have been inspired by him; the satire upon rationalizing divines can also possibly be attributed to him, for he may well have proposed that another pointed attack upon the deists in the fourth book—Pope had attacked them in the *Dunciad Variorum*—would help prevent further misconstruction of the *Essay on Man*. Except for such details, however, there is little that can reasonably be attributed to him. There was, after all, nothing that Warburton could tell Pope about satire or about the follies in polite learning. He had said many times in the *Imitations of Horace* that the Court encouraged vacuity and irresponsibility; and pedantry had been the principal concern of the Scriblerus Club. The substitution of Cibber for Theobald was a natural one for Pope himself to make. The focus of the satire upon groups and classes as opposed to individuals has been charged to Warburton; but the subject matter of the poem lent itself more readily to general rather than specific treatment. Pope was perfectly capable of perceiving an artistic demand of this sort for himself. The interest in concepts that distin-

---

[59] These points have been made by George Sherburn, "The *Dunciad*, Book IV," *University of Texas Studies in English*, 1944, pp. 179–82. For other possible sources of the fourth book see Aubrey Williams, "Literary Backgrounds to Book Four of the *Dunciad*," *PMLA*, LXVIII (1953), 806–13.

guishes the fourth book has also been attributed to Warburton, who, in particular, may be assumed to have been more conversant with educational theory than Pope; but the poet did tell Joseph Spence that "what was first designed for an Epistle on Education, as part of my essay-scheme, is now inserted in the fourth book of the Dunciad." [60] It should also be remarked that as early as 1736 Pope had planned to write some ethic epistles which included subjects brought up in the fourth book:

> If ever I write more epistles in verse, one of them shall be addressed to you. I have long concerted it, and begun it, but I would make what bears your name as finished as my last work ought to be, that is to say, more finished than any of the rest. The subject is large, and will divide into four Epistles, which naturally follow the Essay on Man, viz. 1. Of the extent and limits of human reason and science. 2. A view of the useful and therefore attainable, and of the un-useful and therefore unattainable, arts. 3. Of the nature, ends, application, and use of different capacities. 4. Of the use of learning, of the science of the world, and of wit. It will conclude with a satire against the misapplication of all these, exemplified by pictures, characters, and examples. [61]

It is likely that concepts articulated in the fourth book were borrowed from these plans rather than from Warburton.

We must, therefore, come to the conclusion that Pope's friend did not really exert an important influence upon the fourth book of the *Dunciad;* and, in spite of the poet's apparent willingness to listen to advice on the *Essay on Man* and *Ethic Epistles,* Warburton's influence on these poems was also minor. If the editor laments certain textual changes for which Warburton was responsible, these changes have more to do with presentation than with substance. As Bolingbroke and Swift before him, Warburton may have been responsible for details in Pope's writing; and his conversation may have sharpened some of Pope's statements. But he did not overwhelm his friend, whose last years are a continuation of those which had gone before. If they were not so productive as earlier periods, they did not see the emergence of new interests or new concerns but a continued preoccupation with themes in which he had been absorbed for a number of years and to which he still attempted to give complete and more perfect expression.

VI

Pope's death in 1744 ended the career of one who had thoroughly demonstrated his mastery of the art of verse satire. His achievement is especially notable, for he did not concentrate upon satire until relatively late in his life, and he did not produce a great quantity of satires. Nevertheless, he had convincingly demonstrated gifts that assured his pre-eminence in the genre. His work is distinguished by verbal smartness and variety as well as by acuteness of observation. If there is little of the natural ebullience or good-humored playfulness that has lent charm to the writings of some great satirists, there is the finish that comes from conscious artistry and that gives the aesthetic pleasure always to be derived from a

---

[60] *Anecdotes,* p. 289. One may well believe that some of the speeches before Dullness were adaptations of characters Pope may have sketched, or written, for his ethic epistle on education.

[61] Pope to Swift, March 25, 1736: E-C, VII, 341.

work in which the writer exercises perfect control over himself and his materials.

Although the range of concern in the satires is largely limited to the moral corruptions that may assail persons of importance, the writings taken together represent a distinguished protest against depravity; and, in spite of all his enemies have said about him, there is no real evidence that his satire was consciously motivated by anything other than "the strong antipathy of good to bad." He may sometimes have confused personal animosities with the bad, and the intellectual assumptions of his day may have imposed limitations upon his perceptiveness. Nevertheless, the writing proceeded from what were essentially honest intentions.

And his views were salutary and sane. There was no morbid despair or intense disillusionment in his work; and he remained confident that enlightenment would come through efforts at a rational ordering of human life and conduct. He assumed that social good depended upon the morals of individuals in a society; and Pope's business is therefore private morality. By examining the moral state of persons, he hoped to enlarge prevailing conceptions of pleasure and happiness, and to improve thereby the moral tone of the times. His end was essentially noble. It remains noble, even if at times expressed in savage invective, and even if at times distant from his own actual achievement in conduct.

Some of Pope's Publication Agreements

POPE'S ARRANGEMENTS WITH BENJAMIN MOTTE FOR THE PUBLICATION OF THE POPE-
SWIFT *Miscellanies*.[1]

Whereas it is propos'd to print certain Miscellanies by Dr Swift, Mr Pope and
[*struck out*] Dr Arbuthnot | &c. |[2] in Two or more Volumes to be annex'd to a
Volume under that Title publish'd by Mr Tooke already: I hereby agree to pay for
the Copy of the said Miscellanies, at the rate of Four Pounds for each Sheet as
much as they shall make printed in the present Octavo, and to pay for the said
First Volume already publish'd by Mr Tooke the Sum of Fifty Pounds. Of which
Sum and Sums, Fifty Pounds to be paid down: One Hundred within Two Months
after the Publication of the Two Volumes: One Hundred within Four Months
after the said Publication: and in case of another Volume to be added: the pay-
ment for it at the same rate, to be also made within Two Months after its Publication. In consideration whereof the sole Copy Right to be vested in me. And
whereas there are to be inserted Two or Three Pieces already printed by others, |
to which they have acquir'd a lawful Property from the Author, | the same are
included [*struck out*] intended to be included within this Agreement, and no
part of the said Copy money deducted, except for as much as shall exceed Four
Sheets. Witness my hand. Mar. 29, 1727. ———

[sig.] Benj: Motte

We whose names are hereto signed, do agree to the aforesaid Conditions,

[sig.] Jonath: Swift.
[sig.] Alex^r Pope.

[Memoranda on the verso of the foregoing agreement.]

Apr. 10. 1727.

Rec^d ye Sum of fifty pounds in part of ye foresaid Agreement,

[sig.] A. Pope.

June[3] 12.

1728. This is to acknowledge, that (having given Mr Motte farther time for ye pay-
ment of ye first one hundred 'p^d herein mention'd, which was due last May) I have
Receivd of him a Note of fifty pound to me, payable next October, and another Note of
fifty pound for Dr Arbuthnot, payable next August, in part hereof,

[sig.] A. Pope.

We whose Names are underwritten do hereby acknowledge in behalf of ourselves and
the Revd Dr Swift, that we have receiv'd full Satisfaction of the within nam'd Benjamin
Motte for the Three Volumes of Miscellanies within mention'd now printed: and that
we have granted to the said Benjamin Motte his Executors, Administrators and Assigns

---

[1] From the original in the Pierpont Morgan Library of New York City.

[2] Materials between vertical bars here and elsewhere in this appendix are interlineations made by
the clerk drawing up the agreement.

[3] "June" has been written over the name of another month, apparently "July."

the entire Right and Title to the same for Fourteen Years from the Date of the Publication, and we do promise at the Expiration of the said Fourteen Years [to] renew the said Grant to him or his Assigns for the further Term of Fourteen Years for the Sum of Five Shillings And I the said Benjamin Motte in consideration of an Abatement | already made | of Twenty Five Pounds part of the Two Hundred and Fifty Pounds due by virtue of the within Agreement, for the first Three Volumes do hereby quit claim to any Pretensions I may have by virtue of this Agreement to the Fourth Volume of Miscellanies therein mentioned, and I do hereby acquit the said Mʳ Pope and the other Persons here mentioned from the same. Witness our hands July 1. 1729 ———
                        [sig.] Benj: Motte   [sig.] Alexʳ Pope.

ASSIGNMENT OF THE *Dunciad* TO LAWTON GILLIVER BY LORD OXFORD, LORD BATHURST, AND THE EARL OF BURLINGTON, OCTOBER 16, 1729.[4]

Know all Men by these presents That The Right Honourable Richard Earl of Burlington and Corke The Right Honourable Edward Earl of Oxford and Earl Mortimer and the Right Honourable Allen Lord Bathurst for and in consideration of the Sum of One hundred pounds of lawfull money of great Britain to them in hand paid by Lawton Gilliver of London Bookseller at and before the Ensealing and delivery of these presents the receipt whereof they do hereby acknowledge *Have* and each of them *Hath* granted bargaind sold assignd and transferrd and by these presents *Do* and each of them *Doth* grant bargain sell assign and transferr unto the said Lawton Gilliver his Executors Administrators and Assigns *The Book* intitled *The Dunciad* an *Heroick* poem and the Copy thereof and the sole right and liberty of printing the same *And* also the Prolegomena of Scriblerus *In Witnesse* whereof the said Earl of Burlington Earl of Oxford and Lord Bathurst have hereunto set their hands and Seals this sixteenth day of October in the third year of the Reign of King George the second Annoque Dñi 1729.

Sealed and delivered by the said Earl of Burlington (yᵉ paper being stampt with three six penny stamps) in the presence of us

Sealed and delivered by the said Earl of Oxford
in the presence of us   [sig.] Oxford & Mortimer.
        [sig.] Sam¹ Hopkins
        [sig.] Ed Dewfull

Sealed and delivered by the said Lord Bathurst
in the presence of us   [sig.] Bathurst
        [sig.] Tho Rogers
        [sig.] John Ford

Sealed and Delivered by the Said Earl of Burlington
in The Presence of us   [sig.] Burlington
        [sig.] Wᵐ Kent
        [sig.] John Ferrett

CONTRACT BETWEEN ALEXANDER POPE AND LAWTON GILLIVER, DECEMBER 1, 1732.[5]

Articles of Agreement Indented made concluded and agreed upon this first[6] day of

---

[4] From the original in the British Museum, Egerton MSS. 1951, f. 7.

[5] From the original in the British Museum, Egerton MSS. 1951, f. 8.

[6] The date is followed by a dash in the original, indicating that the document was first drawn up earlier, with sufficient space left that the date of signing might later be included.

December in the year of our Lord One thousand seven hundred and thirty two and in the Sixth year of the Reign of our Sovereign Lord George the Second by the Grace of God of Great Britain ffrance and Ireland King Defender of the ffaith &c. *Between* Alexand<er> Pope of Twickenham in the County of Middlesex Esqr of the one part and Lawton Gilliver of the Parish of St Dunstans in the West in the s^d County of Middlesex Bookseller of the other part.

Whereas the said Alexander Pope intends to publish certain Poems or Epistles in Verse composed by him the s^d Alexander Pope *And whereas* it is intended that the said Lawton Gilliver shall have the sole liberty of printing & selling as many such Poems or Epistles as the said Alexander Pope shall think fit for the space of one year only from the time of entring the same in the Register Book of the Company of Stationers and that in consideration thereof the s^d Lawton Gilliver shall pay unto the said Alexander Pope his Executors and Administrators[7] the sume of ffifty pounds for every such Poem or Epistle which he the said Lawton Gilliver shall so be permitted to print and sell in such manner as hereinafter is mentioned *It is therefore* Covenanted and Agreed by these presents And the said Lawton Gilliver doth hereby for himself his Executors and Administrators Covenant Promise and Grant to and with the s^d Alexander Pope his Executors and Administrators that he the said Lawton Gilliver his Executors or Administrators shall and will accept of the printing and publishing of every such poem or Epistle which he the said Alexander Pope his Executors or Administrators shall permit him the said Lawton Gilliver his Executors or Administrators to print & publish and shall and will print and publish the same respectively And also that he the s^d Lawton Gilliver his Executors or Administrators shall and will pay or cause to be paid unto the said Alexander Pope his Executors or Administrators the sume of ffifty pounds for every such Poem or Epistle as is above mentioned which the said Alexander Pope shall think fit to have published and which he shall permit and suffer the s^d Lawton Gilliver to print and sell as aforesaid at or before the delivery of every such poem or Epistle by him the said Alexander Pope his Executors or Administrators unto | him | the said Lawton Gilliver his Executors or Administrators *And* he the said Alexander Pope for himself his [*illegible word*] Executors and Administrators doth hereby Covenant promise and Grant to and with the said Lawton Gilliver his Executors & Administrators that he the said Alexander Pope his Executors and Administrators shall and will quietly and without any Interruption of him the said Alexander Pope his Executors or Administrators permit and suffer him the said Lawton Gilliver his Executors and Administrators and him and them only to print and sell in what Volume or Size he or they shall think fit every such Poem or Epistle and for which the said ffifty pounds shall be so paid as aforesaid for the space of one <ye>ar to commence from the time of entring every such Poem or Epistle respectively in the said Register Book of the Company of Stationers to and for the sole benefit and advantage of him the said Lawton Gilliver his Executors and Administrators *And* it is also Covenanted concluded and agreed by and between the said Parties to these presents and he the said Lawton Gilliver doth for himself his Executors and Administrators Covenant Promise and Grant to and with the said Alexander Pope his Executors and Administrators that he the said Lawton Gilliver his Executors or Administrators shall and will enter or cause to be entred every and each of the said Poems or Epistles on the delivery of the same to the said Lawton Gilliver in the said Register Book of the Company of Stationers in such manner as Entrys of the like nature are there usually made in the name of him the said Lawton Gilliver to the intent that the said Lawton Gilliver his Executors and Administrators may have the benefit of every such entry for the Space of one year from the time of making every such Entry respectively and for such one year

---

[7] "Executors" and "Administrators," though frequently abbreviated in the original, have been expanded in this transcription.

only And from and after the determination of one year from the time of making every such entry respectively That then the same shall be In trust for the said Alexander Pope and to or for no other intent or purpose whatsoever *And* Lastly the said Lawton Gilliver for himself his Executors and Administrators doth hereby Covenant and Grant to and with the said Alexander Pope his Executors and Administrators that he the said Lawton Gilliver his Executors or Administrators shall and will at the request of the said Alexander Pope | his Executors & Administrators | immediately after the expiration of one year from the Time of every such respective Entry as aforesaid transferr and assign unto the said Alexander Pope his Executors or Administrators or to such person or persons as he or they shall appoint All his right title and interest in every such respective Poem or Epistle for or by reason of the said Entry or otherwise howsoever *In Witness* whereof the s^d Parties to these presents have hereunto interchangeably set their hands & seals the day and year above written —

 Sealed and Delivered (the Paper being
 first duly Stamp'd, in the presence of
  [sig.] Wm Story
  [sig.] Cha Deaves

           [sig.] A. Pope
           [sig.] L. Gilliver

[Gilliver's written acknowledgments on verso of foregoing agreement.]

Jan: 3. 1732–3 I acknowledge to have Receiv'd of Mr Pope his Epistle to the Lord Bathurst of the use of Riches & accept of the printing the same in pursuance to | & | on the Terms of the within written Articles.

           [sig.] L. Gilliver

March 4. 1732/3 I Acknowledge to have receiv'd of Mr Pope his Imitation of Horace Book the Second Satire the first and Accept of the printing it in pursuance to, and on the Terms of the within Articles

           [sig.] L. Gilliver

March 23. 1732/3 I have receivd of Mr Pope his First Epistle (now called an Essay on Man<par>rt 1st) & accept of it in pursuance to, & on the terms of, the within written Articles

Mar: 23. 1732/3 I Acknowledge to have receiv'd of Mr Pope his Second Epistle (now called an Essay on Man p^t 2^d) & accept of it in pursuance to, & on the terms of the within written Articles. And also his Third Epistle

           [sig.] L. Gilliver

Jan:^{y} 1st 1733/4 I Acknowledge to have receiv'd of Mr Pope | his Epistle | to the Lord Cobham and accept of printing the Same in pursuance to & on the terms of the Within written Articles

           [sig.] L. Gilliver

Jany 10. 1733/4 I Acknowledge to have receiv'd of Mr Pope the forth Essay on Man on the Within Written Terms

           [sig.] L. Gilliver

Dec: 1st 1734 I Acknowledge to have Receiv'd of Mr Pope the Epistle to Dr Arbuthnot on the Within Terms

           [sig.] L. Gilliver

Jan: 4. 1734 I Acknowledge to have Receiv'd of Mr Pope The Epistle to a Lady on the Within Written Terms.

           [sig.] L. Gilliver

CODICIL TO THE AGREEMENT WITH LAWTON GILLIVER.[8]

---

[8] From the original in the British Museum, Egerton MSS. 1951, f. 12.

In Case of Mortality, I think proper to Declare my Intention, that whereas Mʳ Gilliver has agreed and covenanted with me to Print certain of my Epistles in Verse seperately, and to pay at the Rate of Fifty pounds for the Liberty of Printing each seperate Epistle for one year: Now This is my Intention, and I hereby desire my Executors Administrators and Assigns, in case I die before all those Epistles be so printed, That He the said Mʳ Gilliver may have the Refusal of all such Epistles as I leave fit for the Press, in order to publish them all together with what were before printed, and with the Dunciad (of which he already has the property and of which he hath lying by an Edition in Quarto and Folio) And if the said Mʳ Gilliver shall not agree with my Executors for the perpetuity of the Epistles, That whosoever shall purchase the perpetuity shall make it a Condition to cause the said Epistles to be printed in the same manner as the abovesaid Edition of the Dunciad, to be bound up, and to go therewith in one Volume: which shall be intituled, The Works of Mʳ Alexander Pope. Volume the Second. In Testimony of this my Intention, I have hereunto subscribed my Hand.

[sig.] A. Pope

The Missing *Dunciad* Manuscripts

If manuscripts of the *Dunciad* were extant, one could trace more closely the genesis of the poem and might achieve a better understanding of Pope's motives and artistic intentions. At present no author's manuscript is known to have survived; but there are at least three printed copies of the poem containing marginalia in the hand of Jonathan Richardson, the younger, who during the period between about 1735 and 1737 was collating Pope's manuscripts and recording the results of his work in printed copies of the poems.[1] One copy of the *Dunciad,* in the Henry E. Huntington Library, has a few notes representing variants occurring in printed editions of the poem; the other two, in the Henry W. and Albert A. Berg Collection of the New York Public Library, are of more interest because they contain numerous readings derived from *Dunciad* manuscripts.[2] At least two manuscripts were involved, for in a note on the title page of the copy of the 1728 edition Richardson wrote: "This Book corrected from the First Broglio MS. as the Ed. 1736 is from the Second."[3] From the usual condition of Pope's manuscripts and from Richardson's term "Broglio," one can infer that the two he worked with contained a tangle of readings representing different states of composition; and since the readings are generally inferior to anything Pope printed in or after 1728, the states must have been early ones. Furthermore, Richardson's collations of other poems where the manuscripts are known to exist were detailed and accurate; and one can reasonably assume that his record of *Dunciad* variants must have been fairly complete.

---

[1] A letter from Pope to Jonathan Richardson, the elder, dated June 17 [1737], suggests that the son's work was then in progress: "I have a particular book here for your son of all my works together, with large margins, knowing how good an use he makes of them in all his books, and remembering how much a worse writer by far than Milton has been marked, collated, and studied by him" (E-C, IX, 506). The "particular book" may have been a copy of the *Works* (1735), which is now in the Henry E. Huntington Library.

[2] One of the copies in the Berg Collection belongs to an edition of the *Dunciad* of 1728 (Griffith 199); the other, to an edition of the *Dunciad* of 1736 (Griffith 405). W. J. Courthope has reprinted some of the marginalia (E-C, IV, 271–97); but what he presents is only a selective compilation of readings in both Berg copies. Editions of Pope's other poems with similar marginalia by Richardson exist in various libraries; and some of Pope's manuscripts have directions, by Pope, telling Richardson what variants he should record and what variants he should neglect. Pope later gave Richardson some of his manuscripts for the pains he "took in collating the whole with the printed editions, at his request, on [Richardson's] having proposed to him the 'making an edition of his works in the manner of Boileau's' " (*Richardsoniana* [London, 1776], p. 264).

[3] The title page of the copy of the 1736 edition bears a complementary note (in Pope's hand?): "This Book is alterd from the Second MS; as yᵉ 1st Ed. 1728 is from the First MS."

The marginalia tell us very little about the earliest form of the *Dunciad*, the character of the sketch snatched from the fire. Moreover, the value of the record is limited because Richardson rarely gives any indication of the approximate order in which various readings occurred to Pope. This lack of specific information is often tantalizing; but Richardson was compiling a personal record for Pope, not for posterity. And he does suggest how much labor Pope lavished on his poem in the effort to

> form with plastic care
> Each growing lump, and bring it to a bear.

Lines were phrased and rephrased; passages were shifted from one context to another as Pope sought to find the setting in which they could shine most brilliantly. In the earlier stages of composition Pope seems to have indulged a fondness for excessive detail; and he was inclined to overwork the scatological wit in the second book. Jonathan Richardson's marginalia demonstrate his untiring attempts to bring such materials under control. For example, when the *Dunciad* was first printed, these lines occur at a climactic point in one of the races:

> A place there is, betwixt earth, air and seas,
> Where from *Ambrosia, Jove* retires for ease.
> There in his seat two spacious Vents appear,
> On this he sits, to that he leans his ear,
> There hears the various vows of fond mankind,
> Some beg an eastern, some a western wind:
> All vain petitions, sent by winds on high,
> With reams abundant this abode supply;
> Amus'd he reads, and then returns the bills,
> Sign'd with that *Ichor* which from Gods distills.
>
> In office here fair *Cloacina* stands,
> And ministers to *Jove* with purest hands;
> Forth from the heap she pick'd her vot'ry's pray'r,
> And plac'd it next him, a distinction rare!
> Oft, as he fish'd her nether realms for wit,
> The Goddess favour'd him, and favours yet.
>
> (1728, ii, ll. 67–82)

The Swiftean tone of these lines is, as it was intended to be, unpleasant; but in an earlier version of the passage Pope had descended to sheer vulgarity:

> Brown Cloacina heard her servant call,
> From her black Grotto, near yᵉ Temple Wall.
> A Place there is between earth, Air, & seas,
> Calld by the Gods the Thund'rer's House of Ease.
> Where in her throne two spacious vents appear,
> On one she sits, to one applys her Ear:
> There lists delighted to yᵉ Jest unclean
> Of Link-boys vile, and watermen obscene.
> Then with Mist's Journals, & with Tanner's Bills
>   Goddesses
> Wipes that rich Ichor which a God distills.

Oft as she fish'd these nether realms for wit,
The Goddess favoured him, and favours yet
                    (Marginalia, 1728, pp. 18–19)

During the manuscript development of the poem an interesting revision took place in the account of the foot race, the first game in the second book. At one time the prize offered by Dullness for success in the contest was a phantom impishly resembling John Gay:

In Fleetstreet fair the Goddess chose y° place,
And mark'd the Barriers, & prescrib'd the Race.
And first (for Dullness, gentle Queen! delights
In Jokes, & feeds her subjects with strange sights)
To nimble Stationers propos'd the Prize,
And sets a Phantome Poet in their Eyes.
Not such as Garrets lodge, of visage thin,
Who like a N^t g^n round him wraps his skin;
But such a bulk as no twelve bards could raise,
Twelve starv'ling bards of these degen'rate days,
Plump as a Partridge; ruddy, round, and fair
She form'd this image of well-bodied air,
With laugh^g Eyes y^t twinkl'd in his head,
Well-look'd, well turnd, well natur'd, & well fed,
So wondrous like that Wootton's self m^t say,
And Kent w^d swear, by G— it must be Gay
                    (Marginalia, 1728, p. 16).

In this account of the race Jacob Tonson, Gay's bookseller, and Edmund Curll, who had published works by "Joseph Gay," a pseudonym designed to exploit John Gay's popularity, run for the prize. Obviously this version differs strikingly from the printed one, in which James Moore Smythe is the phantom poet and in which the race involves Edmund Curll and Bernard Lintot who had published Smythe's play, *The Rival Modes* (1727). In this play had appeared without permission (so Pope alleged) six lines that Pope had written.[4]

It is to be noted that a race between Tonson and Curll for the image of Gay had much more relevance in 1718–20, when Curll was exploiting "Joseph Gay," than it had in 1728. Are we then to see in this episode one fragment that Pope had composed several years earlier, perhaps an episode in the original sketch? It is impossible to answer this question, especially since ordinary prudence would have dictated the change in the passage. For the good-natured jesting about Gay could easily have been misrepresented by dunces who were capable of distorting the allusion and asserting that Pope had turned upon one of his friends. Moreover, the selection of Gay, even in effigy, made it necessary to include Jacob Tonson as one of the participants. To make the venerable Tonson, with whom Pope was friendly and whose work as a publisher was in every way commendable, a participant in the race, would hardly have been just. Nevertheless, it is interesting

---

[4] Norman Ault, *New Light on Pope* (London, 1949), pp. 198 ff., gives a good account of the history of these lines.

to speculate that in this manuscript version we may have a fragment of the *Ur-Dunciad*.

The Berg copy of the *Dunciad* of 1736 provides another interesting view of Pope's tentative plans for his poem. For on the initial flyleaf of this copy, there is a sketch, in Richardson's hand, of a plan for "Canto 2ᵈ." This outline bears no relation to the subject matter of the book as it was printed; but it does summarize the material appearing in the fourth book, ultimately printed in 1742. Theobald is still the hero; and the satire embraces, among other things, universities, virtuosi, Richard Bentley who represents the Cantabrigians, and a "French Refugee Governor with his Pupils," all of whom are portrayed as "telling Dullnes⟨s⟩ & their King Tibbald, what they will perform with ⟨L⟩ives & Fortunes for her, & what they have done in ⟨br⟩inging up yᵉ Youth to such Ends for yᵉ next Age. . . ."

This sketch presents material for the most exciting kind of speculation; but unfortunately there are no grounds for positive claims. The difficulty lies in the impossibility of dating the sketch. It could conceivably represent a proposed revision of the second book drawn up sometime between 1736 and 1740. If the time is correct, then it would seem that Pope may have planned to eliminate the games from his poem and to substitute an attack upon education. The trouble with this explanation is that the notes should be in Pope's autograph rather than in Richardson's, if it were true. Furthermore, one passage appearing on the flyleaf (*Dunciad* [1729], II, ll. 1–12) is an obviously inferior version of the passage as it was first printed in 1729. These difficulties suggest that this summary may represent an early plan for the second book, a plan calling for satire of a Scriblerian sort in the second book, aimed at abuses in learning rather than at the vices of publishers, authors, patrons, and journalists. Lacking more evidence one hesitates to press this extravagant hypothesis too far; one can only regret Richardson's failure to provide more information about the significance of this passage, as well as about that of many others he records. What might have been the principal source of knowledge about the development of the poem is now a source of frustration and debate.

Some Anticipations of the *Essay on Man* in Pope's Letters Before 1729

I am quoting below some of the passages from Pope's letters written before 1729 which in one way or another anticipate ideas and images in the *Essay on Man*. The record is not exhaustive; but it is sufficiently full to support the contention (p. 47) that many ideas in the poem had occurred to Pope long before he began writing his philosophical poem.

Epistle I, ll. 23 ff. This minute, perhaps, I am above the stars, with a thousand systems round about me, looking forward into the vast abyss of eternity, and losing my whole comprehension in the boundless spaces of the extended creation, . . . (To Caryll, Aug. 14, 1713: E-C, VI, 190)

I, ll. 61 ff. It made me reflect that man himself is as blind and unknowing of his fate, as the beast he bestrides: equally proud and prancing in his glory, and equally ignorant whither or to what he is running. (To Martha Blount, Sept. 4 [1728]: E-C, IX, 311)

I, l. 72. What a bustle we make about passing our time, when all our space is but a point! (To Caryll, Aug. 14, 1713: E-C, VI, 191)

I, ll. 77 ff., 189 ff. The greater number of arts to which we apply ourselves are mere groping in the dark; and even the search of our most important concerns in a future being is but a needless, anxious and uncertain haste to be knowing sooner than we can, what without all this solicitude we should know a little after. We are but curious impertinents in the case of futurity. It is not our business to be guessing what the state of souls is, but to be doing what may make our own happy. We cannot be knowing, but we can be virtuous. If this be my notion of a great part of the gravest of sciences, divinity, you may easily imagine how little stress I lay upon any of the lighter arts. (To Caryll, Sept. 20 [1713]: E-C, VI, 195)

I, l. 174. . . . I think myself *paulo minus ab Angelis*. (To Sir Godfrey Kneller, Feb. 18, 1718: E-C, IX, 511. See also Pope to Edward Blount, Sept. 13, 1725: E-C, VI, 385)

I, ll. 285 ff. I believe there is not in the whole course of the Scripture any precept so often and so strongly inculcated, as the trust and eternal dependence we ought to repose in that Supreme Being who is our constant preserver and benefactor. (To Caryll, Sept. 3 [1718]: E-C, VI, 267)

I, ll. 287 f. The separation of my soul and body is what I could think of with less pain; for I am very sure he that made it will take care of it, and in whatever state he pleases it shall be, that state must be right: . . . (To Martha Blount, [1727?]: E-C, IX, 307)

II, ll. 1 ff. Good God! what an incongruous animal is man! How unsettled in his best part, his soul; and how changing and variable in his frame of body!—the constancy of the one shook by every notion, the temperament of the other affected by every blast of wind. What an April weather in the mind! In a word, what is man altogether but one mighty inconsistency? Sickness and pain are the lot of one half of us; doubt and fear the portion of the other! (To Caryll, Aug. 14, 1713: E-C, VI, 191)

II, ll. 19 ff. Nothing can be more kind than the hint you give me of the vanity of human sciences, which I assure you I am daily more and more convinced of; and indeed I have for some years past looked upon all of them no better than amusements. To make them the ultimate end of our pursuit is a miserable and short ambition, which will drop from us at every little disappointment here, and even in case of no disappointment here will infallibly desert us hereafter. . . . Our schemes of government, our systems of philosophy, our golden words of poetry, are all but so many shadowy images and airy prospects, which arise to us but so much the lovelier and more frequent, as we are more overcast in the darkness, wrapt in the night, and disturbed with the fumes of human vanity. (To Caryll, July [13, 1714]: E-C, VI, 213–14)

II, ll. 27 f. I believe you are by this time immersed in your vast wood; and one may address to you as to a very abstracted person, like Alexander Selkirk, or the self-taught philosopher. I should be very curious to know what sort of contemplations employ you. I remember the latter of those I mentioned, gave himself up to a devout exercise of making his head giddy with various circumrotations, to imitate the motions of the celestial bodies. (To Lord Bathurst, Sept. 23 [1719]: E-C, VIII, 327–28)

II, ll. 249 ff. But humanity and sociable virtues are what every creature wants every day, and still wants more the longer he lives, and most the very moment he dies. (To Hugh Bethel, July 12, 1723: E-C, IX, 148)

II, ll. 257 ff. It is really some advantage one receives from knowing the world, that the more one sees of our fellow-creatures, the more willing one grows to part with it and them, which, to own an humble truth to you, is all I ever learned from experience that was to any purpose. (To Caryll, Oct. 11, 1715: E-C, VI, 233. See also Pope to Robert Digby, Sept. 1, 1722: E-C, IX, 79)

II, ll. 275 ff. What is every year of a wise man's life but a censure or critic on the past? Those whose date is the shortest, live long enough to laugh at one half of it: the boy despises the infant, the man the boy, the philosopher both, and the Christian all. You may now begin to think your manhood was too much a puerility; and you will never suffer your age to be but a second infancy. The toys and baubles of your childhood are hardly now more below you, than those toys of our riper and of our declining years, the drums and rattles of ambition, and the dirt and bubbles of avarice. (To Atterbury, [May], 1723: E-C, IX, 58)

III, ll. 131 ff. Indeed it is nature that makes us love; but it is experience that makes us grateful, and, I believe, to thinking minds, gratitude presents as many objects and circumstances to render us melancholy as even hope itself, that great painter of ideas, can do. But, in truth, both what good-natured minds have experienced, and what they expect to experience, fills them to the brim. The better a man is, the more he expects and hopes from his friend, his child, his fellow-creature; the more he reflects backwards and aggrandises every good he has received. His own capacity of being good and kind and grateful, makes him think others have been, or would be so. The only satisfaction this world can afford us under such losses, is to see those whom we believe to have a mutual feeling with us, participate and talk to us. This buoys us up from day to day, till somebody loves us, and buries us, and grieves for us, and there's an end of it. (To Lord Oxford, Nov. 7, 1725: E-C, VIII, 212–13)

III, ll. 246 ff. On the contrary, the superstitious man looks on the great Father of all as a tyrant, and in how miserable a state is he, who lies under perpetual apprehensions of such a power from whom no might can protect, no flight can save, and neither time nor death itself can deliver him. . . . Plutarch has set both the vice and folly of superstitions in the best light I have seen. He observes that these wretches are more impious than atheists, since it is worse to conceive an unworthy opinion of God, than not to believe there is one; as I would rather, says he, it were said there was no such [man] as Plutarch, than that he was passionate, revengeful, and implacable. The superstitious man fears most where others are most secure; he is afraid of heaven, and yet flies to it for succour. . . . In a word, such a wretch must of necessity at once fear God and hate him. (To Caryll, Sept. 3 [1718]: E-C, VI, 266–67)

III, ll. 303 ff. I hope all churches and all governments are so far of God, as they are rightly understood, and rightly administered: and where they are, or may be wrong, I leave it to God alone to mend or reform them; which whenever he does, it must be by greater instruments than I am. (To Atterbury, Nov. 20, 1717: E-C, IX, 12. See also Pope to Lady Mary W. Montagu, [Aug. 20, 1716]: E-C, IX, 346–47. Also Pope to Caryll, July 19, 1711: E-C, VI, 150)

IV, ll. 39 f. Methinks, in our present condition, the most heroic thing we are left capable of doing is to endeavour to lighten each other's load, and, oppressed as we are, to succour such as are yet more oppressed. (To Edward Blount, March 20, 1716: E-C, VI, 370)

IV, ll. 143 f. It is pleasant enough to consider that people who imagine themselves good Christians, should be so absurd as to think the same misfortunes, when they befal others, a punishment of vice, when they happen to themselves, an exercise of virtue. (To Atterbury, Sept. 8, 1718: E-C, IX, 13. See also Pope to Caryll, Sept. 3 [1718]: E-C, VI, 266)

IV, ll. 255 f. . . . I have ever made it my first maxim, never to seek for anything from a good action but the action itself, and the conscious pleasure of a sincere intention. (To Caryll, Dec. 5, 1712: E-C, VI, 174)

IV, ll. 269 ff. But perhaps you will say, the whole world has something to do, something to talk of, something to wish for, something to be employed about: but pray, sir, cast up the account, put all these somethings together, and what is the sum total but just nothing? (To Cromwell, April 27, 1708: E-C, VI, 70)

IV, ll. 319 ff. [Offices of benevolence] often afford the highest pleasure; and those who do not feel that, will hardly ever find another to match it, let them love themselves ever so dearly. At the same time it must be owned, one meets with cruel disappointments in seeing so often the best endeavours ineffectual to make others happy, and very often (what is most cruel of all) through their own means. But still, I affirm, those very disappointments of a virtuous man are greater pleasures than the utmost gratifications and successes of a mere self-lover. (To Bethel, June 24, 1727: E-C, IX, 152. See also Pope to Oxford, Dec. 14, 1725: E-C, VIII, 214)

IV, ll. 323 f. Only what a luxurious man wants for horses and footmen, a good-natured man wants for his friends or the indigent. (To Gay, Dec. 24, 1712: E-C, VII, 410)

IV, ll. 339 f. You see how little glory you would gain by my conversion. And after all, I verily believe your Lordship and I are both of the same religion, if we were thoroughly understood by one another; and that all honest and reasonable Christians would be so, if they did but talk enough together every day, and had nothing to do together, but to serve God, and live in peace with their neighbour. (To Atterbury, Nov. 20, 1717: E-C, IX, 11)

IV, ll. 327 ff. As in the next world, so in this, the only solid blessings are owing to the goodness of the mind, not the extent of the capacity: friendship here is an emanation from the same source as beatitude is there: the same benevolence and grateful disposition that qualifies us for the one, if extended farther, makes us partakers of the other. (To Trumbull, March 12, 1713: E-C, VI, 6–7)

Pope's Quarrel with Lady Mary
and Lord Hervey

Pope's quarrel with Lady Mary and Lord Hervey is shrouded in mystery. Human relations of the kind involved present almost irresistible temptations to side with one or the other of the participants and to overdramatize known events. The traditions surrounding the affair now contain such a fast blend of fact and fiction that separating the truth after two hundred years is a difficult task, especially since the principals were somewhat reticent about the real causes of their differences. But the student of Pope's later poetry should become cognizant of the main facts of the poet's relations with these two contemporaries.

In 1717 an infatuation for Lady Mary had inspired Pope to write *Eloisa to Abelard;* some fifteen years later he was composing devastating couplets at her expense. The chief steps in this disintegrating friendship can be traced, although the open break was long in coming. In 1718, when Lady Mary returned from Turkey with her husband, she began visiting Twickenham; and in 1719 the Montagus rented a house there. At this time relations between the poet and the lady remained most cordial; but by April or May, 1722, there was a growing coolness. For it was then that Lady Mary wrote to her sister, the Countess of Mar, that she was seeing Mr. Pope "very seldom." [1] This remark, though it may invite more than one interpretation, could imply that the friendship had begun to degenerate into indifference; but Professor Robert Halsband has recently argued that sometime between the latter part of 1723 and the autumn of 1724 Lady Mary was still sending letters to the poet. [2] Coolness developed into hostility by 1728, however; for Pope and Swift included in the "last" volume of their *Miscellanies* a poem entitled "The Capon's Tale," in which Lady Mary is advised not to pass her own poems off as the work of others. [3] The *Dunciad*, published the same year, also contained a hit at Lady Mary:

---

[1] *Letters and Works of Lady Mary Wortley Montagu*, ed. Lord Wharncliffe and W. Moy Thomas (London, 1893), I, 461.

[2] "Two New Letters from Lady Mary Wortley Montagu to Alexander Pope," *PQ*, XXIX (1950), 349–52.

[3] Although Norman Ault, *New Light on Pope* (London, 1949), pp. 242–47, presents an interesting argument for Pope's authorship of "The Capon's Tale," there is really no compelling evidence for the attribution. The lampoon has also been ascribed to Swift; but Sir Harold Williams (ed.), *Swift's Poems* (Oxford, 1937), does not admit it to the canon. Regardless of the authorship, the fact that it was published in the *Miscellanies* is significant. It is also significant that prior to their publication the last lines were revised in order to intensify their severity.

> Whence hapless Monsieur much complains at Paris
> Of wrongs from Duchesses and Lady Mary's.[4]
>   (II, ll. 127–28)

The evidence suggests then that the occasion for open war between the two probably occurred between 1724 and 1727, although the trouble was probably preceded
by a period of growing coolness. Lady Mary is the source of several different
explanations of the difficulties working to alienate them during these years.
Samuel Weller Singer found among Joseph Spence's papers a memorandum stat-
ing, "Lady Mary W——— told Lady Pomfret, that when she became much acquainted with the Duke of Wharton [1722], Mr. Pope grew jealous, and that
occasioned the breach between them." [5] Lady Louisa Stuart reported a different
story which she had derived from Lady Mary: ". . . at some ill-chosen time, when
she least expected what romances call a *declaration,* he made such passionate love
to her, as, in spite of her utmost endeavours to be angry and look grave, provoked an immoderate fit of laughter; from which moment he became her implacable enemy." [6] Still another explanation was offered by James Worsdale, the
painter and friend of Sir Godfrey Kneller: ". . . the first cause of quarrel between
her and Pope was her borrowing a pair of sheets from the poet, which, after keeping them a fortnight, were returned to him unwashed." [7] All, or none, of these
accounts may have an element of truth; but it is very unlikely that any one of
them alone explains the outbreak of hostilities. These incidents, or incidents
essentially like them, may have created potential enmity; but the event that brought
the trouble into the open is probably yet to be found.

Popes' own versions of the occasion of the quarrel are distinguished by a degree
of consistency. In "The Capon's Tale" (which may or may not have been written
by him) Lady Mary is specifically charged with passing off her own compositions
as the work of others:

> Such, Lady *Mary,* are your Tricks;
> But since you hatch, pray own your Chicks:
> You should be better skill'd in Nocks,
> Nor like your Capons, serve your Cocks.

In 1729 Pope told William Fortescue that he had left off Lady Mary's "conversation when I found it dangerous"; [8] and four years later, in his *Letter to a Noble*

---

[4] At one point during the preparation of the *Dunciad* Pope thought of treating Lady Mary even
more severely; for he composed these lines:
> See Pix & slip-shod W[ortley] traipse along,
> With heads unpinn'd, and meditating song
> With tresses streamᵍ from poetic dreams,
> And never wash'd but in *Castalia's* streams.
> H[aywoo]d and W[ortle]y; glories of their race!

From manuscript readings recorded by Jonathan Richardson on p. 44 of the copy of the *Dunciad*
(1728), now in the New York Public Library. See above, pp. 120–23.

[5] *Anecdotes,* pp. 236–37 n.

[6] *Letters and Works of Lady Mary,* I, 92.

[7] Sir James Prior, *Life of Edmund Malone* (London, 1860), p. 150.

[8] E-C, IX, 111.

Lord, he obliquely offered a similar explanation:

Your [Lord Hervey's] resentments against me indeed might be equal, as my offence to you both was the same; for neither had I the least misunderstanding with that Lady, till after I was the *Author* of my own misfortune in discontinuing her acquaintance. I may venture to own a truth, which cannot be unpleasing to either of you; I assure you my reason for so doing, was merely that you had both *too much wit* for me; and that I could not do, with *mine,* many things which you could with *yours.* The injury done you in withdrawing myself could be but small, if the value you had for me was no greater than you have been pleas'd since to profess. But surely, my Lord, one may say, neither the Revenge, nor the Language you held, bore any *proportion* to the pretended offence: The appellations of *Foe* to *humankind,* an *Enemy* like the *Devil* to all that have *Being; ungrateful, unjust,* deserving to be *whipt, blanketed, kicked,* nay *killed;* a *Monster,* an *Assassin,* whose conversation every man ought to *shun,* and against whom *all doors* should be shut; I beseech you, my Lord, had you the least right to give, or to encourage or justify any other in giving such language as this to me? Could I be treated in terms more strong or more atrocious, if, during my acquaintance with you, I had been a *Betrayer,* a *Backbiter,* a *Whisperer,* an *Eves-dropper,* or an *Informer?* Did I in all that time ever throw a *false Dye,* or palm *a foul Card* upon you? Did I ever *borrow, steal,* or accept, either *Money, Wit,* or *Advice* from you? Had I ever the honour to join with either of you in one *Ballad, Satire, Pamphlet,* or *Epigram,* on any person *living* or *dead?* Did I ever do you so great an injury as to put off *my own Verses* for *yours,* especially on *those Persons* whom they might *most offend?* [9]

Pope's accounts imply that Lady Mary (and possibly Lord Hervey) had circulated as Pope's a poem of her (or their) own composition, or perhaps a tale of malicious gossip, in which persons whom Pope did not wish to hurt were abused. Unfortunately no one has been able to identify this poem, which may have been passed around only in manuscript. It has been argued that the satire may have been directed at Mrs. Grizel Baillie Murray, who had become a topical figure in 1721 when a footman entered her room and was prevented from criminal assault only by Mrs. Murray's presence of mind. In 1725 Mrs. Murray accused Lady Mary of writing a ballad on the subject entitled *Virtue in Danger; or, Arthur Gray's Last Farewell to the World. Written by a Gentleman at St. James's;* but there is no reason to believe that Pope would have been identified as the "Gentleman at St. James's" or that he was seriously interested in Mrs. Murray's affairs.[10] Nothing else that might establish the validity of Pope's account has been turned up, although there is always the possibility that his remarks may allude to some gossip circulated by word of mouth. We know that during the years when Pope broke with Lady Mary ugly tales about his relations with Martha Blount were being circulated and that Lady Mary would not have hesitated to pass on such stories.[11] If, indeed, she did, we would have sufficient explanation for Pope's

[9] *Works* (1751), VIII, 259–60.

[10] One version of the ballad declares that the poem was written "By a Lady." In a letter to the Countess of Mar, Lady Mary seems to admit her authorship of *Virtue in Danger.* She does not disown the work and hints that there is a secret connected with it which the two of them share (*Letters and Works of Lady Mary,* I, 482–83).

[11] For the story of this gossip, see George Sherburn, *Early Career of Alexander Pope* (Oxford, 1934), pp. 291 ff. One would wish to know more about the "villainous lying tale" Pope refers to in a letter to John Caryll, December 25, 1725 (E-C, VI, 287–88).

later treatment of her as well as for his reluctance to be more specific in his own explanations of the quarrel.

After the publication of the *Dunciad* in 1728, there were more misunderstandings. Among the answers to the *Dunciad* was a short lampoon entitled *A Popp upon Pope* (June 8, 1728), a pamphlet pretending to report that the poet had been barbarously whipped while strolling in Ham-Walks. The report gained a certain currency; and Pope was forced to issue a denial. For some reason he believed the effort to embarrass him was the work, at least in part, of Lady Mary, although there is now no cogent reason to ascribe the satire to her. The following year he learned of the preparation of a severe satire upon himself; and he again suspected Lady Mary of collaborating in it. At least, Dr. Arbuthnot, who remained on friendly terms with both the poet and Lady Mary, undertook to determine the truth; for Lady Mary wrote him on October 17, 1729, in answer to his inquiry:

> I have this minute received your letter, and cannot remember I ever was so much surprised in my life; the whole contents of it being a matter of astonishment. I give you sincere and hearty thanks for your intelligence, and the obliging manner of it. I have ever valued you as a gentleman both of sense and merit, and will join with you in any method you can contrive to prevent or punish the authors of so horrid a villany.[12]

Not content with this explanation, Lady Mary investigated further and reported to Arbuthnot again:

> Since I saw you I have made some inquiries, and heard more, of the story you was so kind to mention to me. I am told Pope has had the surprising impudence to assert he can bring the lampoon when he pleases to produce it, under my own hand; I desire he may be made to keep to this offer. If he is so skilful in counterfeiting hands, I suppose he will not confine that great talent to the gratifying his malice, but take some occasion to increase his fortune by the same method, and I may hope (by such practices) to see him exalted according to his merit, which nobody will rejoice at more than myself. I beg of you, sir (as an act of justice), to endeavour to set the truth in an open light, and then I leave to your judgment the character of those who have attempted to hurt mine in so barbarous a manner. I can assure you (in particular) you named a lady to me (as abused in this libel) whose name I never heard before, and as I never had any acquaintance with Dr. Swift, am an utter stranger to all his affairs and even his person, which I never saw to my knowledge, and am now convinced the whole is a contrivance of Pope's to blast the reputation of one who never injured him.[13]

Explanations of this sort, however plausible, did not satisfy Pope, and ill-will remained. But hostilities were not resumed until 1733.[14] Pope was, after all, pre-

---

[12] *Letters and Works of Lady Mary*, II, 17. The date 1730 suggested for this letter by Lady Mary's editors is surely an error.

[13] *Letters and Works of Lady Mary*, II, 17–19. The libel in question was eventually published in April, 1730, under the title *One Epistle to Mr. A. Pope, Occasion'd by Two Epistles Lately Published.* It was actually written by James Moore Smythe and Leonard Welsted; and it had been announced in *The Universal Spectator*, February 1, 1729, as "the due Chastisement of Mr. Pope for his Dunciad, by James Moore Smythe, Esq; and Mr. Welsted."

[14] After the publication of the *Epistle to the Earl of Burlington* in 1731, Lady Mary may have helped circulate the report that the Duke of Chandos was intended in the portrait of Timon; for

occupied with composition; and Lady Mary, possibly not wishing to quarrel with so effective and bold a satirist as Pope had proved to be, did not, so far as we know, offer any direct provocation. The *Epistle to Lord Bathurst* (published in January, 1733) contained, however, a stroke that those acquainted with court personalities might easily recognize as directed at Maria Skerrett, Walpole's mistress, and Lady Mary:

> Ask you why Phryne the whole Auction buys?
> Phryne foresees a general Excise.
> Why she and Lesbia raise that monstrous sum?
> Alas! they fear a man will cost a plum.
>   (II, ll. 121–24)[15]

Manuscript readings of the *Epistle* recorded by Jonathan Richardson in a printed copy of it now at the Henry E. Huntington Library reveal that the poet in composing the poem had made another attempt to introduce Lady Mary directly. One couplet as published in 1733 reads:

> Or find some Doctor that would save the life
> Of wretched Shylock spite of Shylock's Wife.
>   (ll. 95–96)

As this couplet was printed, specific application is difficult; but in the manuscripts there are two readings demonstrating that Pope had contemplated mentioning a more specific target:

> It might to W[ortle]y, (spite of W[ortle]y's wife)
> Give such a Doctor as would save his Life.

> Or such a Doctor as wou'd save the life
> Of wretched Worldly, spite of Worldly's Wife.[16]

If Pope finally veiled his comments in the *Epistle,* he produced a direct and devastating allusion to Lady Mary in his next poem, his imitation of the first satire of Horace:

> From furious *Sappho* scarce a milder Fate,
> P-x'd by her Love, or libell'd by her Hate.
>   (ll. 83–84)

The stroke was provocative; but Lady Mary, had she been wise, might well have ignored it. Nevertheless, such aloofness may more easily be held to in theory than in practice; and Lady Mary, believing that she had had enough, approached Pope indirectly in an attempt to secure an explanation. Pope's reply, transmitted by

---

in the unpublished answer to critics of the *Epistle, A Master Key to Popery,* Pope referred to a Lady De-la-Wit as helping to spread the gossip. Lady De-la-Wit may, or may not, have been Lady Mary. The *Master Key* was not, however, published.

[15] Quoted from the poem as published in 1733. Later in 1735, when Pope was willing to make the target more generally recognizable, he altered *Lesbia* to *Sappho,* his usual sobriquet for Lady Mary; but informed readers of 1733, knowing of the intimate friendship of Lady Mary and Maria Skerritt, would have had no difficulty recognizing Pope's intentions from the first.

[16] From the marginalia by Jonathan Richardson in a copy of Pope's *Works* (1735) now in the Henry E. Huntington Library.

the Earl of Peterborough in an undated letter, was calculated only to infuriate her.[17] Failing to attain the satisfaction she desired, Lady Mary proceeded to produce her abusive *Verses Address'd to the Imitator of Horace*. This reply, repeating all the commonplaces that had distinguished the attacks of Pope's enemies, was intemperate and uninspired; its exaggerations and broad lines ought not to have impressed anyone. The lampoon sold well, however; and Pope was sufficiently angry to be convinced that henceforth he was entitled to expose her before the public.

Although Lord Hervey was closely associated with Lady Mary in Pope's later satires, he drew the poet's fire a good deal later. Pope had known and admired the celebrated beauty, Molly Lepel, who had become Hervey's wife in 1720; and John Gay had portrayed "Hervey, fair of face" as one of the band joining to celebrate the completion of the *Iliad* translation.[18] Nevertheless, a friendship between the two could not have been a lasting one. Hervey was too much entranced by politics to share any of Pope's serious literary interests; and the latter could hardly have been attracted by either Hervey's personal character or his facile wit. If one can believe Pope's assertions in his *Letter to a Noble Lord* (dated November 30, 1733), the friendship had completed its course to indifference by 1726; but it is doubtful that this coolness was occasioned by anything other than the varying characters and interests of the two men, unless, of course, Pope had been infuriated by Hervey's friendship for Lady Mary. In the *Letter to a Noble Lord* Pope does, it is true, insinuate vaguely that Hervey helped Lady Mary in the unidentified satire or gossip that caused him so much concern; but it is difficult to accept this charge. For if it were true, Pope would surely have dealt with him in his satires of 1727–28, when he struck at Lady Mary.

Real trouble between the two men was brewing in 1732; for Pope thought that Lord Hervey was helping to circulate malicious rumors about his Timon portrait in the *Epistle to the Earl of Burlington*. We don't know whether or not Pope's conviction had any real basis in fact, but he acted as if on surety.[19] He published a short lampoon, an imitation of five lines from Horace's fourth satire of the first book, in the *London Evening Post*, January 22–25, 1732.[20] He also included Lord

---

[17] *Letters and Works of Lady Mary*, II, 22.

[18] *Mr. Pope's Welcome from Greece* (written in 1720).

[19] Hervey did write a private letter to his intimate friend Stephen Fox, in which he declared the *Epistle* to be an execrable performance: "Everybody concurs in their opinion of Pope's last performance, and condemns it as dull and impertinent. I cannot but imagine, by the 18 lines in the last page but one, that he designed ridiculing Lord Burlington as much as he does the Duke of Chandois. It is astonishing to me that he is not afraid this prophecy will be verified, which was told to him a year or two ago,

       'In black and white whilst satire you pursue,
       Take heed the answer is not black and blue' "

(*Lord Hervey and his Friends, 1726–1738*, ed. Earl of Ilchester [London, 1950], pp. 124–25.) Hervey's letter is dated December 21, 1731.

[20] See above, p. 37. As printed in the *London Evening Post* the lines were inscribed to the "Hon. Mr. ------," an allusion to the fact that Hervey's title was a courtesy one. The lines were later included in the *Epistle to Dr. Arbuthnot* (ll. 291–304).

Hervey in his unpublished prose answer to critics of his *Epistle,* the *Master Key to Popery;* and here for the first time he utilized the sobriquet of Fanny.[21]

Pope struck at Lord Hervey again in his imitation of Horace's first satire. The rebuke was not unduly severe—a passing allusion to Hervey's well-known addiction to the composition of verse:

> The Lines are weak, another's pleas'd to say,
> Lord *Fanny* spins a thousand such a Day.
> (ll. 5–6)

Hervey's evil genius prompted him at once to join with Lady Mary in her reply. How much he contributed to the *Verses* is uncertain—Pope himself would not pretend to determine "the exact method of this *Witty Fornication*" [22]—but Hervey undoubtedly furnished some lines. And Pope knew, or thought he knew, that Hervey had arranged for the publication of the reply and had presented the composition to the King and the Queen.[23]

The known facts of the relationship between Pope and his two contemporaries present the picture of a gradually increasing animosity leading to open warfare. We don't know who offered the initial provocations; and we don't have full knowledge of the offenses offered to Pope by Lady Mary and Lord Hervey before 1733, although the kind of affront they may have given, the circulation of slanderous gossip or of manuscript lampoons, is not what is ordinarily passed on to posterity. We do know that Pope was fairly persistent in goading the two of them after 1727, even though he did not really turn upon them until after they had fired a blunderbuss in his direction in 1733. The known facts—and all the facts are not known—suggest Pope as the aggressor; but there are important gaps in our information which render injudicious any effort to make him responsible for the quarrel. The identity of the aggressor is not, however, of primary importance. For the value of the great satirist must ultimately be measured by the truth of his reading of human character rather than by the amount of personal provocation he has received from those he ridicules. The satire on Lady Mary and Lord Hervey is undoubtedly sharpened by hatred; but that Pope has seriously misrepresented anything can well be questioned. He may have grudgingly admitted Lady Mary's intellectual and social gifts; but her sexual promiscuity and the meanness that distinguished her private life were, quite apart from Pope, common knowledge. In the character of Sporus Pope says nothing of Hervey that had not already been said. The aspects of Hervey's character featured in "Sporus" are for the most part true, and despicable.

---

[21] John Butt, " 'A Master Key to Popery,' " *Pope and his Contemporaries: Essays Presented to George Sherburn,* ed. James L. Clifford and Louis Landa (Oxford, 1949), pp. 45–57.

[22] *Works* (1751), VIII, 265.

[23] *Works* (1751), VIII, 279.

Pamphlet Campaigns Concerning Pope, 1728-1744

This appendix contains a selected and chronologically arranged check list of the titles of pamphlets printed in England between 1728 and 1744 and concerned with Alexander Pope; it gives the authorship, where known, and a digest of information in the imprint. To keep the list within manageable limits, I have included only published pamphlets in which the principal business is to defend or to attack Pope. Much of the writing that is the concern of this appendix is ephemeral; and much of it has apparently long since suffered "the martyrdom of jakes and fire." Many pamphlets survive in only one or two known copies; and some seem not to have survived at all. I have included in a separate section at the end those pamphlets, advertised in the periodicals of the time, which probably should appear in the check list but copies of which I have been unable to locate.

An appendix to a study of Pope's later poetry is not the place for a descriptive and analytical bibliography of Popeiana; and many bibliographical niceties have not been observed here. The complicated problem of editions, issues, and re-impressions has not been systematically studied. I have followed the title page of the copy examined in spelling and punctuation, although I have used lower case consistently, except for the initial letter, proper nouns, after periods, and titles within titles. The place of publication is London, unless otherwise indicated; and other information in imprints has been condensed. The day and month of publication have been drawn from advertisements and booklists in contemporary periodicals, although this evidence is not always reliable. Nevertheless, it is generally the only source for dating the ephemera of which this list is largely made up.

I have used the following abbreviations to designate periodicals and other principal sources alluded to in the following pages:

C	*Country Journal; or, The Craftsman*
CS	*Common Sense; or, The Englishman's Journal*
DG	*Daily Gazetteer*
DJ	*Daily Journal*
DP	*Daily Post*
DPB	*Daily Post Boy*
GA	*General Advertiser*
GEP	*General Evening Post*
GM	*Gentleman's Magazine; or, Monthly Intelligencer*
GSJ	*Grub-Street Journal*

LDP   *London Daily Post and General Advertiser*
LEP   *London Evening Post*
LM   *London Magazine; or, Gentleman's Monthly Intelligencer (London Mag-*
           azine and Monthly Chronologer, from 1736)
MC   *Monthly Chronicle*
S/EP   *St. James's Evening Post*
WM   *Weekly Miscellany*
CBEL   *Cambridge Bibliography of English Literature*, ed. F. W. Bateson (New
           York, 1941)
Straus   Ralph Straus, *The Unspeakable Curll* (London, 1927)

1728

April 18 (*MC*)

A collection of several curious pieces lately inserted in the Daily Journal. Containing, [a list of eleven pieces, six of which were attacks upon Pope that had appeared
earlier in *DJ*]. Collected and republished on occasion of the great demand made
for the respective papers in which they were originally inserted, and which are
now no where else to be met with.
    Pr. for T. Warner, J. Jackson, N. Blandford, and H. Whitridge. 1728.

May 13 (*MC*)

The Twickenham hotch-potch, for the use of the Rev. Dr. Swift, Alexander Pope,
Esq; and company. Being a sequel to the Beggars Opera, &c. Containing, [a list
of eight short pieces, most of them concerned with *The Beggars Opera*]. Written
by Caleb D'Anvers.
    Pr. for J. Roberts. 1728

May 28 (*MC*)

[Edmund Curll], A compleat key to the Dunciad.
    Pr. for A. Dodd. 1728. [A 2nd ed., "With a Character of Mr. Pope's Profane
    Writings. By Sir Richard Blackmore," was published on June 4; a 3rd ed.,
    July 2 (Straus, pp. 285–86).]

June 2 (*MC*)

A popp upon Pope: or, a true and faithful account of a late horrid and barbarous
whipping, committed on the body of A. Pope, a poet, as he was innocently walking
in Ham-Walks, near the river of Thames, meditating verses for the good of the
publick. Supposed to have been done by two evil dispos'd persons, out of spite and
revenge, for a harmless lampoon which the said poet had writ upon them.
    Pr. for A. Moore. 1728.

June 11 (*MC*)

[William Bond], The progress of dulness. By an eminent hand. Which will serve
for an explanation of the Dunciad.
    Pr. in the year 1728. [Includes also "Observations on Windsor Forest, the
    Temple of Fame, and the Rape of the Lock, &c." and several brief lampoons.]

June 12 (*MC*)

A compleat collection of all the verses, essays, letters and advertisements, which have been occasioned by the publication of three volumes of Miscellanies, by Pope and company. To which is added an exact list of the lords, ladies, gentlemen and others, who have been abused in those volumes. With a large dedication to the author of the Dunciad, containing some animadversions upon that extraordinary performance.

Pr. for A. Moore. 1728.

June 26 (*MC*)

[James Ralph], Sawney. An heroic poem. Occasion'd by the Dunciad. Together with a critique on that poem address'd to Mr. T[heobal]d, Mr. M[oo]r, Mr. Eu[sde]n, &c.

Pr., and sold by J. Roberts. 1728.

June 26 (*MC*)

An essay on the Dunciad an heroick poem.

Pr. for J. Roberts. 1728.

June 29 (*MC*)

An essay upon the taste and writings of the present times, but with a more particular view to political and dramatick writings. Occasion'd by a late volume of Miscellanies by A. Pope, Esq; and Dr. Swift. Inscrib'd to the Right Honourable Sir Robert Walpole. By a Gentleman of C[hri]st C[hurc]h, Oxon.

Pr. for J. Roberts. 1728.

July 2 (*MC*)

The Popiad.

Pr. in the year 1728. [Includes *A Popp upon Pope*.]

July 18 (*MC*)

[Jonathan Smedley], The metamorphosis: a poem. Shewing the change of Scriblerus into Snarlerus: or, the canine appetite: demonstrated in the persons of P[o]p-e and Sw[if]t.

Pr. for A. Moore. 1728.

July 18 (*MC*)

John Dennis, Remarks on Mr. Pope's Rape of the Lock. In several letters to a friend. With a preface, occasion'd by the late treatise on the profund, and the Dunciad. . . .

Pr. for J. Roberts. 1728.

August 8 (*MC*)

The female dunciad. Containing, [six titles, including "A Faithful Account of the Intrigues, Gallantries and Amours of Alexander Pope" and "The New, Surprizing Metamorphosis; or, Mr. Pope Turn'd into a Stinging-Nettle"].

Pr. for T. Read, and sold by the booksellers of London and Westminster. 1728.

August 12 (*MC*)

[Jonathan Smedley], Gulliveriana: or, a fourth volume of miscellanies. Being a sequel of the three volumes, published by Pope and Swift. To which is added, Alexanderiana; or, a comparison between the ecclesiastical and poetical pope. And many things, in verse and prose, relating to the latter. With an ample preface; and a critique on the third volume of miscellanies lately publish'd by those two facetious writers.

    Pr. for J. Roberts. 1728.

August 16 (*MC*)

[Matthew Concanen?], A supplement to the profund containing several examples, very proper to illustrate the rules laid down in a late treatise, called The Art of Sinking in Poetry. Extracted from the poetical works of the ingenious authors of that accurate piece, and published for the use of their admirers. In two letters to a friend.

    Pr. for J. Roberts. 1728.

August 29 (*MC*)

Characters of the times; or, an impartial account of the writings, characters, education, &c. of several noblemen and gentlemen, libell'd in a preface to a late miscellany publish'd by P[o]pe and S[wi]ft.

    Pr., and sold by A. Dodd, T. Read, and by the booksellers of London and
    Westminster. 1728. [Pope at first attributed this production to Curll and
    Welsted, although he dropped this attribution in *Dunciad* (1735). It is un-
    likely that Welsted, a man of parts, would have descended to the sort of hack-
    writing represented by this pamphlet.]

September 5 (*MC*)

[Elizabeth Thomas], Codrus: or, the Dunciad dissected. Being the finishing-stroke. To which is added, Farmer Pope and his son. A tale. By Mr. Philips.

    Pr. for E. Curll. 1728. [Ambrose Philips was almost certainly not the author
    of *Farmer Pope and his Son*.]

December 12 (*MC*)

[Edward Ward], Durgen. Or, a plain satyr upon a pompous satyrist. Amicably inscrib'd, by the author, to those worthy and ingenious gentlemen misrepresented in a late invective poem, call'd, The Dunciad.

    Pr. for T. Warner. 1729. [Re-issued as *The Cudgel* in 1742. See August 3–5,
    1742.]

1729

April 3 (*MC*)

Thomas Cooke, Tales, epistles, odes, fables, &c. With translations from Homer and other antient authors. To which are added proposals for perfecting the English language.

Pr. for T. Green. 1729. [Contains Cooke's revised version of *The Battel of the Poets,* first published 1725.]

April 17 (*MC*)

[Richard Savage and/or Alexander Pope], An author to be lett. Being a proposal humbly address'd to the consideration of the knights, esquires, gentlemen, and other worshipful and weighty members of the solid and ancient society of the bathos. By their associate and well-wisher Iscariot Hackney. Numb. I. To be continued.

Pr. for Alexander Vint, 1729.

April 30 (*MC*)

[Edmund Curll], The Curliad. A hypercritic upon the Dunciad Variorum. With a farther key to the new characters.

Pr. for the author. 1729.

May 13 (*MC*)

Pope Alexander's supremacy and infallibility examin'd; and the errors of Scriblerus and his man William detected. With the effigies of his holiness and his prime minister, curiously engrav'd on copper.

Sold by J. Roberts. 1729. [At first attributed by Pope (in a letter to Lord Oxford, May 16, 1729) to Thomas Burnet and George Duckett; then in *Dunciad* (1735) attributed by Pope to George Duckett and John Dennis. D. Nichol Smith (ed.), *Letters of Thomas Burnet to George Duckett, 1712–1722* (Oxford, 1914), p. xix, believes it improbable that Duckett had any share in the work; and Edward N. Hooker (ed.), *The Critical Works of John Dennis* (Baltimore, 1939–1943), II, ix-x, does not think Dennis was involved. The work includes several miscellaneous pieces: "A Letter to the Writer of a Letter to my Lord ———— Occasion'd by a Letter to the Publisher of the Present Edition of the Dunciad Variorum"; "A Letter to a Noble Lord: Occasion'd by the late Publication of the Dunciad Variorum"; "The Martiniad, with Notes"; "A Curious Receipt, wherein is disclosed the Art of Writing Poetry with a Small Genius, taken from Martinus Scriblerus's Writings"; and a few brief lampooning verses.]

May 14 (*MC*)

Tom o' Bedlam's Dunciad; or, Pope Alexander the pig. A poem.

Pr. for M. Turner, and sold at the booksellers in London and Westminster. 1729. [The pamphlet has many of the marks of John ("Orator") Henley's style.]

June 6 (*MC*)

A sequel to the Dunciad; being the famous British Sh——rs. A satire.

Pr. for A. Moore, and sold at the pamphlet-shops. 1729.

July 7 (*MC*)

John Dennis, Remarks upon several passages in the preliminaries to the Dunciad, both of the quarto and the duodecimo edition. And upon several passages in Pope's preface to his translation of Homer's Iliad. In both which is shewn, the author's want of judgment. With original letters from Sir Richard Steele, from the late Mr. Gildon, from Mr. Jacob, and from Mr. Pope himself, which shew the falshood of the latter, his envy, and his malice. . . .

    Pr. for H. Whitridge. 1729.

August 7 (*MC*)

[Edward Ward], Apollo's maggot in his cups: or, the whimsical creation of a little satyrical poet. A lyrick ode. Merrily dedicated to Dicky Dickison, the witty, but deform'd governour of Scarborough-Spaw.

    Pr., and sold by T. Warner, and the booksellers of London and Westminster. 1729.

October 23 (*MC*)

[John Roberts], An answer to Mr. Pope's preface to Shakespear. In a letter to a friend. Being a vindication of the old actors who were the publishers and performers of that author's plays. Whereby the errors of their edition are further accounted for, and some memoirs of Shakespear and stage-history of his time are inserted, which were never before collected and publish'd. By a stroling player.

    Pr. in the year 1729.

November 29 (*MC*)

Dean Jonathan's parody on the 4th chap. of Genesis.

    Pr. for Timothy Atkins, and sold by the booksellers of London and Westminster. 1729. [Attributed to Edward Roome in *Dunciad* (1735). Reprinted, with some changes, as *Blast upon Blast* (1742). See below, August 21, 1742.]

1730

January 22–29 (*GSJ*)

[Edward Young], Two epistles to Mr. Pope, concerning the authors of the age.

    Pr. for Lawton Gilliver. 1730.

April 4 (*DJ*)

[Aaron Hill], The progress of wit: a caveat. For the use of an eminent writer. By a fellow of All-Souls. To which is prefix'd, an explanatory discourse to the reader. By Gamaliel Gunson, professor of physick and astrology.

    Pr. for J. Wilford. 1730.

April 28 (*DJ*)

[James Moore Smythe and Leonard Welsted], One epistle to Mr. A. Pope, occasion'd by two epistles lately published.

    Pr. for J. Roberts. [Announced in *Universal Spectator*, February 1, 1728/29, as "the due Chastisement of Mr. Pope for his *Dunciad*, by James Moore

Smythe, Esq; and Mr. Welsted." It was probably circulated surreptitiously as early as October, 1729, when Pope connected Lady Mary Wortley Montagu with it. She denied the charge (*Letters and Works of Lady Mary Wortley Montagu*, ed. by Lord Wharncliffe and W. Moy Thomas [London, 1893], II, 17–19).]

June 30 (*DJ*)

[George Lyttelton], An epistle to Mr. Pope, from a young gentleman at Rome.
>   Pr. for J. Roberts. 1730. [Information about bookseller given in folio ed.; 8vo ed. has imprint reading "Printed in the year 1730."]

August (*GSJ*)

[Matthew Concanen], The speculatist. A collection of letters and essays, moral and political, serious and humorous: upon various subjects.
>   Pr. by J. Watts, for the author. 1730. [*GSJ*, September 3, 1730, writes of the *Speculatist* as being above a month "privately dispersed." A 2nd ed., with the imprint bearing the name of the bookseller "J. Walthoe," appeared in 1732.]

December 1–17 (*GSJ*)

The bays miscellany, or Colley triumphant: containing I. The Petty-Sessions of Poets. II. The Battle of the Poets, or the Contention for the Laurel; as it is now acting at the New Theatre in the Hay-Market. III. The Battle of the Poets. An heroic poem. In two canto's. With the true characters of the several poets therein mention'd; and just reasons why not qualify'd for the laurel. The whole design'd as a specimen of those gentlemens abilities, without prejudice or partiality. Written by Scriblerus Quartus.
>   Pr. for A. Moore; and sold by the booksellers and pamphletsellers of London and Westminster.

1731

January 7–14 (*GSJ*)

Walter Harte, An essay on satire, particularly on the Dunciad. . . . To which is added, a discourse on satires, arraigning persons by name. By Monsieur Boileau.
>   Pr. for Lawton Gilliver. 1730. [A long selection from this didactic poem was printed in *GSJ*, No. 24 (June 13, 1730).]

February 9 (*GSJ*)

An epistle to Mr. Pope, on reading his translations of the Iliad and Odyssy of Homer. To which are added, some examples of the variety of sound in verse, consider'd with Mr. Pope's accuracy in that particular. A short character of Virgil and Homer. And, an epistle to a young poet, concerning Mr. Pope: also, the condition of a good poet.
>   Pr. for J. Wilford. 1731. [Assigned to Walter Harte in *CBEL*.]

March 13 (*DJ*)

Aaron Hill, Advice to the poets. A poem. To which is prefix'd, an epistle dedicatory to the few great spirits of Great Britain. . . .

    Pr. for T. Warner. 1731.

1732

January 3 (*GSJ*)

Leonard Welsted, Of dulness and scandal. Occasion'd by the character of Lord Timon. In Mr. Pope's epistle to the Earl of Burlington. . . .

    Pr. for T. Cooper. 1732.

January 20 (*GSJ*)

[Matthew Concanen], A miscellany on taste. By Mr. Pope. &c. Viz. I. Of taste in architecture. An epistle to the Earl of Burlington. With notes variorum, and a compleat key. II. Of Mr. Pope's taste in divinity, viz. the fall of man, and the first psalm. Translated for the use of a young lady. III. Of Mr. Pope's taste of Shakespeare. IV. ——His satire on Mrs. P[ultene]y. V. Mr. Congreve's fine epistle on retirement and taste. Address'd to Lord Cobham.

    Pr., and sold by G. Lawton, T. Osborn, and J. Hughes. 1732.

January 27 (*GSJ*)

An epistle to Mr. Pope.

    Pr. for H. Whittridge. 1732.

January 29 (*GSJ*)

[Richard Savage (and Alexander Pope?), ed.], A collection of pieces in verse and prose, which have been publish'd on occasion of the Dunciad. Dedicated to the Right Honourable the Earl of Middlesex, by Mr. Savage.

    Pr. for L. Gilliver. 1732. [This miscellany, though not formally advertised as published until late January, may have appeared in late December. The *GSJ*, December 23, 1731, remarks that it is available. The *Collection* contains a dedication written by Savage and unsold sheets of the following poems that had appeared earlier: (1) Edward Young, *Two Epistles to Mr. Pope, Concerning the Authors of the Age;* (2) Walter Harte, *An Essay on Satire, Particularly on the Dunciad;* (3) James Miller, *Harlequin-Horace; or, The Art of Modern Poetry;* (4) George Lyttelton, *An Epistle to Mr. Pope from a Young Gentleman at Rome.* It also includes Richard Savage, *An Author to be Let,* which was reset for this collection and two compilations of journalistic pieces: *Certain Epigrams in Laud and Praise of the Gentlemen of the Dunciad,* and *Essays, Letters, and other Occasional Pieces Relating to the Late War of the Dunces.*]

February 3 (*DJ*)

Leonard Welsted, Of false fame. An epistle to the Right Honourable the Earl of Pembroke....

> Pr. for T. Cooper. 1732.

February 8 (*GSJ*)

On P[op]e and W[elste]d. Occasion'd by their late writings. With advice to a modern poet.

> Pr. for R. P. and sold by E. Nutt, A. Dodd, and J. Jollysse. 1732.

April 5 (*GSJ*)

Mr. Taste, the poetical fop: or, the modes of the court. A comedy. By the author of the opera of Vanelia; or The Amours of the Great.

> Pr. for E. Rayner, and sold by the booksellers in town and country. [Possibly by Eliza Haywood, as is suggested in an attack upon the authoress in *The Neuter; or, A Modest Satire on the Poets of the Age*. See May 29, 1733.]

1733

1733

Lord Willoughby de Broke [Richard Verney], Dunces out of state. A poem. Addressed to Mr. Pope....

> Pr. in the year 1733.

March 1–8 (*GSJ*)

[James Bramston], The man of taste. Occasion'd by an epistle of Mr. Pope's on that subject. By the author of the Art of Politicks.

> Pr. by J. Wright for Lawton Gilliver. 1733.

March 2 (*DP*)

Achilles dissected: being a compleat key of the political characters in that new ballad opera, written by the late Mr. Gay. An account of the plan upon which it is founded. With remarks upon the whole. By Mr. Burnet. To which is added, The First Satire of the Second Book of Horace, imitated in a dialogue between Mr. Pope and the Ordinary of Newgate.

> Pr. for W. Mears. 1733. [The burlesque of Pope's imitation is signed "Guthry," the name of the Ordinary. The sheets were reissued, with a new t.p., sometime in 1734, as *The Case of Alexander Pope*.]

March 6 (*DJ*)

[Patrick M'Doe-Roch, pseud.], The sequel of Mr. Pope's lawcase: or, farther advice thereon: in an epistle to him. With a short preface and postscript. By a Templer.... With notes explanatory, critical and jocose. By another hand, also a brother of the quill. The second edition, revised and corrected, and the notes enlarged.

> Pr. by Anth. Gibbons, for the benefit of the author. 1733. [I have been unable to locate a copy of a "first edition."]

March 9 (*GSJ*)

[Lady Mary Wortley Montagu and Lord Hervey], Verses address'd to the imitator of the First Satire of the Second Book of Horace. By a lady.

> Pr. for A. Dodd, and sold at all the pamphlet-shops in town. [A piracy of this lampoon, *To the Imitator of the Satire of the Second Book of Horace* (Pr. for J. Roberts, 1733), was advertised on the same day in *DJ*.]

March 30 (*GSJ*)

An epistle to the little satyrist of Twickenham.

> Pr. for J. Wilford. 1733.

March 24–31 (*WM*)

On the English translations of Homer: a satire. With the characters of Homer, Virgil and Horace. And the character of a truly accomplished poet. This satire was printed in the year 1721. (With the character of Homer) but is here improved and enlarged.

> Pr. for John Oswald. 1733.

April 3 (*GSJ*)

A proper reply to a lady, occasioned by her Verses Address'd to the Imitator of the First Satire of the Second Book of Horace. By a gentleman.

> Pr. for T. Osborne.

April 13 (*GSJ*)

Advice to Sappho. Occasioned by her verses on the imitator of the First Satire of the Second Book of Horace. By a gentlewoman.

> Pr. for the authoress; and sold by J. Roberts. 1733.

April 18 (*GSJ*)

[Bezaleel Morrice], An essay on the universe: a poem.

> Pr. for John Oswald. 1733.

April 12–19 (*GSJ*)

[David Mallet], Of verbal criticism: an epistle to Mr. Pope. Occasioned by Theobald's Shakespear, and Bentley's Milton.

> Pr. for Lawton Gilliver. 1733.

May 10 (*GSJ*)

[Giles Jacob], The mirrour; or, letters satyrical, panegyrical, serious and humorous, on the present times. Shewing the great improvement of wit, poetry and learning, of arts and sciences, natural phylosophy, the law, physick, religion, morality, modern greatness, dress, fashions, &c. To which is added a legal conviction of Mr. Alexander Pope of dulness and scandal, in the high court of Parnassus.

> Pr. for J. Roberts, and sold at all the pamphlet-shops in London and Westminster. 1733.

May 29 (*GSJ*)

The neuter: or, a modest satire on the poets of the age. By a lady. Dedicated to the Right Honourable Mary Wortley Montague.
    Pr. for T. Osborne, and sold by A. Dodd.

May 29 (*DJ*)

Ingratitude: to Mr. Pope. Occasion'd by a manuscript handed about, under the title of, Mr. Taste's Tour from the Land of Politeness, to that of Dulness and Scandal, &c. &c.
    Pr. and sold by J. Dormer. 1733.

May 31 (*DJ*)

Mr. Taste's tour from the island of politeness, to that of dulness and scandal.
    Pr. for S. Sloe, and sold at the pamphlet-shops of London and Westminster. 1733. [An effort is made in this pamphlet to suggest that it was by Pope. For an attempt to establish Pope's authorship, see Howard P. Vincent, "A Pope Problem," *TLS*, February 14, 1935, p. 92.]

May 31 (*GSJ*)

The wrongheads: a poem. Inscrib'd to Mr. Pope. By a person of quality.
    Pr. for T. Astley, and sold by R. Wellington. 1733.

June 7 (*GSJ*)

[Paul Whitehead], The state dunces: inscrib'd to Mr. Pope.
    Pr. for J. Dickenson. 1733. ["J. Dickenson" in fol. ed.; "W. Dickenson" in sm. 8vo ed. of 1733.]

June 7 (*GSJ*)

The satirist: in imitation of the fourth satire of the first book of Horace.
    Pr. for L. G., and sold by Mrs. Dodd, Mrs. Nutt, and the booksellers of London and Westminster. 1733.

July 6 (*GSJ*)

[Paul Whitehead], The state dunces. Inscribed to Mr. Pope. Part II. Being the last.
    Pr. for J. Dickenson. 1733.

November 1 (*GSJ*)

The art of scribling, address'd to all the scriblers of the age. By Scriblerus Maximus.
    Pr. for A. Dodd. 1733.

November 6 (*GSJ*)

The parsoniad; a satyr. Inscribed to Mr. Pope.
    Pr. for Charles Corbet. 1733.

November 10 (*GSJ*)

[John Lord Hervey], An epistle from a nobleman to a doctor of divinity: in answer to a Latin letter in verse. Written from H[ampto]n C[our]t, Aug. 28, 1733.
    Pr. for J. Roberts. 1733.

November-December

Flavia to Fanny, an eipstle [*sic*]. From a peerless poetess, to a peerless p[eer] in immortal dogrill. Occasioned by a late epistle from Fanny to her governess.

> Pr. for T. Reynolds, and sold by the booksellers of London and Westminster. [The date is suggested on the basis of the obvious references to Lord Hervey's *Epistle from a Nobleman*.]

December 4 (*DJ*)

Tit for tat. Or an answer to the Epistle to [*sic*] a Nobleman.

> Pr. for T. Cooper. 1734. [See February 7–14, 1734, for an enlarged edition of this work.]

1734

1734

The case of Alexander Pope, of Twickenham, Esq; and his counsel learned in the law. Transvers'd to a friendly dialogue between him and the Ordinary of Newgate. By way of allusion to the First Satire of the Second Book of Horace. To which is prefix'd, a dissection and compleat key to Mr. Gay's posthumous opera of Achilles. By Alexander Burnet Esq; The second edition.

> Pr. for W. Mears. 1734. [A re-issue, with a new t.p., of *Achilles Dissected*. See above, March 2, 1733.]

January 4 (*GSJ*)

A most proper reply to the noblemen's Epistle to a Doctor of Divinity. To which is added, Horace *versus* Fannius; or, A Case in Poinct. As reported by Ben. Johnson. And the Belle-man of St. James's Verses.

> Sold by J. Huggonson. 1734.

January 10–17 (*GSJ*)

The tryal of skill between 'Squire Walsingham and Mother Osborne. An eclogue, in imitation of Virgil's Palaemon. To which are added, Horace to Fannius, and An Apology for Printing a Certain Nobleman's Epistle to Dr. S[her]w[i]n.

> Sold by J. Huggonson. 1734.

January 29–31 (*LEP*)

[Robert Dodsley], The modern reasoners: an epistle to a friend.

> Pr. for Lawton Gilliver. 1734.

February (*GM*)

A tryal of skill between a court lord, and a Twickenham 'Squire. Inscrib'd to Mr. Pope.

> Pr. and sold by J. Dormer. 1734.

February 12–14 (*LEP*)

———— Gerard, An epistle to the egregious Mr Pope, in which the beauties of his mind and body are amply displayed. . . .

Pr. for the author, and sold by M. Harris. 1734. [A second edition (with additions) is advertised in *DPB*, April 11, 1734.]

February 7–14 (*GSJ*)

Tit for tat. To which is annex'd, An Epistle from a Nobleman to a Doctor of Divinity. In Answer to a Latin Letter in Verse. Also The Review; or, The Case Fairly Stated on Both Sides. Wherein is shewn the true cause of the foregoing poems.

Pr. for T. Reynolds, and sold by the booksellers in town and country. 1734. [See *Tit for Tat*, December 4, 1733.]

March (*GM*)

The false patriot. An epistle to Mr. Pope.

Pr. for James Roberts. 1734.

March 7–14 (*GSJ*)

An epistle from a gentleman at Twickenham, to a nobleman at St. James's. Occasion'd by An Epistle from a Nobleman, to a Doctor of Divinity.

Pr. for William Guess, and sold at the pamphlet-shops.

November (*WM*)

Robert Dodsley, An epistle to Mr. Pope, occasion'd by his Essay on Man....

Pr. for L. Gilliver. 1734.

1735

February 4 (*DJ*)

An epistle to Alexander Pope, Esq; occasion'd by some of his late writings.

Pr. for J. Wilford. 1735.

February 5–10 (E-C, VI, 354-55)

[Walter Harte], An essay on reason.

Pr. by J. Wright for Lawton Gilliver. 1735. [A 2nd ed. in 1735; a 3rd ed., "corrected," in 1736.]

March 1–4 (*LEP*)

[Thomas Bentley], A letter to Mr. Pope, occasioned by Sober Advice from Horace, &c.

Pr. for T. Cooper. 1735 [For authorship, see James Sutherland (ed.), *Dunciad* (London, 1942), p. 429.]

June 24–26 (*GEP*)

The poet finish'd in prose. Being a dialogue concerning Mr. Pope and his writings.

Pr. for E. Curll. 1735. [Re-issued, along with other Curll pamphlets, in *Post-Office Intelligence*. See December 9, 1735.]

December 9 (*SJEP*)

Post-Office intelligence: or, universal gallantry. Being a collection of love-letters, written by persons, in all stations, from most parts of the kingdom. Faithfully published from their originals, returned into the General-Post-Office in Lombard-Street, the parties to whom they were directed being either dead, or removed from their usual places of abode. With rational remarks upon Mr. Pope's letters, and some of his former and late productions.

> Pr. for E. Curll. 1736. [Includes *Rational Remarks upon Mr. Pope's Letters* and *The Poet Finish'd in Prose.* See June 24–26, 1735.]

1736

March 31 (*LDP*)

Divine wisdom and providence; an essay. Occasion'd by the Essay on Man.

> Pr. by J. Huggonson, and sold by J. Roberts. 1736. [A 2nd ed., corrected, was announced in *LEP,* April 19, 1737; a 3rd ed., in *WM,* September 22, 1739. The title page of the 2nd ed. states that the poem was written by "Mr. Bridges."]

April 7 (*LDP*)

Two epistles of Horace imitated.

> Pr. for T. Cooper. 1736.

May 4 (*DP*)

Bounce to Fop. An heroick epistle from a dog at Twickenham to a dog at court. By Dr. S[wif]t.

> Dublin printed, London reprinted for T. Cooper. 1736. [A sm. 8vo. ed. has imprint: "London: printed, and Dublin re-printed by George Faulkner, 1736." A 2nd ed. (London) came out the same year. Sir Harold Williams (ed.), *The Poems of Jonathan Swift* (Oxford, 1937), III, 1135–36, doubts Swift's authorship; and he cites interesting evidence that Pope himself may have been concerned in this production. See Ault, *New Light,* pp. 342–348.]

1737

April 30–May 7 (*C*)

[Thomas Beach], Eugenio: or, virtuous and happy life. A poem. Inscrib'd to Mr. Pope.

> Pr. for R. Dodsley. 1737. [*GM* lists as published in April.]

August (*GM*)

An epistle to Alexander Pope, Esq; from South Carolina.

> Pr. for J. Brindley and C. Corbett. 1737. [Tentatively attributed to Thomas Dale in *CBEL. LM* lists as published in June.]

August 1 (*DG*)

Joseph Spence, An essay on Mr. Pope's Odyssey. In five dialogues. . . . The second edition.

> Pr. for S. Wilmot, and sold by S. Birt and T. Longman. 1737. [1st ed. published in 1726–27.]

1738

October 24 (*LDP*)

A supplement to One Thousand Seven Hundred Thirty-Eight. Not written by Mr. Pope.

> Pr. for J. Roberts. 1738.

November (*GM*)

[Bezaleel Morrice], The present corruption of Britons; being a paraphrase on the latter part of Mr. P[op]e's first dialogue, entitled, One Thousand Seven Hundred and Thirty-Eight.

> Pr., and sold by Thomas Gray and by the booksellers of London and Westminster.

November 21–23 (*GEP*)

[Elizabeth Carter, trans.], An examination of Mr Pope's Essay on Man. Translated from the French of M. Crousaz, member of the royal academies of sciences at Paris and Bourdeaux; and professor of philosophy and mathematics at Lausanne.

> **Pr. for A. Dodd. 1739.**

November (*LM*)

[Charles Forman, trans.], A commentary upon Mr Pope's four ethic epistles, intituled, An Essay on Man. Wherein his system is fully examined. By Monsieur de Crousaz. . . . Translated from the French original, printed at Geneva, with remarks.

> Pr. for E. Curll. 1738. [Charles Forman was the translator according to the publication announcement in *LM*. The unsold sheets were subsequently included by Curll in *Miscellanies in Prose and Verse, by the Honourable Lady Margaret Pennyman . . . To which are annexed, some other curious Pieces* (Pr. for E. Curll, 1740), published December 6, 1740 (Straus).]

1739

January 31 (*LDP*)

Paul Whitehead, Manners: a satire.

> Pr. for R. Dodsley. 1739.

March (*GM*)

Epidemical madness: a poem in imitation of Horace.

> Pr. for J. Brindley, and sold by Mrs. Dodd and the booksellers of London and Westminster. 1739.

March 1 (*LDP*)

Characters: an epistle to Alexander Pope Esq. and Mr. Whitehead.

> Pr. for T. Cooper, and sold by the booksellers of London and Westminster. 1739.

March 10–17 (*WM*)

William Ayre, Truth. A counterpart to Mr. Pope's Esay on Man, Epistle the First. . . .

    Pr. for R. Minors. 1739.

March 27 (*LDP*)

[William Dudgeon], A view of the necessitarian or best scheme: freed from the objections of M. Crousaz, in his examination of Mr. Pope's Essay on Man.

    Pr. for T. Cooper. 1739.

November 14 (*DP*)

William Warburton, A vindication of Mr. Pope's Essay on Man, from the misrepresentations of Mr de Crousaz, professor of philosophy and mathematicks in the University of Lausanne. By the author of The Divine Legation of Moses Demonstrated. In six letters.

    Pr. for J. Robinson. 1740. [A second edition was announced in *DP*, January 4, 1740.]

1740

April 14 (*DP*)

[————— Lorleach], A satirical epistle to Mr. Pope.

    Pr. for the author, and sold at the pamphlet-shops. 1740. [For authorship, see *N&Q*, 1 series, XI (1855), 378.]

June 24–26 (*LEP*)

William Warburton, A seventh letter, which finishes the vindication of Mr Pope's Essay on Man, from the misrepresentations of Mr de Crousaz, professor of philosophy and mathematicks in the University of Lausanne. . . .

    Pr. for J. Robinson. 1740.

July (?)

The tryal of Colley Cibber, comedian, &c. for writing a book intitled An Apology for his Life, &c. Being a thorough examination thereof; wherein he is proved guilty of high crimes and misdemeanors against the English language, and in characterising many persons of distinction. Together with an indictment exhibited against Alexander Pope of Twickenham, Esq; for not exerting his talents at this juncture: and the arraignment of George Cheyne, physician at Bath, for the philosophical, physical, and theological heresies, uttered in his last book on regimen.

    Pr. for the author, and sold by W. Lewis and E. Curll, Mess. Dodsley, Jackson, Jolliffe, and Brindley, and at all booksellers in London and Westminster. 1740. [The dedication to "Mr. Ralph of Redriff" is signed "T. Johnson."]

October 24 (*DP*)

[James Miller], Are these things so? The previous question from an Englishman in his grotto, to a Great Man at court.

    Pr. for T. Cooper. 1740.

1741

November (*GM*)

[Samuel Johnson, trans.], A commentary on Mr Pope's principles of morality, or Essay on Man. By Mons. Crousaz, . . . in answer to a letter of remarks on his Examen, &c. Containing also [five pieces, including the Abbe du Resnel's translation of the *Essay on Man* into French verse, an interlinear literal English version of that translation, and some annotations by the translator].

> Pr. for E. Cave. 1742. [A copy of this work in the Yale University Library with a title page dated 1739 suggests that it had originally been published in that year but immediately withdrawn. I have found no publication notice of it in 1739. See A. T. Hazen and E. L. McAdam, Jr., "First Editions of Samuel Johnson," *Yale Library Gazette*, X (1936), 45–51.]

1742

July 24–30 (*LEP*)

Colley Cibber, A letter from Mr. Cibber, to Mr. Pope, inquiring into the motives that might induce him in his satyrical works, to be so frequently fond of Mr. Cibber's name.

> Pr., and sold by W. Lewis. 1742.

August 3 (*DP*)

A blast upon Bays; or, a new lick at the laureat. Containing remarks upon a late tatling performance, entitled, A Letter from Mr. Cibber to Mr. Pope, &c.

> Pr. for T. Robbins, and sold at all the booksellers and pamphlet-shops in town and country. 1742. [A 3rd ed. is included in *Lick upon Lick* (February 16, 1744); but I have been unable to discover a 2nd ed. or a reference to its publication.]

August 3–5 (*LEP*)

The cudgel, or, a crab-tree lecture. To the author of the Dunciad. By Hercules Vinegar, Esq;

> Pr. for the author, and sold at his house, the Crab-tree, in Vinegar-yard, near Drury-Lane. 1742. [A re-issue of Edward Ward's *Durgen* (December 12, 1728), with a new title page and with six pages of prefatory matter omitted. The first leaf containing the text of the poem was reset because of the heading *Durgen* on page 1. See Knox Chandler, "Two 'Fielding' Pamphlets," *PQ*, XVI (1937), 410–11. *DP*, July 26, 1742, announces the publication of this pamphlet; but the date seems slightly early.]

August 7–10 (*LEP*)

William Warburton, A critical and philosophical commentary on Mr. Pope's Essay on Man. In which is contain'd a vindication of the said Essay from the misrepresentations of Mr. de Resnel, the French translator, and of Mr. de Crousaz, professor of philosophy and mathematics in the academy of Lausanne, the commentator....

Pr. for John and Paul Knapton. 1742.

August 19–21 (*LEP*)

A letter to Mr. C[ib]b[e]r, on his letter to Mr. P[ope].

Pr. for J. Roberts. 1742. [The BM catalogue and the *DNB* ascribe this work to John Lord Hervey.]

August 21 (*DP*)

Blast upon blast, and lick for lick; or a new lesson for P[o]pe. A parody on the fourth chapter of Genesis. By Capt. H[ercule]s Vinegar.

Pr. for W. Webb, and sold by the booksellers and pamphlet-shops of London and Westminster. 1742. [A revision of *Dean Jonathan's Parody on the 4th Chapter of Genesis* (November 29, 1729). See Knox Chandler, "Two 'Fielding' Pamphlets," *PQ,* XVI (1937), 411–12.]

August 21–24 (*LEP*)

[John Lord Hervey], The difference between verbal and practical virtue. With a prefatory epistle from Mr. C[ib]b[e]r to Mr. P[ope].

Pr. for J. Roberts. 1742. [An effort is made in the prefatory epistle to suggest that the poem itself is by Cibber.]

August 31 (*DP*)

Sawney and Colley, a poetical dialogue: occasioned by a late letter from the laureat of St. James's, to the Homer of Twickenham. Something in the manner of Dr. Swift.

Pr. for J. H. in Sword and Buckler Court, on Ludgate-Hill.

Sept. 30–Oct. 2 (*LEP*)

Scriblerus, [pseud.], The scribleriad. Being an epistle to the dunces, on renewing their attack upon Mr. Pope, under their leader the laureat.

Pr. for W. Webb. 1742.

December (*GM*)

The blatant-beast. A poem.

Pr. for J. Robinson. 1742.

1743

January 11 (*LDP*)

[Colley Cibber?], The egotist: or, Colley upon Cibber. Being his own picture retouch'd, to so plain a likeness, that no one, now, would have the face to own it, but himself.

Pr., and sold by W. Lewis. 1743. [For the authorship, see DeWitt C. Croissant, "A Note on the *Egoist: or, Colley upon Cibber*," *PQ,* III (1924), 76–77.]

February 15 (*DP*)

Colley Cibber, A second letter from Mr. Cibber to Mr. Pope. In reply to some additional verses in his Dunciad, which he has not yet publish'd.

    Pr. for A. Dodd. 1743.

February 18 (*DP*)

Mr. P[o]pe's picture in miniature, but as like as it can stare; a poem: with notes.

    Pr. for G. Lion. 1743.

March 3 (*LDP*)

[John Henley], Why how now, Gossip Pope? Or, the sweet singing-bird of Parnassus taken out of its pretty cage to be roasted: in one short epistle (preparatory to a criticism on his writings) to that darling of the demy-wits, and minion of the minor criticks. Exposing the malice wickedness and vanity of his aspersions on J. H. in that monument of his own misery and spleen, the Dunciad. The second edition.

    Pr. 1736, reprinted in 1743 for J. Roberts. [I have been unable to locate a copy belonging to an "edition" of 1736.]

1744

January 19 (*LDP*)

Colley Cibber, Another occasional letter from Mr. Cibber to Mr. Pope. Wherein the new hero's preferment to his throne, in the Dunciad, seems not to be accepted. And the author of that poem his more rightful claim to it, is asserted. With an expostulatory address to the Reverend Mr. W. W[arburto]n, author of the new preface, and adviser in the curious improvements of that satire. . . .

    Pr., and sold by W. Lewis. 1744.

February 16 (*LDP*)

Lick upon lick; occasion'd by another occasional letter from Mr. Cibber to Mr. Pope. To which is added, (the third edition.) A Blast upon Bays; or, A New Lick at the Laureat: containing remarks upon that tattling performance, Mr. Cibber's first Letter to Mr. Pope, &c.

    Pr. for T. Robbins, and sold at all the booksellers and pamphlet-shops in town and country. 1744. [See August 3, 1742, for 1st ed. of *A Blast upon Bays*.]

June 5 (*GA*)

An elegy on Mr. Pope. Humbly inscrib'd to H. St. John, L. Bolingbroke. By a friend.

    Pr. for Lawton Gilliver, and sold by J. Roberts. 1744.

June 18 (*GA*)

The life of Alexander Pope, Esq; with remarks on his works: to which is added, his last will.

    Pr. for Weaver Bickerton. 1744.

June 18 (*GA*)

The life of Alexander Pope, Esq; with a true copy of his last will and testament.
    Pr. for Charles Corbett. 1744.

June 19 (*GA*)

Discord, or, one thousand seven hundred forty four. By a great poet lately deceased.
Printed from the originall mss. permissu superiorum.
    Pr. for B. Cowse. 1744.

June 22 (*GA*)

An elegy on the death of Mr. Alexander Pope. Being an imitation of the ninth
elegy in the third book of Ovid.
    Pr. for R. Dodsley, and sold by M. Cooper. 1744.

PAMPHLETS WHICH HAVE NOT BEEN LOCATED

September 17, 1728 (*MC*)

The true peri bathoys: or, the art of sinking in poetry, and rising again. In four
cantos. Compar'd with the Dunciad.
    Pr. for S. Chapman, E. Curl, and J. Brotherton.

July 22, 1729 (*MC*)

The Pope-ish controversy compleat.
    [Presumably the five attacks on Pope printed by Curll in 1728–29.]

January 15, 1732 (*GSJ*)

Mr. Pope's poem on taste; with a compleat key and notis variorum.

January 22, 1732 (*GSJ*)

Of Good Nature. An epistle to his G[ra]ce the D[u]ke of C[hando]s.
    [Attributed to the Rev. John Cowper by John Butt, "A Master Key to Popery,"
    Pope and his Contemporaries (Oxford, 1949), p. 43.]

January 28, 1732 (*DJ*)

Malice defeated. A pastoral essay. Occasioned by Mr. Pope's character of Lord
Timon, in his Epistle to the Earl of Burlington: and Mr. Welsted's answer.
    Pr. for J. Millan, and sold by the booksellers of London and Westminster.

1732

An epistle to Mr. Pope; occasioned by his Epistle to the Earl of Burlington.
    [Mentioned by William Ayre, *Memoirs of the Life and Writings of Alexander
    Pope, Esq.* (London, 1745), I, 285, and there attributed to "Joseph Turner."
    Ayre's brief reference does not allow one to identify this pamphlet with any
    one of the others published in January and February, 1732.]

March, 1733 (*LM*)

Sappho to Adonis, after the manner of Ovid.
    [Popeiana?]

June, 1733 (*GM*)

The court dunciad.

   [Popeiana?]

March, 1735 (*LM*)

Tit for tat. Part II. To which is added, The Latin Letter from a Doctor of Divinity to a Noble Lord, Burlesqu'd.

   Sold at the pamphlet-shops.

November 15, 1739 (*LDP*)

One thousand seven hundred thirty-nine, a rhapsody. (Being a sequel to One Thousand Seven Hundred Thirty-Eight by Mr. Pope.)

   Pr. for J. Cooper; Mess. Jackson and Jolliffe, H. Chappelle, and E. Curll.

April 3-6, 1742 (*LEP*)

Bezaleel Morrice, An epistle to the falsely-celebrated British Homer.

   Sold by the booksellers of London and Westminster.

Index

This index does not include all names occurring in the text. Titles of works by major writers of the eighteenth century are ordinarily listed only under the name of the author; titles of works by minor writers of the period are listed both separately and under the name of the author, if known. Members of the nobility are generally listed by title. References to Pope's formal satirical characters (Atticus, Sporus, Sir Balaam, *etc.*) will be found under "Pope, Alexander. Formal satirical characters." Only under the entry "Pope, Alexander" have I attempted a reasonably full analytical index.